At War in the Shadow of Vietnam

At War in the Shadow of Vietnam

U.S. MILITARY AID TO THE
ROYAL LAO GOVERNMENT,
1955–1975

TIMOTHY N. CASTLE

COLUMBIA UNIVERSITY PRESS
New York

Columbia University Press
New York   Chichester, West Sussex
Copyright © 1993 Columbia University Press

Library of Congress Cataloging-in-Publication Data

Castle, Timothy N. (Timothy Neil)
At war in the shadow of Vietnam : U.S. military aid to the Royal
Lao government, 1955–1975 / Timothy N. Castle.
p.   cm.
Includes bibliographical references and index.
ISBN 0–231–07976–1
1. Vietnamese Conflict, 1961-1975—Laos.   2. Vietnamese Conflict.
1961-1975—United States.   3. Laos—Politics and government.
4. Military assistance, American—Laos.   I. Title.
DS558.6.L3C37   1993
327.730594'09'046—dc20
92–44151
CIP

Casebound editions of Columbia University Press books
are printed on permanent and durable acid-free paper.

Printed in the United States of America
c 10 9 8 7 6 5 4 3 2 1

To my mother
Eunice I. Castle

CONTENTS

PREFACE

On August 19, 1990, I looked out the window of a small Thai Airways plane at the scattered rice fields and rusted tin-roofed buildings clustered around the outskirts of Vientiane, the capital of the Lao People's Democratic Republic. As we prepared to land, I recalled distinctly the last time I had flown into Laotian airspace. Seventeen years earlier I had scanned for communist firing positions along the Mekong River from the doorway of a U.S. Air Force CH-53E "Super Jolly Green Giant" helicopter.

From 1971 to 1973 I served as an enlisted man in the U.S. Air Force at Nakhon Phanom Royal Thai Air Force Base in northeastern Thailand. Located a few miles from the Mekong River, and less than seventy-five miles from North Vietnam, the airfield was a constant bustle of helicopters and fixed-wing aircraft. During my second year I was assigned to the 21st Special Operations Squadron (SOS) as a surveillance and intelligence specialist aboard CH-53 helicopters. Although primarily involved in night reconnaissance flights in support of air base defense, I also logged thirty-eight combat sorties over southwestern Laos.[1] The majority of the 21st SOS missions, however, were being flown in support of clandestine operations

in northeastern and eastern Laos. Senior political and military leaders in
Washington believed that U.S. activity in Laos, termed the "secret war"
by journalists, was an important component of America's anticommunist
containment strategy. Around the airfield at Nakhon Phanom, however, we
were concerned with safe and successful flying, not foreign policy issues.
As a twenty-year-old airman I neither knew nor cared about the geostrategic
dynamics that had pulled Laos into such a cataclysmic war.

Five years later, as a civilian graduate student living in a southern
California community with a steadily rising number of Laotian refugees, I
began a concerted study of U.S. involvement in Laos. My 1979 M.A.
thesis focused on the Hmong mountain people of northeastern Laos and
their wartime alliance with the United States.[2] It was a start, but if the true
scope of U.S. activity Laos was to be disclosed and understood, much more
research was necessary. In 1980 I returned to the Air Force as an intelligence officer and began a series of assignments that took me to the Philippines, Singapore, Malaysia, and Thailand. While collecting information in
refugee camps, I saw firsthand the human tragedy of the Indochina war. In
1988, sponsored by the U.S. Air Force Academy, I began work at the
University of Hawaii on a doctorate in Southeast Asian history. Two years
later I spent a month in Laos traveling and interviewing senior Lao communist officials on their wartime experiences. My visit, the first by a U.S.
military researcher since the Vietnam War, was well received by the Lao
government. Following completion of my degree in 1991 I was assigned to
the Air Force Academy as an assistant professor of Asian history.[3] In
December 1991, with funding from the Air Force Academy and the assistance of the U.S. embassy in Laos, I returned to Laos to conduct more
interviews.

The search for an explicated understanding of my small role during the
Vietnam war has therefore developed into an archive-based history that fills
a glaring historiographic gap. The body of literature dealing with this
subject and U.S.–Lao relations in general is embarrassingly deficient. There
have been only two comprehensive scholarly examinations of U.S.–Lao
relations during the Second Indochina War: Charles A. Stevenson's *The
End of Nowhere: American Policy Toward Laos Since 1954* and Martin E.
Goldstein's *American Policy Toward Laos*.[4] Both were published in the
early 1970s, well before the final years of U.S. involvement in Laos.
Moreover, official declassified sources, critical to any thorough analysis,
were especially scarce and difficult to obtain. In his preface Goldstein
expressed hope that materials would soon become available. "One suspects

. . . that presently undisclosed aspects of American participation in Laotian military matters, particularly after 1962, will come to light as time passes and documents become declassified."[5] Goldstein's hopes have been largely unrewarded.

Researchers of contemporary American history have long labored under the U.S. government's cumbersome and overtaxed declassification program. The difficulties of the security review process for documents dealing with Laos are compounded by the number of government organizations involved. The military services are generally willing to declassify their holdings on U.S. military involvement in Laos: there are few operational or weapons secrets contained in Vietnam War–era documents.[6] Resistance to declassification of materials dealing with U.S. military involvement in Laos has come primarily from the Central Intelligence Agency and the Department of State. A request under the Freedom of Information Act, submitted to the CIA on my behalf in 1988 by the U.S. Air Force, resulted in not a single piece of information. The CIA responded that under "the provisions of the CIA Information Act . . . operational files of the CIA have been exempted from the Freedom of Information Act."[7] Likewise, official requests for Department of State materials have met with polite but firm refusals.

How, then, does one go about researching and reconstructing a subject that has long been such a closely guarded secret? Fortunately, a number of retired CIA and State Department officials have written about their experiences in Laos, and many are willing to discuss the topic with serious researchers. U.S. military activities in Laos were well documented, but access to these once highly classified materials is difficult and time-consuming. Fortunately, with the passage of time and an increase in the desire to make known their roles during the Vietnam War, many military personnel who served in Laos will now discuss their duties. There are also a number of Congressional hearings transcripts and studies that examine State Department, CIA, and U.S. military involvement in Laos.

Some of my research tasks, particularly those dealing with classified materials, were simplified because of my status as an active-duty United States Air Force officer. In particular, I was able to gain access to a substantial body of unprocessed primary data at the Air Force historical Research Center at Maxwell Air Force Base, Alabama. This included the opportunity to cull the contents of twenty cartons of documents pertaining to the Air Force management of the CIA's proprietary airline, Air America, Inc. The oral history collection and the declassified end-of-tour reports at

Maxwell AFB were also an extraordinary source of information. In addition, I received access to a number of useful files on Laos at the U.S. Army
Center for Military History in Washington, D.C. The Office of Air Force
History and the Naval Historical Center, both located in Washington, D.C.,
were helpful with historiographic information.

Materials available at the John F. Kennedy Library in Boston, Massa-
chusetts, and the National Archives in Suitland, Maryland, were generally
disappointing. Documents on Laos at the Kennedy library, for the most
part, remain so heavily "sanitized" as to be of negligible value. Exceptions
are the recently available oral history program interviews with Ambassador
W. Averell Harriman. At the National Archives I was able to locate the
U.S. Army records group to which the material of Deputy Chief, Joint
United States Military Advisory Group Thailand (DEPCHIEF) had been
assigned. DEPCHIEF was the covert organization established in 1962 to
"carry out, within Thailand, certain necessary military assistance functions
for Laos."[8] However, a search for the records was unsuccessful. According
to a knowledgeable archivist, during the transfer of Vietnam War–era
materials from the U.S. Army to the National Archives, a vast amount of
data was thoughtlessly destroyed by temporary employees. In all likelihood,
the DEPCHIEF files and other important pieces of the Vietnam War puzzle
were incinerated.

Lacking a complete data base of available official materials on U.S.
involvement in Laos, I turned to many of the participants for information.
This has involved hundreds of letters, scores of telephone calls, and dozens
of face-to-face interviews. I have conducted personal interviews with three
of the four men who served as U.S. ambassador to Laos between 1962 and
1975: Leonard Unger (1962–64), G. McMurtrie Godley (1969–73), and
Charles S. Whitehouse (1973–75). The fourth, William H. Sullivan (1964–
69), who resides in Mexico, has graciously answered my letters. Indeed,
even though we disagree on a number of points, Ambassador Sullivan's
interest and support for this project has been especially noteworthy.

Singular information and assistance came from William E. Colby, former director of Central Intelligence. A number of other CIA veterans of the
Lao operations have also provided valuable recollections. They include B.
Hugh Tovar, chief of station in Laos for many years, CIA case officer John
E. "Jack" Shirley, and James W. "Bill" Lair and Lloyd "Pat" Landry,
the principal architects and managers of the CIA-controlled Thai "volunteer" program for Laos.

I have had extensive contact with U.S. military personnel who were
involved in the Lao aid programs. At the senior command level, I had very

productive interviews with two men who served as commander in chief Pacific (CINCPAC), Admiral Harry D. Felt (1958–64) and Admiral U.S. Grant Sharp (1964–68). General William C. Westmoreland, commander of the U.S. Military Assistance Command Vietnam (COMUSMACV) (1964–68), General John W. Vessey, Jr., who was the first general officer to command DEPCHIEF (1972–73), and his successor, Lieutenant General Richard G. Trefry (1973–74), all provided invaluable information and support for this project.[9] Lieutenant General James D. Hughes, deputy commander of the 7/13th Air Force (1972–73) and Brigadier General Harry C. Aderholt, commander of the Joint United States Military Advisory Group, Thailand (JUSMAGTHAI), (1974–76)—and a special operations advisor for the CIA in Laos during the 1960s—were particularly responsive to my research requests.

At an operational level, I have interviewed scores of officers and enlisted men who were associated with the various Lao support operations. These programs include: DEPCHIEF; the "Ravens," a U.S. Air Force Forward Air Controller (FAC) unit; the "supplemental personnel" assigned to the attaché officers under "Project 404;" and "Waterpump," the U.S. Air Force program established to build a viable Lao air force. I have interviewed and corresponded with dozens of former Air America pilots; their recollections provide a substantial contribution to this study. Significantly, many of these pilots have formed the Air America Association and established an Air America documents repository at the University of Texas at Dallas.

My other critical source of oral history involves numerous interviews with Thai and Lao participants. I have interviewed a number of senior *Force Armée Royal* (FAR) officers, including Major General Vang Pao, the commander of the CIA-supported irregular army in northeastern Laos. I also had a series of discussions with Major General Kong Le, the Lao army officer who staged an extraordinary and short-lived coup against his government in August 1960. During my unprecedented research visit to Laos in 1990 I was able to interview two Pathet Lao generals, Singkapo Sikhotchounamaly and Khamouan Boupha. I also discussed the war years with Sisana Sisane, a senior Lao Communist party official.

In Thailand I found that many of the Thai army's most senior officers had served in Laos or were otherwise involved in the U.S. aid program. Although interviews were difficult to obtain, I did speak with a number of knowledgeable Thai officers, including General Saiyud Kerdphol, formerly supreme commander of the Thai Armed Forces, and Major General Thammarak Isarangura of the Royal Thai Army.

The data I have collected allows me to address fundamental questions, the answers to which have eluded historians. These include: What were the international, regional, and internal Lao political and military issues that brought about the Geneva Conference of 1954? How was Laos affected by the Agreements of 1954? What were the specific actions of the United States as a result of these agreements? The 1962 Protocol to the Declaration on the Neutrality of Laos prohibited "the introduction of foreign regular and irregular troops, foreign paramilitary formations and foreign military personnel into Laos." Also prohibited was the "introduction into Laos of armaments, munitions and war material generally, except such quantities of conventional armaments as the Royal Government of Laos may consider necessary for the national defense of Laos." [10] What were the reactions of the United States, the Soviet Union, the People's Republic of China, North Vietnam, the Royal Lao government, and the Lao communists to these restrictions?

Specifically, in the wake of the 1962 prohibitions, what U.S. programs were established to provide military aid to the Royal Lao government? Why? What were the roles of the Department of Defense, the State Department, the U.S. Agency for International Development, and the Central Intelligence Agency in these activities, and why? Which organization had ultimate authority over these operations, and why? What was the level of cooperation among these various departments of government? At the local level, how were these programs organized and what was the degree of direct U.S. involvement? How did the U.S. military aid programs to Laos evolve from 1955 until 1975? What were the major modifications to the programs? How, and for what reasons, was the Royal Thai government involved in this effort? How effective were the U.S. military aid programs in terms of security for the Lao government?

In an effort to defend the Lao kingdom—and, more important, to disrupt the flow of communist arms, matériel, and soldiers traversing Laos en route to South Vietnam—the United States secretly created and administered a billion-dollar military aid program to Laos. What were the ultimate effects of this involvement in relation to U.S. objectives in the rest of Southeast Asia?

Arriving at answers to these questions has not been easy, and readers may disagree with some, perhaps many of them. They should remember that the views and conclusions expressed by me in this book are personal and do not reflect the official policies or positions of the Department of Defense or of the U.S. government.

ACKNOWLEDGMENTS

During the course of this study I have profited greatly from the expertise, support, and encouragement of many people. I am particularly grateful to Dr. Richard H. Immerman, Temple University of Hawaii. His excellence as a teacher and writer, availability for counsel, good humor, and commitment to a greater understanding of America's role in Southeast Asia made this work a reality. I also want to thank Dr. Thomas W. Gething, Dr. Jerry H. Bentley, Dr. Stephen Uhalley, and Dr. Truong Buu Lam, all of the University of Hawaii; Dr. William M. Leary, University of Georgia; Dr. Robert D. Schulzinger, University of Colorado; and Dr. Sandra C. Taylor, University of Utah.

A number of people within the Department of Defense assisted me in the research and writing of this book. Special thanks to Southeast Asia experts Dr. Timothy W. Wright and Major Anthony J. Litvinas. From the beginning of this project Colonel Martin L. Kaufman has been a valued friend and supporter. I tapped his unique knowledge of American military involvement in Laos, both in operational and support matters, on numerous occasions.

Former Air America employees who have aided me include Leon V. LaShomb, Fred F. Walker, Felix T. Smith, Theodore H. Moore, Thomas G. Jenny, and David H. Hickler. Thanks also to Continental Air Services pilot James M. MacFarlane.

Essential sponsorship for this study came from Lieutenant General Richard G. Trefry, U.S. Army, retired. General Trefry allowed me access to his extraordinarily comprehensive personal papers and helped me gain interviews with a number of knowledgeable senior civilian and military officials. Furthermore, despite his pressing White House duties, General Trefry took a personal interest in my field research and facilitated Defense and State Department approvals for my 1990 visit to Laos.

The recollections, writings, and support of other retired military officers have been indispensable. I am especially indebted to General John W. Vessey, Jr., General John W. Vogt, Jr., General William C. Westmoreland, Admiral Harry D. Felt, Admiral U.S. Grant Sharp, Lieutenant General James D. Hughes, Major General Charles R. Bond, Jr., Major General William C. Lindley, Jr., Major General James F. Kirkendall, Major General DeWitt R. Searles, Brigadier General Harry C. Aderholt, and Brigadier General Roswell E. Round, Jr. Colonel Peter T. Russell, Colonel Strathmore K. McMurdo, Lieutenant Colonal Ronald C. Hartwig, Lieutenant Colonel Dean R. Montanye, Lieutenant Colonel Stuart A. Beckley, Lieutenant Colonel John F. Guilmartin, Jr., and Major Don T. Cherry all provided valuable personal observations of the war in Laos.

Interviews in the United States with Lao and Hmong war participants added a critical perspective. Although my questions often rekindled painful memories, Major General Vang Pao and his family were very accessible and willing to recount their experiences. Similarly, Major General Kong Le retained his good humor through several lengthy interviews. Yang Teng, Moua Thong, Deth Soulatha—and a number of others who wish anonymity—described the war's impact on the Laotian people.

Preparation for my 1990 visit to Thailand and Laos was greatly aided by the suggestions of photo-journalist Roger Warner and Professor Joseph J. Zasloff, University of Pittsburgh. In Thailand General Saiyud Kerdphol, Major General Kanjana Juntranggur, and Major General Thammarak Isarangura provided very helpful information on Thai military involvement in Laos. Thanks also to Mr. Srichow Manitayakoon and Mrs. Nantana Sribunnak. Rich and Karn Arant's thoughtful offer of housing allowed me to live within walking distance of the U.S. Embassy in Bangkok.

My 1990 and 1991 visits to the Lao People's Demcoratic Republic required the concerted efforts of many people. Charles B. Salmon, Jr., Chargé d'Affaires at the American embassy in Laos and his highly efficient staff repeatedly lobbied the Lao government on my behalf. (In July 1992 U.S. diplomatic representation in Laos was reestablished at the level that existed before 1975; Mr. Salmon was appointed ambassador.) Their actions resulted in my obtaining rare interviews with a number of senior Lao government officials and unprecedented travel in northeastern and southern Laos. I particularly enjoyed the hospitality and insights of Karl E. Wycoff, R. Wayne Boyls, Gregory and Pattani Chapman, Rex Dufour, Robert W. Pons, and David C. Joyce. The embassy's Laotian employees, many of whom have signifcant contacts within the Lao government, were always helpful. The U.S. mission in Laos is routinely called upon to perform some of the most important and delicate work in the State Department; their dedicated and effective efforts deserve greater notice.

Within the Laotian government Sisana Sisane, Chairman of the Social Science Research Committee, spent several hours with me discussing his wartime experiences. General Khamouan Boupha, taciturn and insistent on knowing the details of my own military background, was a very difficult person to interview. Nonetheless, the former defense minister presented me with a very clear picture of life during the American bombing campaigns. General Singkapo Sikhotchounamaly, former commander of the communist Lao military, granted me two lengthy interviews. His candid recollections revealed previously unknown information on the fate of U.S military personnel lost in Laos during the war.

I must also express my appreciation to the colleagues, friends, and family members who assisted me throughout this long and often difficult period of research and writing. My greatest respect and thanks to my father, Willis R. Castle. Colonel Michael S. Elliott, my ''elder brother,'' brought to this project an extensive knowledge of Thailand and exceptional writing skills. Grateful thanks also to William R. Gadoury, Patricia Lane, Lieutenant Colonel William J. Williams, Leon and Betty Eberhard, Joy Elliott, Mark A. Borreliz, Major Lorry M. Fenner, Dr. Michael L. Grumelli, and Shella Malolepszy. To my wife, Parinya, and children, Jason and Jamie: thank you for understanding my strange hours, my mood swings, and the closed door to my study.

Last, I dedicate this book to my mother. My chosen path has taken many odd twists and turns, but she has always been there with support and encouragement.

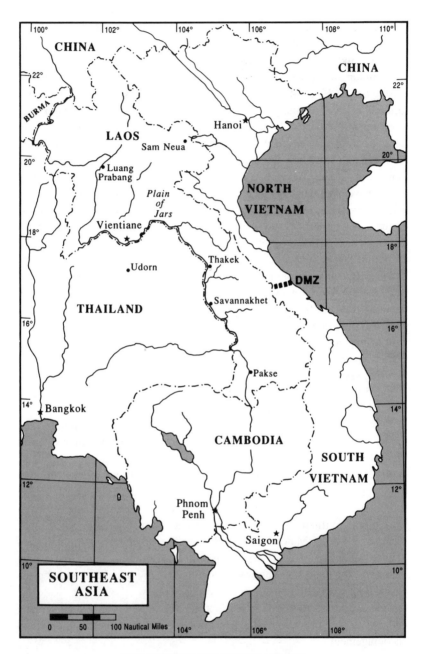

MAP OF MAINLAND SOUTHEAST ASIA

At War in the Shadow of Vietnam

Chapter One

INTRODUCTION

On December 2, 1975, the six-hundred-year-old Laotian monarchy was abolished and the Royal Lao government replaced by the Lao People's Democratic Republic. The demise of this small kingdom in the wake of previous communist victories in Cambodia and Vietnam was a bitter conclusion to America's thirty-year investment in Southeast Asia. The establishment of a communist government in Laos also ended a highly unorthodox and controversial American strategy that, since 1955, had charged the State Department, the Department of Defense, and the Central Intelligence Agency with secretly supplying military assistance to this technically neutral country.

Successive administrations developed and continued this unprecedented policy in response to communist violations of the Geneva Agreements of 1954 and 1962 and crafted it to avoid overt U.S. violations of the same agreements. These decisions spawned a multibillion-dollar U.S. aid program that came to include a complex military logistics network, a civilian-operated airborne resupply and troop movement system, a multinational ground and air force, and the introduction into Laos of a limited number of

U.S. military personnel. Staged primarily from Thailand, the program was made possible by the full cooperation of the Royal Thai government. Remarkably, from 1962 until 1975 the entire operation was commanded by the U.S. ambassador to Laos. As Admiral John S. McCain, commander in chief Pacific (CINCPAC), ruefully observed to his staff, "Laos is a SEC-STATE [Department of State] theater of war."[1] This book attempts to shed light on a secret American military aid program that, obscured in the shadow of Vietnam, fueled a unique and little-known war.

I will concentrate on U.S. military support to the Royal Lao government from the 1962 Geneva Accords, when the covert aid program to Laos was placed under the exclusive control of the U.S. ambassador, until 1975, when the communist victory terminated the program. However, because the policy's genesis can be traced to 1955, this study will also review American activities in Laos prior to the 1962 Geneva Accords.

U.S. military assistance to Laos took many forms and was often undertaken by ostensibly nonmilitary agencies and organizations. An important component of this study is an examination of the USAID Requirements Office (RO) in Laos. Staffed by former U.S. military officers, the RO functioned in the place of a formal Military Assistance Advisory Group (MAAG), which was prohibited by the 1962 Geneva Agreements.

The Central Intelligence Agency had extensive and unprecedented responsibilities in the management of military assistance to Laos.[2] This study will review, to the extent possible, the development and employment of CIA operations in support of the Royal Lao government, including the activities of the 4802d Joint Liaison Detachment (JLD), the CIA's headquarters for Laotian operations. In particular, I will examine the relationship between the 4802d JLD and the Lao irregular army based in northeastern Laos.

The CIA's proprietary airline, Air America Inc., was established, along with the 4802d JLD, at Udorn Royal Thai Air Force Base, Thailand.[3] Air America, operating both fixed-wing and helicopter aircraft, was assigned some of wartime Southeast Asia's most demanding and dangerous flying. The role of Air America in the supply and movement of troops and refugees, as well as in clandestine missions and search-and-rescue operations, was a vital component of the overall U.S. effort.[4]

Royal Thai government cooperation was integral to America's covert aid program to Laos. In addition to providing land for U.S.-built and -operated air bases and army facilities, the Thais established a covert military headquarters that assisted in the recruitment and training of Thai soldiers destined for duty in Laos. I will review the evolution of this U.S.–Thai cooperation and the impact of Thai support on the Lao military assistance program.

Although this is an examination of U.S. military assistance to Laos, I will not concentrate on the massive U.S. air campaigns waged against communist forces and equipment in Laos. The vast majority of these missions were conducted under the authority and direction of the commander of the United States Military Assistance Command Vietnam and his subordinate commands. Notwithstanding the importance of recognizing the U.S. ambassador's involvement in the selection of bombing targets—and his authority to disapprove these operations in Laos—this study will primarily consider those U.S. activities that directly bolstered the fighting capabilities of the Royal Lao government in the kingdom's critical northeastern region.[5]

A discussion of American involvement with the kingdom of Laos must begin with a basic question. Why was Laos important to the United States? A statistical summary of the modern kingdom of Laos is singularly unimpressive. As the prominent Southeast Asia scholar Bernard Fall observed, Laos was "neither a geographical nor an ethnic or social entity, but merely a political convenience."[6] Yet these very factors brought the kingdom to the forefront of international concern and attention. I begin, therefore, with a review of the land and people of Laos and an examination of the political and military factors that caused Laos to become the locus of a major Cold War struggle.

Geography

Laos is a landlocked, sparsely populated, mostly mountainous country located on the Indochinese peninsula.[7] After the 1954 Geneva Accords, the country was bordered on the east by North and South Vietnam (1,324 miles), on the north by the People's Republic of China (264 miles), and on the northwest by Burma (148 miles). On its southern border lay Cambodia (336 miles), and on its western border, Thailand (1,090 miles). The most prominent geographical features are the Annam Cordillera mountain range, which extends northward from the southern portion of Vietnam through Laos and into southern China and Tibet, and the Mekong River, which flows northwest to southeast.[8] Surrounded by more powerful neighbors intent on using its territory to support and wage war, Laos became locked by geographic fate into a long and devastating conflict.

The Plain of Jars, a high, rolling grassland located in the center of northern Laos, is also of particular significance to this study.[9] Dramatically beautiful and surrounded by some of the highest mountains in Southeast Asia, the area has historically been an important crossroads for commerce moving between Vietnam and the Mekong valley. These features have also given the plain an important strategic value. For centuries, armies have crossed through the area en route to wars to the north and south. This pattern continued during the Second Indochina War.

I visited the Plain of Jars in September 1990. Bomb craters, the result of heavy combat in the 1960s and 1970s, were still highly visible throughout the area. Moreover, there are a tremendous number of unexploded and potentially deadly munitions spread about the region. Normal endeavors, like farming and travel, are very dangerous. Deaths and serious injuries among local residents resulting from this hazard are a serious and continuing problem.[10] I will later discuss, in greater detail, military activity in this area.

Government and Society

The Lao constitutional monarchy—abolished by communist directive in December 1975—can be traced to Fa Ngum, who in 1353 became the first king of Lan Xang (Million Elephants).[11] The last sovereign, Savang Vatthana, exercised little power and influence. The constitution promulgated in 1947 vested paramount authority in the prime minister and the Council of Ministers. The National Assembly, elected every five years, was the principal legislative body.[12]

Although a formal census was not taken until 1985, the estimated population of Laos during the period of this study was three million.[13] Its density varied from less than 3 persons per square mile in the mountainous areas to 130 persons per square mile in the lowland areas along the Mekong River. There were forty-four areas officially classified as cities and towns. The five largest were Vientiane, the administrative capital, with a population of some 150,000; Luang Prabang, the royal capital, 25,000; Savannakhet, with about 39,000; Pakse, approximately 37,000; and Khammouane (or

Thakek), more than 13,000. The Royal Lao government administratively defined sixteen provinces and five military regions.[14]

The ethnic configuration of Laos can be usefully divided into four major categories:[15] Lao Lum (Valley), Lao Tai (Higher Valley), Lao Theung (Mountainside), and Lao Sung (Mountaintop). As the names indicate, these groups live separate from one another according to their traditional altitude. Consequently, Laos has historically suffered from an inherent disunity. The Lao Lum, or simply Lao, are a subgroup of the Tai people who originated in southern China. They represent between one-third and one-half of the population and are settled in the lowland areas along both sides of the Mekong River and its tributaries.[16] The Lao Lum comprise the most educated indigenous group and have dominated in the areas of commerce and government. They are predominantly Theravada Buddhists, and their faith directly influences everyday life in Laos. The royal family and all but a few of the ruling elite are ethnic Lao Lum.[17]

The Lao Tai are also a Tai people who migrated to Laos from southern China. Sometimes called the "tribal Tai," they comprise more than a dozen different subgroups; they live primarily in the upland river valleys and plateaus. They subsist by growing irrigated rice, by slash-and-burn farming, and sometimes by dry rice cultivation. In contrast to the Lao Lum, the Lao Tai have accepted little influence from Indian culture and generally avoid urban areas.[18] Some Lao Tai groups practice ancestor worship and there is universal belief among them in the presence and importance of *phi*, or spirits.[19] Lao Tai dialects are similar to the Lao Lum language. In the late 1960s the Lao Tai had an estimated population of 390,000.[20]

The Lao Theung, or "mountainside Lao," are often referred to as the *Kha*, (slave tribes) of Laos. Believed by the Lao Lum to have been the original inhabitants of Laos, they have suffered centuries of discrimination. Traditionally docile, they have been the least represented in the Royal Lao government. The Lao Theung prefer to live on mountain slopes above the Lao Tai and to grow rice by the slash-and-burn method. They practice a variety of religions from Buddhism to ancestor worship. The Lao Theung speak a Mon-Khmer language and had a population of 675,000 in 1969.[21]

The Hmong are the Lao Sung, or "mountaintop Lao." They are members of an ethnic group that has several million members living in the neighboring northern mountain areas of Burma, Thailand, Vietnam, and in the southern mountain regions of the People's Republic of China. Hmong movement out of southern China and into the northeastern mountains of

Southeast Asia is a relatively recent phenomenon. Pressured by the Han
Chinese, the Hmong began to migrate into northern Laos in the 1800s.
More aggressive and warlike than the indigenous peoples of Laos, the
Hmong met little resistance in claiming mountaintop homes throughout
northern Laos.[22]

Estimated in 1971 to number between 300,000 and 500,000 in Laos, the
Hmong prefer to live at elevations of between three and six thousand feet.[23]
Many believe that this protects them from ill health, unfriendly spirits, and
the disdain and discrimination of the lowland Lao Lum.[24] Upland rice,
raised by slash-and-burn farming, is the staple food of the Hmong. They
also cultivate potatoes, corn, and squash and raise chickens, pigs, cattle,
and water buffalo. Their most important crop, and traditional source of
cash, is the opium poppy.[25] Spirits, called Tlan, are an important part of
Hmong life. Although animists, the Hmong do have a concept of a supreme
being called Fua Tai who created all things.[26] The Hmong language is
assigned to the Sino-Tibetan language group.[27]

Submissive by nature and unable to grow more than bare subsistence
crops, the Lao Tai and Lao Theung have historically been dominated and
mistreated by the Lao Lum. In contrast, a valuable cash crop (opium base)
and independent lifestyle allowed the Hmong to live successfully outside
the sway of the Lao Lum–controlled central government. It is, therefore,
not a little ironic that the Hmong would be those called upon to defend their
less resolute countrymen and bear the brunt of communist aggression and
wartime brutality in Laos. What is even more incongruous is that these
proud and enigmatic people would be encouraged to fight not by the Lao
Lum, but by Americans determined to develop an effective indigenous Lao
fighting force.

Three Brothers and Lao Nationalism

Following the Japanese coup de main in March 1945,[28] a group of prominent Laotians led by the viceroy of Laos, Prince Phetsarath, joined to form
a nationalist movement opposed to the reimposition of French colonial
rule.[29] In October, when King Sisavang Vong called for a resumption of
the French protectorate, Prince Phetsarath formed a new government called
Lao Issara (Free Laos) to resist a French return. Phetsarath was aided in this
new government by his two younger brothers, Prince Souvanna Phouma
and Prince Souphanouvong.[30]

The Lao Issara, however, were no match for the returning French armed forces, and, by September 1946, Paris had regained control of the kingdom. The princes were forced to flee to Thailand where they established a government in exile.[31] In Bangkok, however, diverging personal ambitions soon split the group into three factions. Phetsarath was an "ambitious and shrewd aristocrat" who sought to place himself on the Lao throne. Souvanna Phouma, the pragmatist, doubted the wisdom of military action against the French and instead prepared quietly for a return "to a reconciled and unified nation, whose independence he felt was drawing near." Souphanouvong was "fiery, and quick-tempered . . . [and] advocated open war."[32] Moreover, to the distress of many Laotians, Prince Souphanouvong had increasingly involved himself with the communist Viet Minh movement in Vietnam.[33]

By late 1949 the royal brothers had gone their separate ways and the Lao Issara government in exile was formally dissolved. Souvanna Phouma accepted an offer of amnesty, returned to Laos, and within two years became prime minister. Phetsarath, piqued by King Sisavang Vong's refusal to reinstate his title of viceroy, chose to continue his exile.[34] Souphanouvong, resolute in his resistance to the French, obtained Viet Minh assistance and formed a guerilla organization called the Progressive People's Organization.[35]

In mid-August 1950 Souphanouvong convened a revolutionary congress at the Viet Minh headquarters north of Hanoi and proclaimed the formation of a new resistance government called the Land of Laos, or Pathet Lao. The political arm of this government would eventually be known as the Lao Patriotic Front (Neo Lao Hak Sat). Souphanouvong had made a momentous decision to join with the Viet Minh. From this point forward, the Vietnamese communists would support the Pathet Lao as military allies and ideological mentors.[36]

Indochina, America, and the Cold War

Post–World War II communist gains in Eastern Europe had convinced Washington that France should be returned to the status of a "Great Power." According to diplomatic historian George Herring, the "building [of] stable and prosperous Western European governments that could stand as bulwarks against Russian expansion" became critical to U.S. security objectives in Europe. In order to insure French support of American objectives in Europe, the United States pledged not to interfere with a French return to Indochina.[37] Seeking to bolster its new containment strategy in Europe, America ignored the national aspirations of the Vietnamese people and, in all likelihood, lost an opportunity to avert the devastating Franco–Viet Minh War.[38]

Moreover, during the next several years it became obvious that communist activity in Indochina was just as menacing, and certainly more lethal, than the spread of communism in Europe. By 1949 French forces had suffered more than thirty thousand casualties in their largely unsuccessful war against the communist Viet Minh.[39] The United States' concern was expressed on December 30, 1949, when National Security Council (NSC) Study 48/2 declared

> The United States on its own initiative should now scrutinize closely the development of threats from Communist aggression, direct or indirect, and be prepared to help within our means to meet such threats by providing political, economic, and military assistance and advice. . . . Particular attention should be given to the problem of Indochina.[40]

Seeking to stem the "Red Tide," the United States was moving quickly toward an interventionist policy in Southeast Asia.

America's Indochina involvement was increased when, on January 29, 1950, the French government established Vietnam, Laos, and Cambodia as autonomous "associated states" within the French Union. A week later the United States granted recognition to the new governments, opening the way for direct U.S. military and economic assistance.[41] Meanwhile, by early 1950, anticommunism was becoming a staple of American politics. Senator Joseph R. McCarthy and others were attacking the administration for the "loss" of China. Communism, it seemed, was on the march. In the *Saturday Evening Post,* influential journalist Stewart Alsop warned

> The head pin was China. It is down already. The two pins in the second row are Burma and Indochina. If they go, the three pins in the next row, Siam, Malaya, and Indonesia, are pretty sure to topple in their turn. And if all the rest of Asia goes, the resulting psychological, political and economic magnetism will almost certainly drag down the four pins of the fourth row, India, Pakistan, Japan and the Philippines.[42]

This alarmist scenario, coupled with the disclosure that in 1949 the Soviets had successfully tested an atomic device, jolted American priorities and prompted President Truman to request a review of foreign policy goals. The result was NSC Memorandum 68, "probably the longest, most detailed and perhaps the most important policy paper ever produced by the National Security Council." The memo, first drafted on April 7, 1950, concluded that "the cold war is in fact a real war in which the survival of the free world is at stake." On June 27, 1950, as part of Washington's response to the June 25 invasion of South Korea, President Truman announced that the United States would establish a military mission in each of the "associated states."[43] It was a fateful decision that ultimately led the United States into its most hotly debated and misunderstood war.

Bankrolling the French

On December 23, 1950 the United States, France, and the associated states of Vietnam, Laos, and Cambodia signed the Pentalateral Mutual Defense Assistance Pact and established procedures for the transfer of U.S. military aid to French forces in Indochina.[44]

"By 1952 the United States was bearing roughly one-third the cost of the war, but was dissatisfied with the results and found itself with no influence over French military policy."[45] Nevertheless, the United States felt compelled to continue military and economic aid to France. Explains Professor George G. Herring, "America's Indochina policy continued to be a hostage of its policy in Europe. . . . The French repeatedly warned that they could not furnish troops for European defense without generous American support in Indochina."[46] As a result the French continued to receive ever-increasing amounts of U.S. military aid.[47]

U.S. support notwithstanding, when Dwight D. Eisenhower became president in 1953 the war was going badly for the French. "In the campaign of 1952, the Republicans had attacked the Democrats for failing to halt the advance of [c]ommunism, and they were even more determined than their predecessors to prevent the fall of Indochina."[48] In early April 1953, however, the People's Army of Vietnam, having successfully captured the northern Tonkin provinces, turned west into Laos. The Viet Minh force consisted of four divisions commanded by General Vo Nguyen Giap and some two thousand Pathet Lao soldiers under the leadership of Prince Souphanouvong. These forty thousand men faced ten thousand Lao and three thousand French troops.[49] Giap hoped to capture the royal city at Luang Prabang, while at the same time attacking French and Lao positions on the Plain of Jars. The capture of Luang Prabang would deal a great psychological blow to the French and the Lao, and the loss of the plain would pose a direct threat to Vientiane. Yet another Viet Minh army would cross central Laos, reach the Mekong River, and thereby split the country in two.

The communist forces were successful in capturing the Lao border province of Sam Neua, and on April 19 Souphanouvong established his rebel headquarters in Sam Neua City. The army then moved toward the royal capital, where they met unexpected French resistance and the onset of the monsoon rains. These delays seem to have convinced the communist leadership that an attack was too dangerous, and they withdrew.[50]

Notably, the CIA's proprietary airline at that time, Civil Air Transport (CAT), provided important assistance to the beleaguered kingdom. From May 6th until July 16, 1953, a dozen CAT pilots, flying U.S. Air Force C-119 transports with French markings, dropped military supplies to French forces operating in Laos.[51] Thus, Civil Air Transport, later to become Air America, began its twenty-two year involvement with the hazardous mountains and jungles of Laos.[52]

The Viet Minh and Pathet Lao attack into Laos "shattered" President Eisenhower's confidence in the French and led him to believe that "if Laos were lost, the rest of Southeast Asia would follow and the gateway to India would be opened."[53] Over the next few months the "military and political situation in Indochina drastically deteriorated." By January 1954, the French had positioned approximately 13,000 men around the valley of Dien Bien Phu; the Vietnamese ringed the area with 49,500 combatants and 55,000 support troops.[54] In February the Viet Minh forces succeeded in placing their heavy weapons along the rim of the valley and looked down on the trapped French forces in anticipation of victory.[55] The French were faltering and, despite the objections of the United States, "in early 1954 agreed to place Indochina on the agenda of an East-West conference scheduled to meet in Geneva."[56]

President Eisenhower and his hard-line secretary of state, John Foster Dulles, were now forced to consider the possibility of a negotiated settlement in Indochina. They feared such a resolution would surrender Indochina to the communists and open the way for further communist gains in Asia and the Pacific. On the other hand, both were convinced that unilateral military intervention by the United States would be a grave mistake. Ultimately, President Eisenhower decided to wait for developments at the Geneva talks and on April 29, 1954, the National Security Council decided "to hold up for the time being any military action on Indo-China."[57] A week later, following a siege that lasted fifty-six days and resulted in the loss of more than eight thousand Viet Minh and two thousand French Union soldiers, General Giap's forces captured Dien Bien Phu.[58] The French Indochina empire had been dealt a mortal blow. Moreover, the United States would now have to consider the consequences of a communist government in Vietnam, and what steps might be taken to support "free world" countries in the region.

Geneva 1954

On May 8, 1954 representatives from France, the Soviet Union, the United States, the People's Republic of China, Great Britain, the Democratic Republic of Vietnam under Ho Chi Minh, the Republic of Vietnam under Bao Dai, and the kingdoms of Laos and Cambodia assembled in Geneva to work out a solution for Indochina. After much anguish and discord, the conferees agreed to partition Vietnam along the seventeenth parallel, with the Ho government in control of all territory north of the line. Addressing the future of Laos, Sir Anthony Eden, the British foreign secretary, declared that "Laos should remain as an independent and neutral buffer between China and Siam. It is therefore essential that the United States should not attempt to establish any military influence [there]. Any attempt to do so was bound to provoke some countermove by China."[59]

The conferees agreed, and on July 20, 1954, Laos was "reaffirmed as a unitary, independent state with a single government in Vientiane. A cease-fire was to take effect on August 6, and within 120 days all "Vietnamese People's Volunteers" were to leave the country. The Pathet Lao "were to regroup in the two northern provinces of Sam Neua and Phong Saly pending integration into the Lao army or demobilization . . . [and] all foreign powers except France were prohibited from establishing or maintaining bases in Laos."[60]

Predictably, the settlement in Geneva received a chilly reception in Washington.[61] At a news conference on July 21 President Eisenhower seemed anxious to distance the United States from the agreements. The president said he was "glad" that a consensus had been reached to end the bloodshed, but that the "agreements contain features which we do not like." The president was clearly thinking about the legitimization of the Ho Chi

Minh government and its effect on the rest of Southeast Asia. He pointed
out the United States was "not itself [a] party to or bound by the decisions
taken by the Conference."[62]

Thailand, America, and a Military Buildup

Indeed, the United States was moving quickly to counter the communist
gains in Vietnam. On August 20, 1954, President Eisenhower approved
National Security Council Policy Statement 5429/2, which said the United
States was to "make every possible effort, not openly inconsistent with the
U.S. government position as to the [Geneva] armistice agreements, to
defeat communist subversion and influence and to maintain and support
friendly non-Communist governments" in the region.[63] The kingdom of
Thailand "was to hold a central position in the new American strategy for
the region."[64] The policy statement recommended the United States provide military and economic assistance to the Thais and "concentrate efforts
on developing Thailand as a support of U.S. objectives in the area and as a
focal point of U.S. covert and psychological operations in Southeast Asia."[65]
The stage was set for the United States and the kingdom of Thailand to
expand covert activities against communist efforts in Southeast Asia.[66]

The Southeast Asia Collective Defence Treaty and the Pacific Charter,
signed in Manila on September 8, 1954, were a further demonstration of
America's measured response to communist expansion in Southeast Asia.
Under what was commonly called the Manila Pact, the United States,
Britain, France, New Zealand, Australia, Pakistan, the Philippines, and
Thailand agreed to form a regional defence organization called the Southeast Asia Treaty Organization (SEATO).[67] Although the Geneva Accords
prevented Laos, Cambodia, and South Vietnam from joining the association, a separate protocol extended SEATO protection to the former colo-
nies.[68]

The Manila Pact and the establishment of SEATO were seminal events
in the history of Thai-American relations. According to Thai specialist
R. Sean Randolph, "Thailand broke with its past by investing its future in
an explicit and only slightly qualified alliance with the United States."
Bangkok would now look to Washington for the "firmest possible American guarantee of Thailand's security."[69]

Foreign aid was an important lever against the spread of communism in
Southeast Asia, and the United States carefully structured its foreign aid to

Thailand to meet this specific security aim. According to international economist Robert J. Muscat the primary objectives of U.S. aid to Thailand "concerned no less than the integrity of the Thai state in the face of regional threats." [70] The result was the development, beginning in 1950, of a "two pronged economic and military aid relationship" between the United States and Thailand. [71]

The basis for this strategy was a September 19, 1950, "Economic and Technical Cooperation Agreement" and the October 17, 1950, "Mutual Defense Assistance Agreement." The first agreement quickly produced $8 million in economic aid and the establishment of a U.S. Operations Mission (USOM) to assist in Thai development. Within a month the Thai government was being assisted by "fifty technical experts working in the fields of agriculture, irrigation, transportation, communication, commerce, education, and public health." In October, the World Bank awarded Thailand a $25.5 million loan to assist "in the rehabilitation of the country's transportation and irrigation network." [72]

Military aid was substantial as well. A U.S. Military Assistance Advisory Group (MAAG) was assigned to Bangkok to "facilitate and supervise the training of the Thai armed forces and the distribution of military assistance." This assistance amounted to "$4.5 million in 1951, $12 million in 1952, and $56 million in 1953." [73]

The signing of the Manila Pact engendered ever greater military assistance. From 1954 to 1962 the United States provided Thailand approximately $97 million for "upgrading and construction of minimal facilities at seven Royal Thai Air Force bases, ten Royal Thai Army base camps, two Royal Thai Army hospitals, two Royal Thai Naval bases, and . . . ammunition-storage facilities." [74] Thailand was well on its way to becoming a "launching pad" for America's anticommunist stand in Southeast Asia.

Chapter Two

NEUTRALITY THAT DOESN'T WORK

On July 21, 1954, a day after signing the Agreement on the Cessation of Hostilities in Laos, the kingdom of Laos declared that it was "resolved never to pursue a policy of aggression and will never permit the territory of Laos to be used in the furtherance of such a policy." [1] This noble objective was doomed to fail.

Attempting to Make Geneva Work

The Geneva settlement affirmed political independence for Laos but did little to offer the kingdom military protection from the Pathet Lao and the North Vietnamese. However, because the Lao communists showed no inclination toward combat without Vietnamese assistance, the domestic threat could be relieved by assimilating the Pathet Lao leaders into the political process. Since the twenty-five thousand-man Royal Lao Army was no match for the People's Army of Vietnam (PAVN), the Lao government could only hope that international pressure would deter North Vietnamese aggression.[2]

Reconciliation between the Vientiane government and the Pathet Lao proved difficult. Major quarrels over election laws—and the dispatch of government soldiers to Pathet Lao "assembly areas" in Phong Saly and Sam Neua provinces—caused the Lao communists to boycott the general elections of 1955.[3] Nevertheless, Souvanna Phouma, who had become prime minister on March 21, 1956, pursued rapprochement with Souphanouvong, and in August the brothers issued two joint declarations. The first called for a joint commission to "work out details of a cease-fire, the administration of the provinces of Phong Saly and Sam Neua, and the integration of the Pathet Lao fighting forces into the Royal Army." The second agreement declared the intention to form a "National Union Government that would include representatives of the Pathet Lao."[4]

Further meetings in December 1956 produced agreement on the rights of the Pathet Lao to "conduct political activities like any other Laotian political party" and the promise that "after the formation of the coalition government, the administration as well as the fighting forces in the provinces of Phong Saly and Sam Neua would be placed under the authority of the new government."[5] Despite considerable dissent within the Lao National Assembly a coalition government was formed in November 1957, and the two provinces were formally returned to Royal control.[6] Prince Souphanouvong and Phoumi Vongvichit, another key Pathet Lao leader, assumed prominent positions in the new administration.[7] The Lao government had taken a decided turn toward the Left, a political change that caused American officials considerable discomfort.

The U.S. Presence in Laos

In September 1954 Charles W. Yost became the first U.S. ambassador to Laos.[8] Four months later the United States established a United States Operations Mission and set about to quickly bring American know-how to bear on the myriad problems of Laos.[9] Over the next year the USOM funded eleven nonmilitary projects at a cost of about $1.4 million. These programs included planned improvements in the areas of agriculture, public health, civil administration, and education.[10] The primary focus of USOM spending, however, was defense related.[11] "The ratio of funds devoted to

military and internal security purposes as compared to the amounts obligated to economic and technical assistance was approximately 4 to 1.''[12]
This responsibility created numerous problems for a small embassy which
was not structured or staffed to administer a military assistance program.

The difficulties at the U.S. mission in Laos posed a diplomatic dilemma
for Washington. Article Six of the Geneva settlement on Laos banned ''the
introduction into Laos of any reinforcements of troops or military personnel
from outside Laotian territory.''[13] The Eisenhower administration judged
the placement in Laos of a U.S. Military Assistance Advisory Group
(MAAG), the standard method of managing foreign military aid programs,
a contravention of the Geneva provision.[14] Consequently, while the United
States was determined to provide military aid to the kingdom of Laos,
Washington could not openly appear to violate the Geneva agreement.

The Program Evaluations Office

The predicament was solved in December 1955 when the U.S. State Department placed the management of American military assistance to Laos
under the control of a thinly disguised, but politically defensible, military
aid organization called the Program Evaluations Office (PEO). This decision set the precedent for nearly two decades of covert U.S. military aid to
the Royal Lao government.

The PEO was initially staffed by reserve, retired, and former U.S.
military personnel who were given U.S. State Department Foreign Service
Reserve Officer (FSRO) rank.[15]

> The mission of the PEO was two-fold: first to advise the US Ambassador
> and USOM on the military needs of the RLG [Royal Lao government]
> and assist in preparing the requests for MAP [Military Assistance Pro-
> gram] funds, and second to provide end-use observers for the military
> material already furnished to Laos. . . . PEO operated as a separate
> agency, with the Chief of PEO (CHPEO) acting as a member of the
> Country Team and reporting directly to the Ambassador. On purely
> military matters CHPEO reported directly to Commander in Chief, Pacific
> (CINCPAC), and DOD [Department of Defense], with information to the
> Ambassador.[16]

In February 1957, Brigadier General Rothwell H. Brown, U.S. Army,
retired, who had previously held senior MAAG positions in South Vietnam

and Pakistan, was appointed CHPEO. The organization expanded its activities to include "preparation of training plans and programs [and] improvements in training aids and instructor methods." The PEO, grudgingly respectful of the Geneva Accord prohibition against non-French military training units in Laos, perforce worked through the authorized French Military Mission (FMM).[17] This unsatisfactory arrangement would soon change.

From Left to Right

Laos held its national elections in May 1958, and the Pathet Lao and their supporters won thirteen seats in the fifty-nine seat Lao Assembly.[18] The U.S. Embassy, which had been working hard to prevent any communist representation in the government,[19] was greatly disturbed by Souvanna's earlier cabinet appointments and then stunned by the left-wing election victories. The U.S. Embassy halted all economic aid to Laos on June 30, forcing Prime Minister Souvanna Phouma from office.[20]

Phoui Sananikone, a pro-West diplomat, succeeded Souvanna in August 1958 and formed a cabinet that included four members of the anticommunist Committee for the Defense of National Interests (CDNI), also known as *les Jeunes*.[21] In the shuffle Phoui dropped Souphanouvong and Phoumi Vongvichit from the new government and appointed Souvanna Phouma ambassador to France.[22] The United States responded by resuming aid in October.[23]

On February 11, 1959, Phoui announced that his government considered "the application of the Geneva Agreements as fully accomplished and that, therefore, Laos was no longer bound by its provisions."[24] Three months later, in a move designed to weaken the Pathet Lao, the prime minister ordered the integration of the Pathet Lao military forces into the Royal Lao army.[25] On instructions from Souphanouvong the rebels refused and declared their intention to fight. This act of defiance prompted the Lao government to place Souphanouvong and several of his supporters under house arrest in Vientiane.[26]

By July 1959 the Pathet Lao had consolidated its military forces and launched an offensive against the Lao government.[27] Souphanouvong and fifteen other Pathet Lao leaders were then charged by the government with treason and placed in a jail just outside the capital. Souvanna's attempt to bring the Pathet Lao into the political process had failed, and the right-wing instigated purge reignited the civil war.[28]

The Heintges Plan

In November 1958 the Pentagon sent Brigadier General John A. Heintges, U.S. Army, to Laos to study the situation and recommend changes. After completing a comprehensive review in February 1959, General Heintges replaced General Brown as commander of the Program Evaluations Office.[29] Heintges favored an increased role for the PEO and deftly coordinated a new military assistance plan with Lao and French officials in Vientiane. Formal discussions of the plan in Washington and Paris resulted in the signing, in late May, of a U.S.-French Memorandum of Understanding. On July 23 the Lao government, at Washington's urging, publicly "requested" increased military aid from the United States.[30]

The Heintges plan allowed the U.S. a greatly expanded and more direct role in Lao military training. One important provision permitted U.S. "civilians" to act as "deputies" to French supervisors in the four Lao military regions. The United States could finally get men into the field where, Washington hoped, they could introduce the *Force Armée Royale* to more effective American training methods. The plan essentially elbowed aside the French Training Mission.[31]

To carry out the expanded mission the Departments of Defense and State approved

> Seventeen additional PEO personnel spaces and authority to contract for the services of an additional 103 ECCOIL technicians. By the end of 1959 the authorized strength of the PEO was 175 plus 190 contract personnel and 149 temporary-duty (TDY) Special Forces personnel for a total authorized strength of 514. Of the total of 514 authorized at the end of 1959, 428 were on hand, an actual strength 21 times greater than a year earlier.[32]

The Filipino technicians were employees of the recently formed Eastern Construction Company in Laos (ECCOIL). Headed by "Frisco" Johnny San Juan, a Filipino with close ties to Philippines President Ramon Magsaysay, the ECCOIL cadre were combat veterans of World War II and of Philippine government campaigns against the communist Huk guerrillas. They were a "third country" element which would remain an important part of the U.S. military aid program to Laos for many years to come.[33]

The other major new component in the U.S. strategy was the deployment in Laos of U.S. Army Special Forces Field Training Teams (FTTs). Twelve eight-man modified "A" teams and a control detachment from the 7th Special Forces Group at Fort Bragg, North Carolina, arrived in Laos between the 24th and 31st of July, 1959. Although the FTTs remained in Laos for no more than six months before being replaced by fresh U.S. Green Berets, their in-country presence and the plan they sought to implement represented a critical change in U.S. policy toward Southeast Asia.[34] Unfortunately, the six-month tours hampered efforts to build foreign language proficiency and important professional relationships between the Special Forces soldiers and their trainees.[35]

The CIA and les Jeunes

In December 1959 a political crisis erupted in the Phoui Sananikone government. The prime minister, troubled by the growing strength of the Lao right-wing, decided to remove the CDNI members of his cabinet. With CIA encouragement, the Lao army reacted by seizing control of the government. Brigadier General Phoumi Nosavan, one of the CDNI members Phoui sought to remove, emerged as the leader of the coup.[36] The general orchestrated the formation of a new government, and Kou Abhay, head of the King's Council and a Phoumi supporter, became prime minister on January 7, 1960.[37]

National elections were held as scheduled in April 1960, but the Lao army and the CIA ensured that there was no repeat of the earlier Pathet Lao victories. In the communist stronghold of Sam Neua, the Pathet Lao candidate "received a total of 13 votes to the successful candidate's 6,508." In southern Laos, a Pathet Lao candidate received four votes to the opposition's 18,189, "although there were at least 5 members of his immediate family eligible to vote for him."[38] According to Arthur Dommen, "CIA agents participated in the election rigging, with or without the authority of the American Ambassador." A U.S. embassy officer reported that he had seen "CIA agents distribute bagfuls of money to village headmen."[39] Following the right-wing victory, Prince Somsanith, a close associate of General Phoumi, was named by the king to succeed Kou Abhay as prime minister.[40]

The Great Escape

One of the new regime's first scheduled tasks was to bring Souphanouvong and the other confined Pathet Lao leaders to public trial. However, Souphanouvong and his comrades escaped on May 23rd and made their way to

Sam Neua province. According to prisoner Sisana Sisane, the Pathet Lao leaders simply "prepared the guards with political education" and were able to slip away.[41] Since the jail was located within the headquarters of the Lao provost marshal (chief of the military police), the escape was viewed by most diplomatic observers as yet another embarrassing demonstration of the Royal Lao government's ineptitude. But was it?

Major General Oudone Sananikone of the Royal Lao Army, writing in 1978, said "the escape was engineered and ordered by none other than Phoumi Nosavan himself. A truck was provided, the gate was unlocked, the guards assisted, and the Pathet Lao leaders drove out of Vientiane."[42]

It is impossible to know what really happened that day. Souphanouvong and his fellow prisoners were skilled political propagandists quite capable of eliciting support from both common soldiers and senior Lao army officers. A public trial would have created unwanted problems for General Phoumi and the new government.[43] It seems likely, therefore, that the escape was the result of long talks with sympathetic guards and the agreeable and mostly nonviolent nature of the high command of the Lao army.

The Phoumi-controlled government virtually guaranteed the United States a commanding influence in Laotian affairs. By early August 1960 Washington was optimistic about the future of Laos and quite unsuspecting of the next bizarre turn in Lao politics.

The Kong Le Coup

In addition to the threats of internal rebellion and external invasion, long-standing political intrigue and bickering among the Lao military and civilian elite seriously undermined the stability of Laos. The king was no more than a compliant figurehead who routinely acquiesced to the prevailing authority in Vientiane. Real power in Laos was vested in about twenty powerful lowland Lao families.[44]

Throughout the summer of 1960 Captain Kong Le,[45] an aggressive American-trained FAR battalion commander, became increasingly exasperated with his government.[46] On August 9, 1960, reacting to widespread corruption and the indifferent treatment of common soldiers, Kong Le and his U.S. Special Forces-trained paratroop battalion seized control of Vientiane. Kong Le declared he would end corruption in the military and political bureaucracies and stop the Lao civil war. Most of all, he wanted an end to foreign interference in his country. He later claimed "American aid had corrupted many government officials. The goal of U.S. aid was good, but the program created too many opportunities for corruption. It had to be stopped."[47] Kong Le insisted the government of Laos return to a "policy of genuine neutrality" which, he believed, would allow the country to avoid being overpowered by foreign influences.[48]

The coup met little resistance. A day earlier Prime Minister Somsanith, General Phoumi, and most of the Lao cabinet had flown to Luang Prabang for a conference with King Savang Vatthana.[49] General Phoumi, upon learning of the coup, first flew to Bangkok for consultations with Prime Minister Sarit Thanarat of Thailand and then went to his personal power base in the southern Lao town of Savannakhet to prepare for counteraction. Somsanith and the cabinet ministers awaited developments in Luang Prabang.[50]

Arthur Dommen portrays the initial U.S. reaction to the coup as indecisive and ambiguous. The State Department "advised Ambassador Brown to take such action as would remove Kong Le from the scene as expeditiously as possible," but provided "no specific orders" and then sent "conflicting suggestions."[51] Consequently, newly arrived Ambassador Winthrop G. Brown exerted little calming influence over the spreading chaos.

Kong Le, recognizing his political and administrative limitations, sought assistance from Souvanna Phouma in the formation of a new government. The prince responded favorably, but insisted that the National Assembly agree to any change in the government. Under pressure from Kong Le and Souvanna supporters, the Assembly voted on August 13 to replace Somsanith with Souvanna.[52] Prince Somsanith stepped down and Souvanna formed a new cabinet on August 16.

General Phoumi, however, was unwilling to accept the change. Despite a visit from Souvanna and an initial pledge that Phoumi be a member of the new cabinet, the general decided to stage his own coup.[53]

Two Governments

On September 10, 1960, General Phoumi Nosavan announced the formation of a "Revolutionary Committee" headed by fellow southerner Prince Boun Oum. Phoumi abrogated the Lao constitution and, with the assistance of a Thai-imposed blockade of Vientiane, prepared to retake control of the government.[54] The United States—faced with a legitimate government in

Vientiane headed by a neutralist, and a rebel group in Savannakhet led by a right-wing general friendly to the U.S.—initially took a wait-and-see attitude.[55]

Nevertheless, Souvanna pressed the United States, which had already suspended cash-grant aid to Vientiane at the time of the coup, to overturn the Thai blockade. The United States refused, and on October 4 Souvanna announced his intention to establish diplomatic relations with the Soviet Union. The prince then further damaged his relations with the United States by inviting the Pathet Lao to participate in discussions aimed at a new coalition government. The Pathet Lao responded favorably and ordered its units to "avoid clashes with the forces loyal to Souvanna Phouma, in the interests of combining in the fight against General Phoumi's troops." Concurrently, "the Pathet Lao capitalized on the internal conflict . . . [and seized] full control of the villages and territories in the mountainous areas."[56]

The United States halted all military aid to the Vientiane government on October 7 and announced that the former ambassador to Laos, J. Graham Parsons—now Assistant Secretary of State for Far Eastern Affairs—would conduct personal negotiations with Souvanna. Parsons arrived in Vientiane on October 12 and presented the prime minister with three conditions for U.S. support: a cessation of negotiations with the Pathet Lao; a guarantee that Souvanna would negotiate with General Phoumi; and the relocation of the Royal Lao administrative government to Luang Prabang where, Washington believed, the king could exert a conservative influence. Souvanna Phouma immediately rejected the conditions and decided to look elsewhere for assistance.[57]

The following day Souvanna began negotiations with Aleksandr N. Abramov, the recently arrived Soviet ambassador to Laos. They reached an agreement "in principle," and the prime minister announced in late October that he would be "very happy" to receive Soviet assistance. The United States actively began efforts to topple the Souvanna Phouma government.[58]

A "Rump" PEO

U.S. forces and matériel were an important part of General Phoumi's plan to retake the Laotian capital. Shortly after the Kong Le coup the U.S. Embassy established a Deputy Chief Program Evaluations Office in Savannakhet and manned it with about fifteen officers and twenty-five enlisted men. Following Souvanna Phouma's decision to negotiate with the Pathet

Lao, the U.S. Embassy ordered this southern PEO to "arrange for organizing, training, and equipping Phoumi's forces and to produce a campaign plan whose details were essentially US but were presented to Phoumi's subordinate commanders as Phoumi's plan." [59]

Air America, no stranger to Laos and covert activity, was ordered by the CIA to deliver supplies to General Phoumi's forces in southern Laos. According to an official U.S. Air Force history, "substantial deliveries were made by [Air America] contract C-46s and C-47s to the royalist base at Savannakhet." [60] The Phoumi forces were also augmented by the arrival of two hundred Lao paratroops who had just completed training in Thailand. The PEO brought the men to Savannakhet in contravention of Souvanna's orders. [61]

The Soviet and Chinese Factor

In early December Russian planes began ferrying fuel and military equipment into the Lao capital. [62] Quinim Pholsena, a member of Souvanna's cabinet, had signed a deal with the Russians in which it was agreed that "in exchange for a formal alliance between Kong Le's troops and the Pathet Lao, the Russians would airlift into Laos arms and supplies for the resistance against General Phoumi's American-supplied troops. [63]

According to the U.S. State Department, "the Soviets made at least 34 flights to Vientiane between December 3 and December 14, 1960." [64]

The People's Republic of China (PRC) was not a disinterested party in this Lao government version of "musical chairs." American involvement in both the ouster of the earlier Souvanna government and the coup against Phoui Sananikone had confirmed PRC suspicions about U.S. motives in the region.

The impending collapse of the neutralist-oriented Kong Le–Souvanna Phouma government was viewed by Peking as yet another blow to Chinese communist influence in Laos, with a corresponding gain for the United States. In November Souvanna had agreed "to accept aid from Peking and Hanoi and to send an economic and cultural delegation to both capitals." A Phoumi-dominated government would reverse this policy, and the Chinese foresaw an even stronger undesirable American presence in Laos. [65]

Phoumi's Victory

By late November 1960 General Phoumi's army, with the support of U.S. advisors, Thai technicians, and Air America, had begun a march up National Route 13 toward Vientiane.[66] On December 9, as Phoumi's troops came within striking distance of the capital, Souvanna delegated his powers to the "High Command of the Army" and left for exile in Phnom Penh, Cambodia.[67]

On December 12 General Phoumi gathered thirty-eight members of the National Assembly in Savannakhet. The representatives passed a motion of no confidence in Souvanna's now exiled administration, and the next day the king approved a change in government. Prince Boun Oum became prime minister. The United States announced its full support of the new government and stated that Phoumi was "politically free" to retake Vientiane.[68]

Phoumi's units launched their attack on December 13 and, after three days of heavy artillery fire in which more than five hundred civilians were killed or injured, the Kong Le forces withdrew from the city.[69] An American diplomat celebrated with a champagne party, while the Russian ambassador "watched a group of Phoumi's soldiers pull down and destroy the Soviet flag."[70]

A Neutralist–Pathet Lao Base on the Plain of Jars

Kong Le and his men easily made their way north along National Route 13. Resupplied by Soviet IL-14 aircraft, the neutralists captured the small town of Vang Vieng, located fifty-five miles from Vientiane. On December 31 several Soviet aircraft landed at Vang Vieng, picked up the rebels, and successfully parachuted Kong Le and his soldiers onto the southern edge of the Plain of Jars. The combined Pathet Lao–Kong Le forces then drove the Royal government soldiers off the plain. "By 3 January 1961, every strategic road junction on the plain was under the control of pro-communist troops." The Soviets quickly adjusted their airlift to the plain.[71]

Lieutenant Colonel Butler B. Toland, Jr., U.S. Air Force attaché to Laos, obtained the first photographic evidence of this escalation in Soviet aid on December 16, 1960. Colonel Toland, flying a USAF VC-47 from Luang Prabang to Vientiane, happened to sight a Soviet aircraft circling near Vang Vieng. He closed on the IL-14 and, from a distance of about one hundred feet, photographed the transport as it dropped supplies. A few minutes later the Soviet plane turned north, and Toland flew on to Vientiane.[72]

A week later two USAF assistant air attachés were flying the VC-47 on a reconnaissance mission over the Plain of Jars when the aircraft was struck by .50 caliber machine gun rounds fired from a suspected communist position. "The radio operator was struck by a ricocheting bullet. About 14 or 15 holes were sustained in the aircraft."[73] This was the first incident in Southeast Asia of a USAF aircraft flown by active-duty military pilots being struck by communist ground-fire.[74]

Moving Toward Superpower Confrontation

On the international political front, Washington and Moscow were trading allegations of interference in Laotian affairs. In a diplomatic note of December 13 the Soviets charged the United States with "flouting the sovereign rights of the Laotian government headed by Prince Souvanna Phouma and with extending overt support to the rebel forces of Phoumi Nosavan." The U.S. responded on December 17 by condemning the "Soviet action in airlifting weapons and ammunition in Soviet planes to rebel military forces fighting the loyal armed forces of the Royal government."[75] Three days later the United States increased its airlift support to Laos. At the direction of the Joint Chiefs of Staff (JCS), the U.S. Navy transferred four H-34 helicopters to Air America and readied a U.S. Marine Corps maintenance and mobile-training team to assist the CIA in resupplying the FAR.[76]

Just as U.S. aerial support to General Phoumi's forces was an important factor in reclaiming Vientiane from Kong Le, the Soviet airlift was equally significant in resupplying the Pathet Lao and their new neutralist allies. During the final two weeks of 1960 the Soviets "flew more than 180 sorties into Laos in support of Kong Le and the Pathet Lao."[77] The airlift was quite exceptional. According to Soviet Deputy Foreign Minister Georgy M. Pushkin, the Soviet airlift was, "apart from the Second World War . . . the highest priority Soviet supply operation since the Revolution."[78]

By December 1960 the conflict in Laos had, tragically, developed into a war supported by competing external forces. Moreover, the increasing levels of Soviet and American air power in Laos underscored the unyielding determination of Moscow and Washington to support their surrogates, even at the risk of a direct superpower confrontation in the mountains and jungles of Laos.

Chapter Three

CONFLICT, DIPLOMACY, AND COVERT OPERATIONS

On December 31, 1960, senior military and intelligence advisors gave President Dwight D. Eisenhower a very disquieting briefing on Laos. The Soviets were maintaining their extraordinary airlift of military aid to the Pathet Lao–neutralist forces on the Plain of Jars. Intervention in Laos by the Chinese or the North Vietnamese, or both, seemed a distinct possibility. Despite hundreds of millions of dollars in U.S. military and economic aid the Royal Lao government appeared on the verge of losing control over more than half the kingdom. Eisenhower declared at the conclusion of the meeting, "We cannot let Laos fall to the [c]ommunists even if we have to fight . . . with our allies or without them." [1] Laos had become a potential flash-point for international conflict and the president "regretted deeply" that his administration had "left a legacy of strife and confusion in Laos." [2]

Kennedy Inherits Laos

On January 19, 1961, President-elect John F. Kennedy held a final transition meeting with President Eisenhower during which the two focused on "points of crisis, and especially on the mounting crisis in Laos." Eisenhower expressed his view that Laos was the "key to Indochina." If necessary, the United States should "intervene unilaterally" to prevent a communist takeover.[3] The talk confirmed Kennedy's earlier concerns over U.S. involvement in the Lao muddle.[4] When he became the thirty-fifth president of the United States the next day, the strife in Laos became the first foreign policy challenge for Kennedy's new team of "action intellectuals."[5]

Meeting the communist threat to Laos was a problem that consumed a striking amount of the new president's time. Arthur M. Schlesinger, Jr., then a special assistant to President Kennedy, has written that in "the first two months of his administration he [Kennedy] probably spent more time on Laos than on anything else."[6] According to Walt W. Rostow,

> Kennedy was not about to see Laos fall to the communists; but every experience of the situation in his first weeks of responsibility drove him to the conclusion that American forces should not engage there, if there was any way to avoid it. . . . Kennedy's task, as he saw it, was to convince the communists that he would, in fact, fight if necessary to avoid a communist takeover while seeking a political settlement.[7]

Laos, a country with little intrinsic value, had become an important chip in a deadly serious superpower poker game. According to the *Pentagon Papers,* the CIA concluded in early 1961 that the other governments of Southeast Asia were inclined "to regard the Laotian crisis as a symbolic test of strengths between the major powers of the West and the Communist bloc."[8] Kennedy was cognizant that in capitals from Saigon to Moscow his reaction to events in Laos was being carefully monitored and evaluated.[9]

The Phoumi-Souvanna Gambol

The New Year in Laos was marked by the continued political posturing of General Phoumi and Prince Souvanna Phouma. On January 4, 1961, the Boun Oum government received a vote of confidence from the Lao National Assembly, and the king formally accepted Boun Oum and his cabinet. General Phoumi, the dominant personality in Vientiane, became deputy prime minister and minister of defense.

Souvanna Phouma, from his exile in Phnom Penh, rejected the investiture as illegal and continued to receive Soviet support and encouragement for his neutralist forces.[10] The prince insisted that his centrist philosophy alone could bring together the Phoumists, neutralists, and the Pathet Lao to create a united Laotian government. Seeking support for his position and responding to a plea for reconciliation from King Savang Vatthana, Souvanna returned to Laos on February 20.

The prince flew by Soviet aircraft to the Plain of Jars and convened a strategy meeting with his cabinet in the small town of Khang Khay. Souvanna found, settled in among the rebel Lao soldiers, Czech and North Vietnamese "information offices," an "economic and cultural delegation" from Beijing, a North Vietnamese tent hospital, a full Soviet embassy, and a dozen Russian aircraft maintenance personnel. Russian 37 mm. radar-directed antiaircraft guns protected the entire area. The Plain of Jars, as Arthur Dommen aptly writes, "was becoming a mirror image of the PEO compound in Vientiane." [11]

Following the cabinet discussions Souvanna established contact with General Phoumi's representatives, and the parties agreed to a summit meeting. Souvanna and Phoumi met in Phnom Penh in mid-March, but the talks produced little substance. In a joint announcement the leaders declared their strong opposition to foreign interference and their desire for a genuinely neutral Laos. [12] The words had a fatuous ring, however, as Phoumi returned to a government financed and armed by the United States, and Souvanna's legitimacy was propped up by an alliance with the Pathet Lao and their communist advisors.

Signaling Resolve

In early February 1961 President Kennedy formed an interagency task force to examine U.S. policy toward Laos. The group included Assistant Secretary of State J. Graham Parsons, Deputy Assistant Secretary of State John Steeves, Assistant Secretary of Defense for International Security Affairs Paul H. Nitze, NSC staffer Walt W. Rostow, and others from the military, the State Department, and the CIA. The task force held extensive meetings and in a February 28 memorandum from Walt Rostow, provided the president with an interim assessment of the situation:

> The good general [Phoumi Nosavan] has been politicking rather than using his forces to increase our bargaining position in the negotiations ahead. . . . It is believed that the time may not be inappropriate for us to make a show of strength and determination, since the Soviet air supply continues unabated. [13]

On March 9, 1961, the task force, along with Admiral Felt, CINCPAC, met with the president and recommended a "seventeen-step escalation ladder" of possible American responses to the communist's movements in Laos. The most drastic option called for the occupation of southern Laos by sixty thousand U.S. soldiers. The troops would be supported by air cover and, in the event of Chinese or Vietnamese reaction, nuclear weapons would be available for use against the Communists.[14]

Apart from confronting the immediate problems associated with the crisis in Laos, the presidential meeting exposed institutional differences in strategy and coordination between the Departments of State and Defense. On March 10 a concerned Walt Rostow wrote the president:

> the Department of State has an understandable instinct to conduct pure diplomacy with minimum involvement with the CIA and the military until an acute crisis occurs. The tendency is then to turn the problem over almost wholly to those who control force, and to get the hell out. This is the pattern which produces the uneasy relations between State and the Pentagon which surfaced yesterday.[15]

The president agreed, and the lessons learned during the debate on Laos would soon lead Kennedy to undertake unprecedented changes in the implementation and management of U.S. foreign policy.

At the conclusion of the March 9 meeting President Kennedy decided to start up the "escalation ladder" and ordered an Okinawa-based U.S. contingency force, Task Force 116, to "alert" status. He also directed that units of the Seventh Fleet stand by in the South China Sea and the Gulf of Siam.[16] The Soviets, according to a presidential aide, would now have to decide whether to opt for "a cease-fire and neutralization . . . or American intervention."[17]

The Kennedy White House, after more than two months of study and debate, was setting the stage for direct U.S. military intervention in Laos. But the "action intellectuals" had also decided concurrently to pursue an unconventional solution to the Lao imbroglio.

Preparing for a Covert War

During the March 9 conference Kennedy authorized the transfer of sixteen U.S. Marine Corps H-34 helicopters to the CIA for use by Air America.[18] On March 22 three hundred U.S. Marines assigned to Task Force 116 arrived at Udorn, Thailand, fifty miles south of Vientiane, to organize a helicopter repair and maintenance base. Six days later the H-34's were flown from a U.S. Navy ship to Bangkok.[19] The following day, military and Air America pilots flew the helicopters to Udorn. Air America thereby established its extraordinary Thailand headquarters, precipitating an operation which was to become the cornerstone of American activities in Laos.[20]

The presidential orders of March 1961 inaugurated a policy that would characterize American military activity in Laos for more than a dozen years: extensive CIA paramilitary operations supported by Thailand-based, covert U.S. military agencies.

The FAR Farce

The possibility of American military intervention in Laos evinced a well-founded Pentagon conviction that the Royal Lao Army (FAR) was incapable of defending the kingdom. Recent intelligence reports showed that Pathet Lao soldiers, joined by North Vietnamese "advisers," were easily achieving daily territorial gains against the Royal Lao government.[21] The U.S. military believed, however, that with improved training the FAR could be prepared to fight limited engagements. Thus, while the White House ordered U.S. troops readied for possible deployment into Laos, the PEO increased its efforts to strengthen Phoumi's army.

Building a combat effective Lao army was a difficult task. Leadership and morale in the FAR was extremely poor; it was not unusual for the Lao general staff to send units into the field without proper training or equipment. The Franco-American military training program, an uneasy arrangement at best, had ceased to exist in February 1961 when the French withdrew from the plan.[22]

Continued rebel successes and the loss of the French instructors prompted the PEO to request 9 more Special Forces Field Training Teams and an additional 121 ECCOIL technicians. By March 1961 the PEO had posted American advisers to many of the FAR combat units and was conducting much-needed training in rear areas.[23] Nevertheless, the FAR battalions remained in a highly precarious state.

> Instances were reported of the collapse of [FAR] units that had no US advisors with them or whose advisors did not stay with the CO [commanding officer] through the engagement. In cases where it was reported

that the advisors withdrew, they were immediately followed by the officers of the unit, after which the unit itself panicked.[24]

As a result, in mid-April 1961, CINCPAC recommended to the Joint Chiefs of Staff that American advisors be authorized to "participate in combat operations . . . should the situation so require." Previous guidance on this subject seems to have been intentionally ambiguous, but most advisors understood the importance of avoiding situations where "capture seemed imminent." While the response of the JCS is not known, from this point forward "US advisors appear to have increasingly stayed with [FAR] units during combat operations."[25]

The apparent policy change acknowledged the willingness of the United States to accept the risks of American soldiers in Laos being captured, injured, or even killed. Unfortunately, and perhaps inevitably, the decision quickly cost American lives.

The Loss of Team Moon

On March 9, 1961, communist soldiers captured a vital road junction between Luang Prabang and Vientiane. FAR units, ordered to counterattack the enemy, responded in panic by "throwing away their guns and fleeing for safety to the surrounding mountains."[26] In the wake of the debacle U.S. Special Forces FTT 59, "Team Moon," was assigned to rebuild and advise the dispirited forces.

The Royal troops were returned to the offensive, and heavy fighting continued along Route 13 for more than a month. On April 22, following a "heavy and accurate artillery barrage," Pathet Lao soldiers overran Team Moon's position. Sergeants Bischoff and Biber were killed by grenade and machine gun fire. Captain Moon and Sergeant Ballenger were captured. Moon, after two escape attempts, was executed by his guards. Ballenger was released by his captors sixteen months later.[27]

It was painfully obvious that the FAR, after receiving some $350 million in U.S. assistance and being bolstered by American advisers, was still no match for the Vietnamese-assisted Pathet Lao–neutralist forces.[28]

From PEO to MAAG

Captain Moon and his men did not die as "civilian" advisors. On April 19, 1961, President Kennedy had authorized the Program Evaluations Office to operate openly as a uniformed Military Assistance Advisory Group (MAAG).

> As long as the US was "officially" abiding by the 1954 Geneva Agreements and the French were in the military training picture, it was useful for the US to staff the PEO on a semicovert basis. Since in 1961 these conditions no longer prevailed there was no reason to continue what had been in effect an open secret.[29]

Still, it was no coincidence that the order came on the heels of the failed Cuban refugee invasion of Cuba. "Fearing that the communists in Asia might interpret his decision [to abort the operation] as irresolution," Kennedy authorized an immediate change to a MAAG.[30]

Brigadier General Andrew J. Boyle, U.S. Army, who had succeeded General Heintges in January 1961, became the chief of MAAG, Laos. The U.S. Army Special Forces units in Laos also received a name change. Previously, the teams had been known by various code-names ("Foretell," "Monkhood," "Molecular," "Footsore") or simply by the name of the team leader. From this point forward the soldiers were designated "White Star Mobile Training Teams" (WSMTTs).

The White Star advisors, about 150 men divided into twelve different teams, were assigned to all levels of the Laotian military. Their duties "ranged from individual weapon instruction to basic and advanced unit training . . . supervision of artillery training, construction projects, [and] assistance in communication and logistics."[31] White Star teams were also engaged in training "irregular forces to carry out guerilla and antiguerilla operations."[32]

"Rose Bowl" and U.S. Intelligence Collection

As the Lao military and political situation continued to whirl in confusion, the White House ordered an increase in U.S. intelligence collection in Laos. The decision-makers were particularly concerned over the paucity of information on the communist build-up on the Plain of Jars.[33] But the 1954 Geneva Agreements prohibited the United States from sending to Laos its most capable intelligence-collection aircraft. As mentioned earlier, airborne intelligence gathering in Laos was initially conducted by a single VC-47 airplane assigned to the USAF air attaché to Laos.

The USAF improved the situation in early January 1961 by dispatching to Laos a specially configured SC-47 reconnaissance aircraft, dubbed "Rose Bowl." The new plane had a larger crew, a substantially increased fuel capacity, radio direction-finding equipment, and a K-17 camera.[34]

During January and February Rose Bowl flew almost every day taking "miles of photography." Concurrently, the airmen were "scanning radio bands" in an attempt to pinpoint the location of a communist radio beacon. For some time the crew had been frustrated by the ability of the Soviets to land their IL-14s at Xieng Khouang in bad weather. "We'd go up there in the worst kind of damn weather . . . watch them and they'd make a circle and start an approach and go down. We knew of course that it was a radio . . . we [just] couldn't pick it up."[35]

On March 23, 1961, the Rose Bowl crew was scheduled to fly to Saigon for rest and relaxation. Instead of proceeding directly to Saigon the aircraft commander decided to make a reconnaissance run over the Plain of Jars. The SC-47, according to two different sources, violated standing orders and flew over Xieng Khouang airfield at an altitude of thirty-five hundred feet. The airplane was hit by gunfire, caught fire, and immediately crashed to the ground. Major Lawrence R. Bailey, Jr., a U.S. Army attaché catching a ride to Saigon, was the only survivor. Bailey was captured by the Pathet Lao and imprisoned in Sam Neua for seventeen months.[36]

The SC-47 shoot-down prompted the Pentagon to deploy the more advanced and less vulnerable RT-33 jet reconnaissance aircraft to mainland Southeast Asia. The United States concealed the effort by painting Lao markings on a borrowed Philippine Air Force RT-33. RT-33 surveillance missions, called "Field Goal," began from Udorn, Thailand, on April 24, 1961. Three weeks later, in an effort to strengthen regional air defenses, the U.S. moved six F-100 fighter aircraft from the Philippines to Bangkok.[37]

Public Posturing

As Major Bailey was being interrogated by his communist captors, President Kennedy began an unprecedented television address and press conference on Laos.[38] The White House shrewdly scheduled the talk for the American dinner hour and arranged for the president's remarks to be broadcast live world-wide over the Voice of America. It was a strong message calculated to "convey to the Communists his mounting concern and resolution."[39]

Implicitly reciting the lessons of Munich, he highlighted the growing seriousness of the Lao crisis and expressed his hope for a settlement.

> My fellow Americans, Laos is far away from America, but the world is small. . . . The security of all Southeast Asia will be endangered if Laos loses its neutral independence. Its safety runs with the safety of us all. I want to make it clear to the American people, and to all the world, that all we want in Laos is peace, not war—a truly neutral government, not a cold war pawn—a settlement concluded at the conference table, not on the battlefield.[40]

Having initiated military measures to emphasize his determination to prevent a communist takeover in Laos, the president publicly announced a moderate course.

Asia scholar Usha Mahajani has, nevertheless, expressed the view that Kennedy's press conference was actually designed "to prepare the American people for U.S. military intervention in Laos." According to Mahajani, "The invasion of Cuba, planned for April, was expected to be a resounding success. . . . Kennedy envisaged a similar triumphant operation in Laos."[41]

Operation "Millpond"

Dr. Mahajani was referring to intervention by Task Force 116, and these forces were certainly positioned for action in Laos. Recent evidence, however, reveals that Kennedy also had ordered the CIA to undertake "deniable" bombing operations against communist positions on the Plain of Jars. Flown as part of "Millpond", the attacks were planned to coincide with what became the ill-fated Cuban Bay of Pigs operation.[42]

In March 1961 approximately a dozen unmarked U.S. B-26 bombers were flown by a mix of Air America pilots and reserve and "recently discharged" active duty U.S. Air Force pilots to Takhli, Thailand, located about 120 miles north of Bangkok.[43] Fear of a security leak kept the B-26s grounded most of the time and the pilots confined to the airfield, which they dubbed "The Ranch." For more than a month the men reviewed flying tactics, studied target folders, and occasionally flew C-46 cargo planes on ammunition resupply missions into Laos.[44]

Operation Millpond was supervised by U.S. Air Force Major Harry C. "Heinie" Aderholt. Major Aderholt was the commander of the 1095th Operational Evaluation Training Group, an Air Force organization that specialized in "cooperative efforts" with the CIA. At this same time Aderholt was also controlling covert C-46 airlift operations into Laos and coordinating—with the CIA and Air America—the surveying and establishment of small landing strips known as "Lima sites."[45] The Lima sites, scattered throughout Laos, would soon become essential to Air America's covert efforts in airborne resupply and troop movement.

Finally, on the evening of April 16, 1961, the B-26 pilots were given commissions in the Royal Laotian Air Force, blood chits with some gold coins, and officially told they were about to attack the Plain of Jars. The next morning, just hours before the planned take-off time, the strikes were abruptly cancelled. Major Aderholt told the men that events in Cuba had forced cancellation of their primary mission.[46]

Failure in Cuba notwithstanding, the Takhli B-26s remained prepared for action. In Laos, early on April 26, 1961, General Boyle cabled CINC-PAC and warned that the Lao government forces were "on the ropes." According to one historian the general believed the Pathet Lao would be stopped by nothing "short of open U.S. or SEATO intervention backed by B-26s." Later in the day, Ambassador Brown cabled the State Department and requested "formal authority to authorize air strikes to deprive the enemy of key objectives."[47] Although the White House immediately convened a meeting to "coordinate U.S. moves," extant records do not mention what response, if any, was sent to Brown and Boyle.[48]

For another three months the B-26's remained on alert at The Ranch, occasionally flying reconnaissance missions over northeastern Laos. One of these missions, flown on or about May 1, resulted in a near shoot-down. Two "former" U.S. Air Force pilots, Ronald L. Allaire and Claude W. Gilliam, having without incident photographed the town of Nape, quickly turned and began a second pass over the town center. A 37-mm antiaircraft gun began firing and the B-26 was struck in the left horizontal stabilizer and elevator. The uninjured crew managed to avoid an international incident by flying the aircraft back to Takhli.[49] By August the B-26s had been flown to storage on Okinawa, and the pilots returned, variously, to the "real" U.S. Air Force, to Air America, and to other flying jobs. This phase of Millpond was closed down.[50]

While the public must await further details on the connection between the Bay of Pigs affair and the CIA's Thailand-based B-26 operations, there is no question that the Cuban disaster caused President Kennedy to question the wisdom of direct U.S. military intervention in Laos.[51] According to Kennedy confidant Theodore C. Sorenson,

> That operation [the Bay of Pigs] had been recommended principally by the same set of advisors who favored intervention in Laos. But now the President was far more skeptical of the experts, their reputations, their recommendations. . . . He relied more on his White House staff and his own common sense.[52]

The president's decision to cancel the air strikes in Laos did not, however, affect his affinity for clandestine initiatives in the area. CIA paramilitary operations in Laos, with strong Thai support, were becoming an important component of U.S. military assistance to the Royal Lao government.

Thai Military Assistance to Laos

The Kong Le coup, as previously noted, created considerable anxiety within the kingdom of Thailand. The Thais believed "any neutralist government in Laos would be fundamentally incapable of resisting communist pressures without the active military and economic support of the West."[53] Lao neutralism, as interpreted in Bangkok, meant an anti-Communist position. Prime Minister Sarit was, therefore, only too pleased to support General Phoumi's return to power.

But, as they had declared since 1955, the Thai government remained convinced that communist encroachment in Laos would be halted only by SEATO intervention. A formal Thai request for direct military action was discussed during the March 26–27, 1961, SEATO Ministerial Conference. Although supported by U.S. Secretary of State Dean Rusk, the appeal was shelved due to strong French and British opposition.[54] The rejection prevented a multilateral military reaction to communist activity in Laos and made any overt military action by Thailand or the United States politically onerous. Deterred from a public course of action, Bangkok and Washington decided to expand their cooperation in covert military aid programs to Laos.

Small groups of Lao soldiers had, unofficially, been trained at Thai military bases since 1957. The U.S.–funded instruction occurred on a random basis and mostly involved Lao airborne companies and logistics specialists.[55] This was changed in April 1961 when, under Project EK-

ARAD, the Royal Thai Army began accepting entire FAR battalions for military training in Thailand. In May the United States and Thailand agreed to expand the program to include basic training for officer candidates and recruits, specialized artillery training, and basic pilot training for the Royal Lao Air Force. By the end of the year the Thai military had graduated five Lao infantry battalions, two artillery batteries, one hundred officer candidates, over two hundred recruits, and more than a dozen pilots.[56]

The Thai military also deployed advisors to Laos. During May and June Thai artillery experts assisted the U.S. Army in FAR fire-direction training. In addition, under a "Thai Volunteer Program," pilots, medical technicians, radio operators and mechanics from the Thai armed forces and police were given discharges of convenience. The men were then issued Lao identity papers, hired by U.S. entities, and sent to Laos as "civilian experts." From mid-1961 until March 1962 the "volunteer" operation maintained about sixty Thai specialists in Laos.[57] The Lao government was further aided by another long-standing covert U.S.–Thai program.

Sea Supply

In 1951, at the direction of the U.S. National Security Council, the CIA and the Thai National Police began a joint project to build a paramilitary force that would "operate in small-unit patrols, parachute behind enemy lines, commit sabotage, and engage in espionage and surveillance."[58] The NSC intended the program to halt the activities of Chinese-inspired insurgents along Thailand's long, mostly undefended borders.[59] Control of the project was assigned to the CIA's Bangkok cover organization, the Overseas Southeast Asia Supply Company or, as it was more commonly known, "Sea Supply."[60]

Under the direction of James W. "Bill" Lair, Sea Supply established a camp at Lop Buri, eighty-five miles north of Bangkok, and began airborne training for selected members of the Thai police.[61] The results were encouraging and, with Thai permission, the CIA extended the program to include members of the Royal Thai Army, Air Force, and Navy. Over the next two years more than four thousand men graduated from the Sea Supply school.[62]

In 1953 the school was relocated to Hua Hin, ninety miles south of Bangkok and across the street from the king of Thailand's southern palace. For the next four years the CIA trained Thai Royal Guard battalions in airborne and counterinsurgency operations.[63] Beginning in 1958 the pro-

gram's graduates were being formed into hundred-man Police Aerial Rein-
forcement Units (PARU) within the newly created Thai Border Patrol Police
(BPP).[64] A measure of the realistic nature of their training was that the men
completed the program by parachuting into insurgent-contested areas. Having taken advantage of Maoist dictums, the graduates were now prepared to
work alongside their own people, with all the advantages of familiar terrain
and community support. Highly trained and mobile, the PARU were argu-
ably Thailand's most versatile fighting force.[65]

When the Kong Le forces seized power in Laos, CIA and Thai officials
assigned PARU specialists to General Phoumi's lead battalions. In November and December 1960 PARU communications and medical technicians,
working with U.S. Army advisors, played an important role in Phoumi's
capture of Vientiane.[66] It was not surprising, therefore, that CIA would call
on the PARU for other operations in Laos.

Claiming the Lao Highlands

A special contingent of CIA case officers, accompanied by PARU squads,
were ordered into Laos in early 1961.[67] The first group included John E.
"Jack" Shirley, Lloyd "Pat" Landry, and Anthony "Tony" Poe. At the
U.S. Embassy the CIA station chief, Gordon L. Jorgensen, explained their
mission. The Lao government controlled little territory north of Vientiane.
If and when settlement talks occurred, ostensible proof of Vientiane's
country-wide political and military authority would be critically important.
In order to strengthen a demonstration of Royal government control Shirley,
Landry, and Poe were told by Jorgensen to begin immediately the recruit-
ment and military training of northern Laos' Hmong population. Using the
Hmong, the CIA would try to ensure that Vientiane could claim control of
the highlands.[68]

Hmong cooperation, however, was not easily gained. The Hmong were
fighters, but they fought only in defense of their own land and lifestyle.[69]
Disdained by most lowland Lao as "dirty, drug addicts," the mountaintop
people, in turn, viewed the Lao Lum with contempt. The Hmong felt no
allegiance to a country controlled by lowlanders.[70] Therefore, as CIA case
officers and their PARU interpreters/assistants moved from village to village, their message to the tribesmen was simple: "The Vietnamese will
soon come to take your land. We [the U.S.] will give you the means to
fight and defend your homes."[71]

The response was generally favorable. The Hmong enjoyed having the new weapons, and there was no CIA effort to move the tribesmen away from their homes. Within a few months, using a basic three-day instruction cycle, several thousand men had received CIA training and weapons.[72]

Searching for Turks

The CIA's enlistment of disparate hill tribes provided the Royal Lao government with an increased presence in northern Laos. Nevertheless, the agency believed that the effort was at best a passive delaying tactic. Washington did not initially envision the Hmong as an offensive force. Laos, experts agreed, would be controlled by the side with the most capable and determined armed forces. Despite considerable PEO/MAAG efforts, the FAR had a consistently poor combat record and showed few signs of impending meaningful improvement. Said one NSC staffer, "We discovered the Laotians were not Turks . . . they would not stand up and fight."[73]

But what about the Hmong? The CIA knew the Hmong could be aggressive warriors. Still, would they fight for anything more than their own mountaintops? Could the Hmong be trained in military tactics and the use of the heavy weapons (e.g., machine guns, recoilless rifles, mortars) necessary to engage the well-armed communist forces? Moreover, what about leadership? The performance of the FAR had proved the folly of a well-armed army led by inept and apathetic officers. Did the Hmong represent a source of manpower that could be used to bolster the Royal Lao Army? The CIA believed it had positive answers to all these questions.

The Emergence of Vang Pao

The Hmong of Xieng Khouang province were seriously concerned when the Pathet Lao–Kong Le forces seized the Plain of Jars in December 1960. A collective system was anathema to the Hmong. The Pathet Lao and Vietnamese often conscripted Hmong villagers for use as porters and guides and frequently seized Hmong opium crops.[74] There was also the distinct possibility that the high plain would become the scene of major fighting.

Lieutenant Colonel Vang Pao, a Hmong FAR officer native to Xieng Khouang, decided the Hmong should move from the plain to a more secure area.[75] The CIA, which had contact with Vang Pao through a PARU officer, agreed to back the plan.[76] Supported by Air America aircraft, Vang Pao relocated some two hundred Hmong villages to seven pre-selected sites in the mountains ringing the Plain of Jars.[77] A military headquarters was established by Vang Pao at Phadong, located about six miles south of the plain, and the CIA, PARU, and White Star advisors set to work.[78]

> By May 1961 the CIA had equipped some five thousand Meo [Hmong] fighting men and had established a logistics pipeline entirely separate from that supporting other [Royal Lao] government forces. Vang Pao meanwhile cemented the loyalty of widespread Meo [Hmong] villages northeast of the plain, visiting them by light aircraft and arranging for air delivery of food and arms.[79]

The CIA's "discovery" of an indigenous Lao fighting force was an encouraging development. Nevertheless, the Hmong could do little to solve the kingdom's real security problem. External communist support fueled the Kong Le–Pathet Lao forces, and until this association was served the Royal Lao government would remain in jeopardy.

Pursuing Diplomacy

In March and April 1961 President Kennedy signaled the communist world his resolve to preserve the Boun Oum government, with U.S. military force if necessary. Kennedy recognized, however, that a peaceful resolution between the two superpowers would allow Washington and Moscow to move on to other more important foreign policy problems. Moreover, many in the White House believed that a skillful handling of the Lao crisis would enhance Kennedy's stature as a statesman. The president, therefore, took steps to assure the Soviets that he preferred a diplomatic solution.

On March 26 and 27 President Kennedy met with British prime minister Harold Macmillan and Soviet foreign minister Andrei A. Gromyko, respectively. During the meetings Kennedy repeated his determination to defend Laos while, at the same time, stressing his desire for a peaceful settlement.[80] The talks set off a flurry of worldwide diplomatic activity, and the Soviet Union and Great Britain, co-chairs of the 1954 Geneva Conference, were successful in arranging the reactivation of the International Control Commission and the establishment of a May 11 truce date.[81] While the diplomats worked behind the scenes to bring about a peaceful resolution to the Laotian dilemma, the Pathet Lao launched another offensive against

Royal Lao positions.[82] Two weeks before the cease-fire was to begin, President Kennedy was again forced to contemplate increased U.S. military intervention in Laos.

In an April 27 meeting Walt W. Rostow, speaking for the Lao Task Force, advised the president to send a limited number of troops to Thailand. Ambassador W. Averell Harriman, who would head the U.S. delegation to Geneva, concurred and said the presence of U.S. troops in Thailand would strengthen the American negotiating position. The JCS agreed with deploying troops but believed a "show of force" had to be backed up with a strong offensive capability. The JCS did not want to begin the operation without the commitment of "120,000–140,000 men, with authority to use nuclear weapons if necessary."[83]

Kennedy left the meeting greatly concerned over the military's belligerent "all the way" attitude and what seemed to him careless planning for various contingencies. The Bay of Pigs debacle was, no doubt, still fresh in his mind.[84] The president also knew there would be little SEATO support and virtually no Congressional backing for any large scale U.S. military action in Laos. Moreover, Kennedy was being told that South Vietnam, not Laos, was the preferable setting for a United States stand against communist expansion in Southeast Asia.[85]

Indeed, convincing evidence suggests that by this time Kennedy, if forced into a major confrontation with the Communists in Asia, had decided Vietnam would be the battleground. In an oral history interview on August 5, 1970, William H. Sullivan, recently returned from almost five years as ambassador to Laos, described the Kennedy White House view:

> The attitude was that Laos was a secondary problem; Laos was a poor place to get bogged down in because it was inland, had no access to the sea and no proper logistics lines . . . that it was rather inchoate as a nation; that the Lao were not fighters, et cetera. While on the other hand if you were going to have a confrontation, the place to have it was in Vietnam because it did have logistical access to the sea and therefore, we had military advantages. It was an articulated, functioning nation. Its troops were tigers and real fighters. And, therefore, the advantages would be on our side to have a confrontation and showdown in Vietnam and not get sucked into this Laos operation.[86]

Nonetheless, by May 1, 1961, Kennedy had decided to initiate U.S. military action in Laos. Fortuitously, just as the president was about to order a SEATO alert, the communists publicly agreed to a cease-fire. U.S.

military action was cancelled and the cease-fire in Laos took effect on May 11.

Five days later the following countries convened a second Geneva Conference: the P.R.C., Cambodia, France, Laos, the U.S.S.R., Britain, the United States, South Vietnam, North Vietnam, India, Canada, Poland, Burma, and Thailand.[87] A June 3–4 meeting in Vienna between President Kennedy and Premier Khrushchev seemed finally to defuse the issue between the two superpowers. In a joint statement the leaders said they had "reaffirmed their support of a neutral and independent Laos chosen by the Laotians themselves, and of international agreements for insuring that neutrality and independence."[88]

A major Soviet-American military confrontation in Laos had been averted, and it was now up to the diplomats at Geneva to bring a settlement to the troubled kingdom of Laos. But, as the peacemakers went to work in Geneva, the combatants in Laos were finding it difficult to maintain the cease-fire.

The Hmong Factor

Not surprisingly, the first serious cease-fire violations in Laos occurred between the Kong Le–Pathet Lao troops on the Plain of Jars and Vang Pao's Hmong forces located at Phadong. Well before the cease-fire, CIA officers, PARU, and U.S. Army White Star advisors had arrived at Phadong to train and organize the Hmong soldiers.[89] The close proximity of the opposing forces—a half dozen miles—bred distrust and security concerns. Shortly after the cease-fire was initiated, Pathet Lao gunners, with North Vietnamese support, began attacking Phadong with 75mm artillery fire. The shelling continued until June 6, when the Hmong were driven out of the area.[90] In protest, Western delegations suspended the Geneva talks for five days.[91]

Vang Pao reassembled his forces southwest of Phadong at the village of Pha Khao and continued guerilla operations. Once again, CIA, PARU, and White Star advisors set to work training the Hmong army. The task was made easier when, on August 29, 1961, President Kennedy approved National Security Action Memorandum 80. The memo called for:

> An immediate increase in mobile training teams in Laos to include advisors down to the company level, to a total U.S. strength of 500, together with an attempt to get Thai agreement to supply an equal amount

of Thai for the same purpose. An immediate increase of 2,000 in the number of Meos [Hmong] being supported to bring the total to a level of 11,000.[92]

By October the president's decision had raised the number of U.S. Army Special Forces in Laos to 300 men, with another 112 being prepared for deployment to the kingdom.[93]

The U.S. would continue to train General Phoumi's lowland troops, but Vang Pao's Hmong army was becoming the most important indigenous fighting force in Laos. By the summer of 1962, the general and his U.S. advisors had founded a permanent military headquarters in the Long Tieng valley, located thirty-five miles southwest of the plain.[94] Known by the CIA and Air America as Lima Site 98 or Lima Site 20A, Long Tieng would soon become the focal point of America's secret war in Laos.

Project Mad River

The movement of CIA, PARU, and White Star advisors, as well as the supply of the Hmong soldiers and their families, was a major task and would have been impossible without the aerial services of Air America. Under contract to the U.S. International Cooperation Agency (ICA), the CIA proprietary airline had been flying H-19 and H-34 helicopters in Laos for some time. The initial ICA contract specified that Air America was to "furnish approximately 35 personnel for the operation and maintenance of four H-19 aircraft." The arrival of four H-34 helicopters in December 1960 changed the contract terms and Air America was held responsible for "furnishing between 85 and 140 personnel."[95] As discussed earlier, Air America received an additional sixteen H-34s in March 1961 and based them at Udorn, Thailand. Shortly thereafter, under Project Mad River, the U.S. Air Force contracted Air America to fly and maintain the H-34s.[96]

On May 19, 1961, General Boyle, the chief of the U.S. MAAG in Laos, dispatched a classified message to the headquarters of the Air Material Force Pacific Area (AMFPA), the U.S. Air Force's Far East procurement agency. The message requested that AMFPA undertake secret contract negotiations with Air America in Taipei, Taiwan.[97] According to AMFPA civilian contracting officer James Spencer, the general provided the following guidance: "I want airplanes to fly where I want them, when I want them, and with no interference. Now get me a contract that will give me what I want as soon as possible."[98]

The contract requirements were unusual, to say the least, but after a favorable legal review the Air Force decided that Air America could be provided a sole source contract. The contract justification read:

> The Department of the Air Force proposes entering into a contract with Air America, Inc., on a sole source basis for the furnishing of services by the contractor to provide, establish, manage, operate, and maintain a complete flying and maintenance service, inclusive of all facilities, supplies, materials, equipment, and support services not furnished by the U.S. Government to permit utilization by the U.S. Government of helicopter aircraft at points in Southeast Asia as designated by the Chief, MAAG, Laos, in support of the Royal Lao Government.[99]

The justification went on to state that the contract was required for services "in the interest of National Defense, which because of military considerations, should not be publicly disclosed and for which Air America, Inc., is the only known source." Procurement action started on May 31 and was completed by June 7, 1961. This initial Mad River contract, dated July 1, 1961, paid Air America slightly more than $2.5 million for the first year of the H-34 operation.[100]

Flying for Project Mad River was dangerous work. On May 15, 1961, an H-34 emergency landing enabled the Pathet Lao to capture a "temporary" Air America pilot, a "temporary" Air America flight mechanic, and an American television reporter. Two weeks later an H-34 crashed while moving supplies near Phadong, killing two "temporary" Air America pilots and seriously injuring a MAAG passenger.[101]

Deadlock

The fall of Phadong caused only a temporary delay in the Geneva negotiations, and further serious cease-fire violations were discouraged by the June-to-October rainy season. Because Kennedy and Khrushchev settled the major issue of external intervention at Vienna, and since the Americans, Soviets, and Chinese were agreed in their support of a neutral Laos, the delegates turned their attention toward procedural problems.[102] Their work could not proceed, however, without the formation of a recognized Lao government.

In late June and again in early October Souvanna Phouma, Souphanouvong, and Boun Oum met to work out an agreement on a new coalition government. The princes agreed that Souvanna would head the new government, but the division of cabinet positions, particularly those of defense and interior, could not be settled. Souphanouvong suggested a compromise that would give the two ministries to Souvanna, but Boun Oum, fearing the close relationship between the two brothers, balked.[103]

Meanwhile, the Geneva delegates were becoming impatient with the Laotians. The diplomats had finished drafting the necessary documents; all that remained to be done to reach a final agreement was the seating of a new Lao government. In December Great Britain and the Soviet Union urged the three princes to find a solution. Boun Oum now refused even to hold meetings with Souvanna and Souphanouvong.

Washington, which at the urging of Ambassador Harriman now backed Souvanna as prime minister, began to apply diplomatic pressure on the Vientiane government.[104] When this friendly persuasion failed to work, the United States cut off economic aid to Boun Oum. Four days later the prime minister consented to new discussions; aid was resumed. Boun Oum and Phoumi, nevertheless, continued to reject Souvanna's control of the defense and interior portfolios. The talks deadlocked.[105] The situation in Laos then took another turn toward superpower confrontation.

The Nam Tha Debacle

Despite warnings from his American advisers, in early 1962 General Phoumi began to mass troops in the northwestern Lao town of Nam Tha. According to one knowledgeable source, Phoumi sought to provoke an attack that would result in the communist capture of a key Lao city. The bizarre plan, Phoumi hoped, would result in U.S. military intervention on his behalf and in America's rejection of Souvanna Phouma and the neutralists.[106]

The general received his wish the first week of May 1962 when minor Pathet Lao movements at Nam Tha forced five thousand of Phoumi's best troops to "stream in panic across the Mekong into Thailand."[107] The *New York Times* reported that the Kennedy administration felt the Royal government had provoked the attack.[108] Nevertheless, the president felt obligated to demonstrate U.S. support in the face of what reporters described as a serious communist offensive.

On May 15, 1962, in an effort to gain some bipartisan leverage, Kennedy met with his White House predecessor. Eisenhower agreed to support a hard-line position, and later the same day Kennedy announced the movement of about three thousand U.S. troops to Thailand.[109] Kennedy "wanted a political use of military forces, not the start of a regular military operation which might generate its own forward momentum, as in Korea."[110] The "signal" seemed to have the desired effect. On May 25 Premier Khrushchev announced that "Moscow continued to support the establishment of a neutral Laos, thereby convincing the United States that Russia was doing what she could to prevent the Pathet Lao [actions]."[111] Communist activity subsided, and the U.S. forces deployed in Thailand advanced no farther. Cooperation between Moscow and Washington had once again averted direct American military intervention in Laos.

Souvanna Prevails

The miserable performance of General Phoumi's army left the rightists in near political and military collapse. Boun Oum and Phoumi decided to salvage what they could in a new government. On June 11, 1962, Souvanna, Souphanouvong, and Boun Oum announced the formation of a coalition government. Souvanna was to become prime minister and minister of defense, and Souphanouvong and Phoumi were named deputy premiers. Cabinet positions were divided as follows: neutralists, seven seats; right wing, four seats; Pathet Lao, four seats; and four seats uncommitted. Two weeks later the Souvanna government took office and a delegation was dispatched to Geneva.[112]

On July 23, 1962, the irrepressible Souvanna Phouma watched as the foreign ministers of fourteen nations signed a Declaration and Protocol on the Neutrality of Laos.[113] It was a time for celebration and happiness, not unlike a similar occasion eight years previous. However, as with the Geneva agreements of 1954, Laos would have a very difficult time remaining neutral and independent of outside influences. Despite another international accord Laos remained ensnared by the political and territorial ambitions of communist neighbors, the security concerns of Thailand and the United States, and geographic fate.

Chapter Four

THE GENEVA FACADE:
SEE, HEAR, AND SPEAK NO EVIL

The 1962 Geneva agreements satisfied President Kennedy. He had avoided a major U.S.–Soviet confrontation and was free to pursue with Premier Khrushchev more important matters. And, as the U.S. focus in Southeast Asia shifted to Vietnam, Laos was quickly and largely forgotten by the American public.

The conflict there, however, was far from resolved. As the United States prepared to withdraw American military personnel from Laos in accordance with the Geneva agreements, it became clear there would be no similar North Vietnamese compliance. Kennedy, at the strong urging of Averell Harriman, nevertheless decided to carry out the departure. The president did not challenge the communist violations with direct military action, deciding instead on a policy of covert U.S. military support to the Royal Lao government. Ten years later presidential advisor Walt Rostow observed, "I would judge Kennedy's failure to move promptly and decisively to deal with the violation of the Laos Accords the greatest single error in American policy of the 1960's." [1]

The Pushkin-Harriman Understanding

On July 23, 1962, fourteen nations pledged their cooperation and assistance in "build[ing] a peaceful, neutral, independent, democratic, unified and prosperous Laos." [2] Soviet-American unanimity was, however, considered the linchpin of any successful agreement on Laos. Soviet Deputy Foreign Minister Georgi Pushkin had repeatedly provided personal assurances to U.S. representative W. Averell Harriman that Moscow fully endorsed Washington's desire for a neutral and independent Laos. The Pushkin-Harriman understanding, according to a knowledgeable former U.S. State Department official, included the following points:

> The USSR would be responsible for compliance by the Communist side, including North Vietnam and the Pathet Lao. The UK and US would be responsible for the non-Communist side. . . . The USSR would ensure that Hanoi would observe Lao neutrality to include preventing North Vietnamese use of Laos as a corridor to South Vietnam. [3]

American-Soviet cooperation was underscored when, following the signing of the Geneva agreements, Ambassador Harriman summoned Leonard Unger, U.S. ambassador-designate to Laos, to Geneva for a face-to-face meeting with Sergei Afanasseyev, the new Soviet ambassador to Laos. Ambassador Unger recalls that Harriman and Pushkin told the two Vientiane-bound diplomats to "work together and make it [Geneva agreements] work." [4]

Harriman's Decision

There was no doubt in Unger's mind that Harriman believed he had a firm commitment from Pushkin, and this confidence in the Soviet position was communicated by Ambassador Harriman to President Kennedy. [5] Still, as the October 1962 deadline for the departure from Laos of all foreign regular and irregular troops approached, [6] there was no indication that the North Vietnamese were leaving Laos in any great numbers. [7]

The continued communist presence created some sentiment within the Kennedy administration to delay U.S. compliance with the agreements until the Vietnamese removed their forces from eastern Laos. Averell Harriman, who was now assistant secretary of state for Far Eastern affairs, would have

none of it. Together with Roger Hilsman, Harriman advised the president
to comply fully with the Geneva agreements. Writes Hilsman:

> We felt . . . that the Communists continued to pursue their goal of
> gaining control of all of Laos, but that for the time being, at least, they
> intended to do so primarily through political means and generally within
> the terms of the Geneva agreements. The North Vietnamese would un-
> doubtedly insist on maintaining some military presence in Laos, both to
> backstop the Pathet Lao position and to maintain their hold on the infiltra-
> tion routes into South Vietnam. But our judgment was that the Commu-
> nists would make an effort to keep this military presence small and
> inconspicuous and would use the infiltration routes circumspectly. Harri-
> man, especially, felt strongly that the United States should comply with
> both the letter and the spirit of the agreements in every detail. If the
> Geneva agreements and the political situation in Laos failed, he wanted it
> to be the Communist side that had to pay the political cost. If the
> Communists broke the agreements and the United States had to intervene
> with force, he wanted to make sure we had all the international political
> support we could get.[8]

President Kennedy, hearing no serious opposition to these judgments, decided to complete the U.S. military departure from Laos.

Withdrawing from Laos

The United States, which since the May 1961 cease-fire had steadily increased the size of its MAAG in Laos, was required to withdraw slightly
more than 1,200 U.S. and third country personnel. About 100 of these men
were Thai "volunteers," 424 were contract technicians of the Eastern
Construction Company in Laos (ECCOIL), and the rest were members of
the U.S. armed forces.

The Pentagon, in order to make the most effective use of the remaining
training time with the Royal Lao Army and Hmong irregular forces, ordered
a phased departure of the MAAG personnel. Thai specialists departed Laos
on August 22, a month later the U.S. completed an evacuation of the
ECCOIL employees, and in mid-September a few American military personnel began to depart the country. According to Admiral Felt, CINCPAC,
Washington ordered the U.S. MAAG to maintain a sizable contingent in

Laos up until the deadline and to "go out with flags flying high."[9] On October 6 Major General Reuben H. Tucker, III, Chief, MAAG Laos, and 127 MAAG personnel formally departed the kingdom of Laos.[10]

North Vietnamese compliance with the accords, as expected by the CIA, was patently spurious. On October 7 the official North Vietnamese news agency reported that "the Vietnamese military personnel which were previously sent to Laos at the request of the Royal Lao Government have all been withdrawn from Laos."[11] According to William Colby, then chief of CIA clandestine operations in the Far East,

> there had been some 7,000 North Vietnamese troops in Laos at the time of the Accord. But during the so-called count-out [conducted by the International Control Commission] only forty went through the formalities of leaving the country. Since they had never been acknowledged as being there, they could hardly in theory be officially counted out, but our intelligence showed that they were there nonetheless.[12]

The Pathet Lao, whose fighting men were estimated to number some 16,000 at the beginning of the cease-fire, had now increased their armed forces to about 19,500.[13] As the Royal Lao government supposedly inaugurated a new era of guaranteed peace and neutrality, there was little real prospect for either.

A Wary Beginning

In July 1962 Leonard Unger took charge of one of the most demanding U.S. diplomatic posts in the world. He was particularly well qualified for the position, having arrived in Vientiane after a four-year stint as deputy chief of mission at the U.S. Embassy in Bangkok. Ambassador Unger held the people of Southeast Asia in high regard, spoke Thai, and counted many influential Thai leaders as personal friends.[14] Unger's keen awareness of Thai politics did not mix well with his "marching orders" from Averell Harriman.

Bangkok was extremely skeptical of the Souvanna Phouma coalition government's ability to withstand communist domination. The Thai, as always, were deeply concerned over the security of their extensive borders and the degree to which China and North Vietnam might exploit a weak Laos to infiltrate and overwhelm Thailand. Earlier in the year Thai Foreign Minister Thanat Khoman had received what he considered to be a firm U.S.

commitment to defend Thailand, with or without SEATO approval, against communist attack. Issued on March 6, 1962, and popularly known as the Rusk-Thanat Communique, was the affirmation by U.S. Secretary of State Dean Rusk "that the United States regards the preservation of the independence and integrity of Thailand as vital to the national interest of the United States and to world peace." [15] The pledge, backed by the May 1962 deployment of American troops to Thailand, convinced Bangkok the U.S. was determined to fight Communist advances in Laos.

But when the United States appeared willing to accept a formidable North Vietnamese presence in Laos, Thai government officials expressed doubts about America's long-term role in Southeast Asia. During a conversation with Ambassador Unger, Foreign Minister Thanat expressed "no enthusiasm for the Harriman plan in Laos and said neutralization would not work." But Harriman "had the president's ear," and Unger had no choice but to hope for the best and implement Harriman's policy. [16]

However, as the deadline approached for the withdrawal of all foreign troops, Harriman could no longer ignore the communist violations. William Colby personally provided Secretary Harriman a weekly briefing on CIA operations in the Far East. Colby recounts that, since July, Harriman had made it very clear to Colby that he expected the CIA to comply fully with the agreements.

> He insisted on knowing in detail our activities there, and of approving or disapproving every step we took so as not to permit any differences to arise between CIA's policies and his. But gradually our weekly intelligence reports became more ominous. The North Vietnamese troops were not only still there, they were moving out to expand the area they and their Pathet Lao puppets controlled, pushing the tribal Meo [Hmong] away from their settlements, or absorbing those who did not flee, as well as attacking the neutralist forces. [17]

Harriman relented, and Air America was allowed to resupply secretly the Hmong irregulars with small amounts of ammunition and food. CIA case officers in Laos were told that "it was only to be used for defensive fighting . . . not [for] initiating actions against the North Vietnamese or the Pathet Lao." [18]

The Lao coalition government, as permitted in the Protocol to the Declaration on the Neutrality of Laos, was also seeking U.S. military defensive materials. According to Article Six, "the introduction into Laos of armaments, munitions, and war material generally, except such quantities of

conventional armaments as the Royal Lao government may consider necessary for the national defense of Laos, is prohibited."[19] On September 10,
1962, Prime Minister Souvanna Phouma sent a letter to Ambassador Unger
requesting repair parts and supplies for U.S.–furnished equipment, training
ammunition, petroleum, oils and lubricants, building supplies, and cloth-
ing. Unger responded on October 12:

> My formal affirmative reply to this request will be forthcoming shortly,
> upon completion of certain internal administrative procedures within the
> United States Government in Washington. As I have informed you orally,
> a small office has been established within and under the full control of
> the United States AID Mission to Laos. This unit . . . is responsible for
> determining jointly with the . . . Royal Lao Government the required
> quantities and types of materials . . . specified in your letter, and for
> seeing to their shipment to Laos.[20]

Six days after the American MAAG had formally departed Vientiane the
U.S. ambassador was acknowledging a new military assistance program to
Laos.

The Rebirth of Covert U.S. Military Assistance

Ambassador Unger's letter of October 12 to Prime Minister Souvanna
Phouma disclosed the existence of a new office within the USAID mission
to Laos. Unger, like his predecessor some seven years earlier, had no
embassy infrastructure for conducting a military assistance operation. In
1955 the U.S. State Department had finessed Article Six of the 1954
Geneva Agreements by creating a Program Evaluations Office. In October
1962 the United States faced a similar constraint: Article Four of the 1962
Geneva Protocol provided that "the introduction of foreign regular and
irregular troops, foreign para-military formations and foreign military personnel into Laos is prohibited."[21]

The Kennedy administration, as a result of Averell Harriman's forceful
recommendation, intended to comply fully with the Geneva agreements.
But the growing awareness in Washington that the Soviets were unable to
enforce Pushkin's promises brought the agreements into a more pragmatic
focus. According to Douglas S. Blaufarb, CIA station chief in Vientiane
from 1964 to 1966,

the U.S. position with respect to the [1962] Accords was that, in order to preserve the essence of an independent and neutral Laos, certain limited and carefully controlled departures from the implementing protocols had to be undertaken. These would be discussed with Souvanna Phouma in advance and his views would be respected.[22]

The creation of a "small office," as it was termed by Ambassador Unger, was one of America's first "controlled departures" from the agreements. Ostensibly under the control of the USAID program and designated the "Requirements Office" (USAID/RO), the unit was established to act as the in-country component of a highly classified, Thailand-based, joint U.S. military assistance organization.[23]

DEPCHIEF

As early as August 1962 President Kennedy approved plans for a new covert U.S. military assistance program to Laos.[24] The day after General Tucker withdrew the U.S. MAAG from Laos he established and took command of Deputy Chief, Joint United States Military Assistance Advisory Group, Thailand (DEPCHJUSMAGTHAI). Deliberately placed within the structure of the U.S. Military Assistance Advisory Group in Thailand— DEPCHIEF, as it was commonly known—was in fact an entirely "separate entity" with orders to undertake the "planning, programming, requisitioning, receipt and storage in Thailand, [and] onward shipment to Laos" of U.S. MAP [Military Assistance Program] materials.[25] If questioned by the press, military authorities were ordered to say that DEPCHIEF was a supplement to the ongoing U.S. MAP effort in Thailand, "particularly in the fields of civic action and counter-subversion."[26]

DEPCHIEF was headquartered at the Capital Hotel in Bangkok and reported directly to CINCPAC. Personnel initially consisted of approximately thirty-nine officers, seventy-eight enlisted men, and a handful of carefully selected Thai civilian employees. Organizationally DEPCHIEF was divided into five divisions: Air Force, Comptroller, Logistics, Intelligence, and Plans and Training. Detachments were located at a 380-acre munitions storage facility located five miles south of Udorn (code-named "Peppergrinder"); at the Air America facility at Udorn Air Base; and at the Thai port of Sattahip. DEPCHIEF also operated a large warehouse (code-named "Redcap") at Bangkok's Don Muang airport.[27]

The USAID Requirements Office, an integral element of DEPCHIEF, was staffed by about thirty retired U.S. military officers and enlisted men. The Americans were supplemented by recently returned third-country technicians who "assisted the FAR logistics organization with maintenance skills not available to the FAR."[28] With few exceptions, Thailand-based DEPCHIEF personnel were not allowed in Laos, thus making the Requirements Office the "eyes and ears" of the U.S. military assistance program to Laos. Military responsibilities notwithstanding, DEPCHIEF, and particularly the RO, operated under the tight control and authority of the U.S. Ambassador to Laos.

The Kennedy Letter

Leonard Unger went to Vientiane at a time when the president had just delegated unprecedented authority to U.S. diplomatic posts abroad. In the aftermath of the Bay of Pigs failure President Kennedy decided to shake up the State Department. According to Arthur Schlesinger, "Kennedy had come to the Presidency determined to make the Department of State the central point, below the Presidency itself, in the conduct of foreign affairs."[29] In a period of just four months the president had been confronted with foreign policy crises in Laos and Cuba. Kennedy found the State Department sorely deficient in providing him critically important counsel, and the president began calling the State Department "a bowl of jelly."

On May 29, 1961, in an effort to correct these deficiencies and improve the operation of America's diplomatic missions, President Kennedy sent a letter to each American ambassador abroad that said, in part:

> You are in charge of the entire U.S. Diplomatic Mission, and I expect you to supervise all of its operations. The Mission includes not only the personnel of the Department of State and the Foreign Service, but also representatives of all other United States agencies. . . . As you know, the United States Diplomatic Mission . . . does not . . . include United States military forces operating in the field where such forces are under the command of a United States area military commander.[30]

The letter "gave every ambassador for the first time the authority to know everything the CIA people were doing in his country (even if not always the way they were doing it)."[31] And, in the special circumstances that existed in post-October 1962 Laos, where the United States was engaged in military activities without an "area military commander," the ambassador acquired unprecedented military power.[32]

The U.S. ambassador to Laos became the immediate controlling authority for

> all the functions of a Military Assistance Advisory Group, some of the functions of a U.S. military command, and numerous unconventional activities in support of irregular troops, including a requirement for airborne logistics . . . in circumstances which prohibited an avowed military presence of the type normally considered essential.[33]

The Kennedy letter became, with significant consequences for U.S. policy in Laos, a holy writ for a series of strong-willed U.S. ambassadors in Vientiane.

Internal Dissension

The 1962 Geneva Agreements removed the specter of international confrontation in Laos, but accomplished little toward resolving the kingdom's internal problems. Souvanna Phouma was left with the impossible task of presiding over a coalition government comprising three armed camps. In late 1962, to the surprise of few, the tripartite government of Laos began to unravel.

For nearly two years Pathet Lao military commanders had shared their Soviet-supplied equipment with Kong Le and his neutralist army. In October 1962, anticipating the end of the Soviet airlift, the Pathet Lao began denying resupply to the neutralists. At the same time the communists were agitated by Souvanna's arrangements for American military shipments to the Phoumi army and his approval of aid to the Hmong irregulars.

The prince reacted to the Pathet Lao action by requesting U.S. resupply flights to Kong Le's forces in the Plain of Jars. The Pathet Lao viewed these flights as "subversive" and on November 27 a neutralist antiaircraft artillery unit, acting on the orders of a procommunist officer, shot down an Air America C-46 transport plane. Kong Le was outraged by the treachery, but was prevented by the Pathet Lao from taking any action against the gunners. Shortly thereafter about four hundred neutralists defected to the Pathet Lao.[34]

The Pathet Lao and the neutralists then embarked on a bitter series of military clashes and assassinations in both the Plain of Jars and Vientiane.

Ketsana Vongsavong, a close associate of Kong Le and Souvanna, was killed on February 12, 1963, allegedly by communist agents. On April 1 a soldier believed to be loyal to Kong Le evened the score by gunning down Foreign Minister Quinim Pholsena, a left-leaning neutralist. The killing of Quinim and memories of their earlier imprisonment prompted Souphanou- vong and several other Pathet Lao officials to leave Vientiane for the safety of their Khang Khay headquarters. Meanwhile, shooting between the Pathet Lao and the neutralists had forced Kong Le to move his troops to the extreme western third of the Plain of Jars. The coalition cabinet was, in effect, at an end.[35]

Moscow Backs Out

Although the North Vietnamese were in Laos to stay, Hanoi's Soviet patrons had decided it was time to move on. Following the signing of the 1962 Accords, Premier Khrushchev told Prince Souphanouvong that the "main task" in Laos was now "political." In August Aleksandr Abramov, the departing Soviet ambassador to Laos, told a senior ICC official that the formation of the tripartite government and the signing of the Geneva agree- ments were "great achievements of the policy of peaceful coexistence and important links in East-West dialogue."[36] On December 2 the Soviets officially ended their Lao airlift by turning over nine IL-2 transport aircraft to the coalition government. The planes were to be divided evenly among the three factions. Pointedly, the Soviets also gave the North Vietnamese the larger IL-14s used during the airlift. Although the Soviets would con- tinue to maintain an embassy in Vientiane, Moscow had deliberately for- feited any important role in Laotian affairs.[37]

The Soviet exit from Laos has a number of plausible explanations. Charles Stevenson ascribes the Soviet withdrawal to preoccupation with the missile crisis in Cuba and the Sino–Indian border war.[38] The Kremlin leaders were also hopeful that diplomatic success in Laos would pave the way for the reopening of the Berlin negotiations.[39] Whatever their motives, the Soviets no longer considered Laos worthy of high-level discussions. In July 1963 Averell Harriman, in Moscow to negotiate a nuclear test ban treaty, raised the issue of Pathet Lao and North Vietnamese violations of the Geneva agreements. Khrushchev, according to Harriman, brushed off the subject and said, "It's time to go to dinner; we haven't got time to talk

about Laos. Why do we want to bother with Laos? I have no interest in
Laos."[40]

A Plausibly Deniable Army

Washington clearly did not share Moscow's attitude toward Laos. Tightly
controlled CIA "defensive" shipments to the Hmong during the summer of
1962 eventually gave way to the creation of a U.S.–organized Hmong
paramilitary program. The CIA became the program's executive agent and,
at the direction of the president and the National Security Council, began
recruiting, training, and directing a tribal army.

According to William Colby, the decidedly military task was given to
the CIA "to avoid the necessity for uniformed U.S. involvement in Laos."[41]

> The lowland-bound Royal Lao Army, despite American military aid, was
> not going to go outside the narrow limits of the Mekong plain to engage
> the Communists. And the American military . . . had no desire to set up
> the long logistics lines a regular American military force would require in
> Laos.[42]

Turning the job over to the CIA, as Ambassador Colby would readily
agree, also provided an important measure of plausible deniability.[43] Under
questioning in 1975 by a U.S. Senate intelligence oversight committee,
Secretary of State Henry Kissinger provided two reasons for assigning the
operation to the CIA: "One, to avoid a formal avowal of American participation there for diplomatic reasons, and the second, I suspect, because it
was less accountable."[44]

The CIA was well prepared for the assignment. Following contact with
Vang Pao in 1961, CIA officer James W. Lair sent his headquarters an
eighteen-page cable outlining the Hmong paramilitary potential. Desmond
FitzGerald, then CIA Far East chief and a long-time proponent of paramili-
tary operations, agreed that the Hmong offered the best hope for an indige-
nous Lao fighting force. By mid-1963 the CIA had instituted a vigorous,
Thailand-based, offense-oriented paramilitary training program for Vang
Pao's men.[45]

Initially, CIA case officers selected 750 Hmong and sent them to the
PARU center at Hua Hin, Thailand, for training in guerilla warfare tactics
and in the use of modern weapons and radios.[46] The Hmong were returned

to Laos and soon saw action against communist-held Hmong villages throughout northeastern Laos. Once freed from Pathet Lao control, the villages were fortified and defended by Hmong soldiers. Lima sites, the unimproved landing strips surveyed by Major Aderholt and others, were also built alongside the villages to accommodate aerial resupply flights.[47]

In addition, in the coming months and years many of these young men would be transported by Air America and U.S. military aircraft into communist-controlled areas of northeastern Laos and western North Vietnam. The mission of these ten-to-twelve–man "Road Watch" teams was to observe and report back to CIA case officers on Pathet Lao and North Vietnamese activity. When such actions were deemed useful, the Hmong also carried out harassment raids on enemy forces and, when reinforced, engaged in set battles.[48] The significant partnership that developed between these Hmong "Road Watch" teams and American airpower will be examined in chapter six.

Flying Rice and Weapons

The war in Laos and the development of the irregular army considerably disrupted the Hmong villagers. Military service, even for short periods of time, caused family hardships and neglect of crops and livestock. Isolated village outposts required dependable resupply of food and military matériel. CIA advisors quickly recognized that if the Hmong army was to be successful, the agency would have to ensure that the soldiers and their families received regular deliveries of food and military equipment. According to a senior CIA official,

> the knowledge that their families would be cared for . . . was a factor in persuading the tribesmen to join the irregulars, for in those hills the only protection for a village rests with the men of that village. Thus a tribesman was unlikely to accept a commitment to serve as a full-time soldier away from his home unless he was assured that his family would be cared for in his absence.[49]

The air link to the Hmong had to be expanded.

In January 1962 the original Air America-MAAG contract regarding Laos operations had been modified by the U.S. embassy to include the services of seven U-6 "Beaver" single-engine aircraft. Two months later the embassy again changed the contract to provide for the services of four multi-engine airplanes: a C-45, a C-46, a C-47, and a DC-4.[50] The agreement does not mention U-10 Helio-Couriers, but these Short Take-Off and Landing (STOL) aircraft were also being widely used in Laos.[51] Thus, in the post-Geneva 1962 period, Air America was well equipped to handle increasingly diverse and perilous missions.

The creation of the rough dirt and grass Lima sites, which numbered nearly three hundred by 1970, provided mountaintop or mountainside landing zones throughout Laos.[52] However, the strips were often treacherous to land on, and the absence of navigational aids called for extraordinary flying skills. Aircraft landings and take-offs often occurred within minimum flight restrictions, and mistakes could easily result in an aircraft and its crew slipping off the side of a three thousand-foot cliff. Parachute drops of supplies were conducted in areas without Lima sites, or where it was judged unsafe to land. This also required considerable expertise on the part of crewmen in the rear of the aircraft, called "kickers," who shoved out pallets of food and military supplies, and sometimes even live animals, to villagers waiting below.[53]

In addition to Air America the U.S. government also hired Bird and Sons, a small civilian contract airline, to fly supplies and men in and out of Laos. The airline, which began operating in mainland Southeast Asia in 1958, employed about fifty-five pilots who flew a variety of small and medium transport planes out of Vientiane and Udorn. Bird and Sons, like Air America, flew both CIA and USAID operations.[54] In September 1965 Bird and Sons was sold to Continental Air Lines and was renamed Continental Air Services, Incorporated (CASI). The new company continued the policy of flying both covert and overt missions.[55]

USAID Laos

Most of the work performed in Laos by Air America and the other contract air carriers represented the final stage of a complex pipeline supplying U.S. military and economic aid to Laos. This could not have been successful without the full support of USAID Laos. Ostensibly a nonmilitary agency, USAID Laos was intimately involved in the distribution of military assistance. The decision to use USAID for military functions was, according to a 1970 statement by USAID Administrator John A. Hannah, unprecedented, and the agency preferred "to get rid of this kind of operation."[56]

USAID Laos was, of course, also involved in more traditional "nation-building'' projects in such areas as education, health, and road construction.[57] But in Laos all these efforts had military applications. Placing the Requirements Office within USAID was, therefore, not only expedient but also practical. USAID's involvement in military affairs also offered DEPCHIEF and CIA a useful financial association, as will be examined below.

Notwithstanding the importance of facilitating bureaucratic paperwork, USAID Laos' greatest contributions to Lao security took place in the field. One of USAID's most significant efforts—and an example of the relationship between economic development and military security—was the Refugee Relief Program. In a 1972 assessment of the program, Douglas Blaufarb noted that

> USAID refugee relief has been much more than the name suggests. It is a fully-integrated and quite essential element of the [CIA] tribal program. Particularly in the Meo [Hmong] region it has strong field representation . . . and it participates closely with Vang Pao and the CIA in Meo [Hmong] operations. It has access to the same aircraft used by CIA for air transport. Through a small group of AID personnel and a larger number of Lao employees . . . [USAID] maintains an up-to-date status report on the refugee population, location, and needs, and prepares a daily schedule of supply deliveries.[58]

CIA officers, Air America crews, and USAID employees were, quite literally, standing elbow to elbow in the management of the emerging covert war in Laos.

The Continuing Thai Connection

Bangkok's cooperation and support continued to be indispensable to American covert operations in Laos. Thai airfields provided secure maintenance and support facilities for U.S. civilian and military aircraft flying into Laos. PARU teams and Royal Thai Army artillery units were busily engaged in training Hmong and Lao soldiers, both in Laos and Thailand. DEPCHIEF programs, particularly those relating to logistics storage and transport of materials to Laos, were made possible through the efforts of the Thai military.

It was not surprising therefore that, as U.S. and Thai involvement in Laos escalated, the CIA decided to formalize its relationship with the Thai military. In late 1962 the CIA established at Udorn, Thailand, the 4802d

Joint Liaison Detachment (JLD).[59] Headed by James Lair, the JLD formed a close working relationship with a Thai military unit called "Headquarters 333."[60] The two organizations, comprising thirty-five to forty Americans and a slightly greater number of Thais, acted as a joint U.S.–Thai command center for covert military and intelligence-collection activities in Laos.[61] In the years to come the 4802d and Headquarters 333 would oversee a spiraling U.S.–Thai commitment to Lao defense.

The Geneva Agreements of 1962 resulted in a superpower sleight-of-hand. Moscow, unable to enforce Pushkin's pledge to halt North Vietnamese trespass of Laos, decided to turn a blind eye to the kingdom. Washington—increasingly concerned with Vietnam and confident Moscow would not intervene in Laos, so long as U.S. ground forces did not enter the country—embarked with Thailand on a complex, covert military assistance program to Laos.

Unquestionably, in late 1962, with good reason, the United States and Thailand were in direct violation of the Geneva agreements. But, so long as the U.S.–Thai activity was conducted "quietly," the superpowers chose to ignore the obvious.

Chapter Five

SECSTATE THEATER OF WAR

According to pronouncements from the Western world, the war in Laos was limited to minor skirmishes. But minor or not, the blood I saw was real. There was the nineteen-year-old boy who had stepped on a land mine. He had been a soldier since he was fifteen. I saw another boy with part of his face shot away. I saw the blood, I saw the look in the eyes of the wounded, frightened soldiers. I felt that knot in my stomach that comes when war is no longer something you read about in newspapers.[1]
> —Father Matt J. Menger, Sam Thong, Laos, 1963.

Pushing from Both Ends

Throughout 1963 and into early 1964 the United States, at Prime Minister Souvanna's behest, continued to resupply the rightist and neutralist armies. DEPCHIEF processed military aid shipments through Bangkok and up to the Thai-Lao border, where the material could be trucked or airlifted to the waiting forces. Similarly, a Hanoi-administered military assistance program used Vietnamese truck convoys and Soviet-built transport aircraft to keep supplies moving from the Communist bloc to the Pathet Lao. More than three hundred Vietnamese "construction workers" on the Plain of Jars appeared to be analogous to the DEPCHIEF and USAID/RO employees laboring in Bangkok and Vientiane. Unlike the United States, however, the North Vietnamese had maintained a significant number of ground troops inside Laos. By mid-May 1963 Hanoi had deployed eleven battalions of the People's Army of Vietnam (PAVN), comprising about five thousand troops, to protect north-south cross-border trails. These units also provided support to the Pathet Lao.[2]

Meanwhile, the Lao internal military and political situation moved toward complete fracture. Neutralist troops on the western side of the Plain of Jars, now joined by rightist forces, were frequent targets of Vietnamese artillery fire. On June 6, 1963, Souvanna publicly charged Pathet Lao–North Vietnamese collusion in the attacks and, two weeks later, halted government funds to Souphanouvong's faction. The action was significant because Souvanna had previously honored an agreement with North Vietnam not to acknowledge the presence of PAVN forces in Laos in exchange for their withdrawal after the Geneva accord.[3]

In Vientiane right-wing police harassed the remaining Pathet Lao officials and their small security detachment. As a result, tripartite meetings on the Plain of Jars in December 1963 and direct talks between Souvanna and Souphanouvong in Sam Neua during mid-January 1964 explored the possibility of establishing Luang Prabang as a new "demilitarized" seat of government. The plan failed to materialize, however, as the Pathet Lao, in late January, launched a military campaign in central Laos, and fighting erupted between rightist/neutralist forces and communist positions on the Plain of Jars.[4] It was obvious that the three Lao factions were intent on using military means to solve a manifestly political problem.

Seeking goodwill, in early April Souvanna paid official visits to Peking and Hanoi. The Chinese, who had previously championed Souvanna's neutralist position, received the prime minister with suspicion and cool formality. During an official banquet Premier Chou En-Lai accused American "imperialists"—and, by association, Souvanna—with violating the Geneva agreements. A subsequent joint Chinese-Lao communique was less strident, with Chou calling for an internal Lao political settlement among the Pathet Lao, the neutralists, and the right wing.[5]

The prime minister's call on the Hanoi leadership was not nearly as sociable. Throughout the visit one of Souvanna's aides was held virtually incommunicado, and General Giap, commander of the PAVN, tersely told the prince that the Vietnamese "could not tolerate the presence of troops on the Plain of Jars other than those of the Pathet Lao."[6] The North Vietnamese were not in a negotiating mood.

Upon returning home Souvanna arranged a meeting on the Plain of Jars with Prince Souphanouvong and General Phoumi. Hoping to provide a safe locale for all members of the coalition government, Souvanna once again suggested that the three leaders declare Luang Prabang a "demilitarized" area. Failing to gain any agreement, the dejected prime minister, now threatening resignation, returned to Vientiane. The following day, April 19,

1964, Souvanna was arrested by two right-wing generals, Kouprasith Abhay and Siho Lamphouthacoul.[7]

Ending the Tripartite Coalition

The events in Vientiane on the morning of April 19, 1964, marked a
milestone in recent Lao history. Their importance was comparable to that
of the events of August 8, 1960. The attempt by the rightist officers to
take matters into their own hands . . . shook the foundations of the
coalition government. How . . . could one believe that there was goodwill when supporters of one of the three parties were declaring flatly that
they had replaced the tripartite government?''[8]

It was a question the United States was loathe to answer. DEPCHIEF and
USAID/RO were working hard to train and supply the right-wing, and to
some extent the neutralist, military elements of the Lao government. Now,
with the right wing seizing power, Washington was forced to rebuke its
Vientiane favorites or face a total breakdown of the tripartite government.

Ambassador Unger, who had been attending a diplomatic conference in
South Vietnam, rushed back to Laos and quickly communicated America's
displeasure to the offending generals. Unger, supported by the other Western ambassadors, also urged King Savang Vatthana and General Phoumi to
assist in the restoration of the Souvanna government. Faced with over-
whelming Western opposition and a likely termination of military and
economic assistance, on April 22 Kouprasith and Siho released Souvanna.
The next day, in exchange for several political and military changes within
the government, the generals agreed to support Souvanna's return to power.[9]

Oddly enough, while the right wing was now in the ascendancy, General
Phoumi emerged from the coup a loser. Siho and Kouprasith regarded
Phoumi's power as excessive and wanted a share of the general's lucrative
opium, gold, and gambling interests. On May 2, acquiescing to Kouprasith
and Siho, Souvanna personally replaced Phoumi as minister of defense,
established a military committee to reorganize FAR command and control,
and announced plans to merge the rightist and neutralist military factions.[10]

The United States supported the solution, feeling the need to back the
generals while ensuring Souvanna's presence as the symbol of a ''neutral''
government. Souphanouvong, correctly foreseeing a de facto–rightist takeover and an end to any neutralist influence within the coalition, demanded

that his brother reinstate the tripartite government. But Souvanna, under pressure from the right wing, was no longer in a position to allow neutralist or Pathet Lao representation in his cabinet. On June 3, 1964, Souphanou-vong declared that the Pathet Lao no longer recognized Souvanna as prime minister, thereby ending any further pretense of communist participation in the Royal Lao government.[11]

Returning to the Battlefield

Warfare is a dynamic process that continually engenders new killing tech-nology. A successful and professional military must constantly update its weaponry or risk destruction by a technically superior armed force. Tech-nology alone, of course, cannot ensure military dominance. It does, none-theless, offer a means by which even small countries may prevail in the face of more powerful, but less technologically advanced, adversaries.

Despite years of American efforts the Royal Lao military was not, and in all likelihood would never be, a match for the PAVN. It was predictable, therefore, that the United States would eventually decide to boost the Lao government's military capability against the communists by providing the FAR with more advanced weapons and, in particular, combat-capable air-craft.

The upgrading of the Royal Lao Air Force (RLAF) began in August 1963, when the United States gave the Souvanna government six T-28 airplanes and provided a U.S. Air Force Mobile Training Team (MMT) for initial instruction and maintenance services at Vientiane's Wattay airfield.[12] The intended use of, and U.S. control over, these airplanes is outlined in a October 26, 1963, message from the U.S. State Department to Ambassador Unger:

> We are not rpt [repeat] not yet prepared to authorize use of T-28's . . . except in response to certain clearly aggressive PL actions. Reaffirm, however, previous authorization for T-28's to attempt intercept and down any NVN illegal supply flights. Do not rpt not approve use of bombs for cratering Route 7. Washington approval should be requested for types of other possible uses you would recommend for bombs.[13]

In the words of the U.S. Air Force attaché in Vientiane at the time, "They had six T-28s with .50 caliber guns. They had never dropped a bomb, and that was the extent of the tactical Lao Air Force. I don't believe they were able to keep more than three of those six in commission at any one time." [14] It was apparent that if the United States wanted a combat-effective Lao air force it would have to provide the Lao a higher level of training and repair support. Such activity in Laos, however, would have been an obvious violation of the Geneva agreements.

Project "Waterpump"

On December 6, 1963, CINCPAC recommended to the secretary of defense that a T-28 Air Commando detachment from the USAF Special Air Warfare Center at Eglin Air Force Base, Florida, be deployed to Udorn, Thailand, to "provide realistic operational experience to RLAF aircrews and to provide a ready operational force to augment the RLAF as required." [15]

In mid-March 1964 thirty-eight U.S. Air Force officers and enlisted men of Detachment 6, 1st Air Commando Wing—code-named "Waterpump"— arrived in Saigon. Half the group remained temporarily in Vietnam to assemble four crated T-28s, while the rest departed for Thailand. Using Air America equipment at Udorn, the detachment established a T-28 maintenance facility and immediately began a T-28 ground-and-flight school for Thai and Lao pilots. The pilots were well-qualified flyers, but most had difficulty mastering American bombing tactics. By mid-May Waterpump, augmented by additional T-28s from South Vietnam, had more than a dozen graduates flying daily bombing and reconnaissance missions over Laos. For identification, and as a measure of competence, the American flyers were called the "A Team," while the Thai pilots were designated the "B Team," and the Lao were the "C Team." [16]

To coordinate this activity the State Department established a primary Air Operations Center (AOC) at Wattay and a secondary AOC at Lao Air Force headquarters in Savannakhet. The Waterpump team provided the AOCs with communications equipment and map, targeting, and pilot-briefing rooms. Waterpump personnel in civilian clothes staffed the Wattay AOC; they were required to return to Thailand every evening. Eventually this restriction was relaxed, and the men were allowed to reside in Vientiane. A similar situation existed at Savannakhet, where a U.S. Air Force assistant air attaché was placed in command. In addition to manning the AOCs, Waterpump airmen, who were designated "civilians" by the U.S.

embassy in Vientiane, assisted the Lao air force at Wattay and Savannakhet with maintenance and bomb-loading tasks.[17]

On April 27, while Vientiane was embroiled in political turmoil, the Pathet Lao launched a heavy attack against Kong Le's forces. According to Charles Stevenson, the assault was carried out in response to Souvanna's violation of the Geneva accords, and after a series of FAR and Hmong operations against communist positions along the border and on the southern edge of the Plain of Jars.[18]

Washington's reaction was to follow the Kennedy strategy: President Johnson ordered a troop alert on Okinawa and directed the Seventh Fleet, already in the South China Sea, to prepare for military action.[19] Of more immediate importance, the Waterpump-supported Thai and Lao pilots were ordered to begin a stepped-up bombing and reconnaissance campaign against communist positions on the plain. While this aerial assault averted what might have been Kong Le's complete destruction, by May 16 the neutralists had been driven from the plain, and thousands of Hmong villagers were streaming south.[20]

The Issue of U.S. Aerial Reconnaissance

The performance level of the Thai and Lao pilots, as had been demonstrated during their training at Udorn, was competent, but far below that which American pilots could provide and which Washington now desired. During a National Security Council meeting on April 29, 1964, security aides showed President Johnson U-2 reconnaissance photographs that "revealed major improvements in road networks [in Laos], the effect of which is to improve Hanoi's ability to back up forces in Laos or in South Vietnam." The North Vietnamese construction spread from Route 12, located east of Thakek, down to Tchepone, a Laotian town situated directly west of the demilitarized zone between North and South Vietnam.[21] Therefore, while the fighting on the Plain of Jars represented a serious escalation of Lao hostilities, it was also a useful catalyst for increased U.S. military reconnaissance of communist infiltration along the Laotian–South Vietnamese border.[22]

This intelligence opportunity was discussed on May 18, 1964, in an urgent telephone conference involving senior White House, SECSTATE, DOD, and CIA officials in Washington, and Ambassador Unger in Vienti-

ane. Unger had just reported via cable to the State Department that Souvanna had rejected an American request for low-level jet reconnaissance
flights over Laos. According to Unger's message, Souvanna requested the
flights not take place at this time, "believing such action would be exploited
by [the] communists (and perhaps others) as direct military intervention."
Unger concurred with the prime minister that the overflights were not a
good idea.[23]

Nevertheless, seeking to bolster a *reclama* to the prince, the Washington
group recounted to Unger the advantages of reconnaissance activity over
Laos: [a] way of pinpointing targets . . . morale effect in conjunction with
increasing and more effective T-28 operations . . . noncombat operation
designed to give him [Souvanna] facts on situation.'' The officials added,
"We believe all these warrant operation in themselves, but also have in
mind golden chance to route aircraft over Tchepone area on way north."
The Washington policymakers then told Unger:

> We do not have in mind authorizing this [overflights] at once if Souvanna
> opposed, but are considering groundwork from which we might proceed
> in day or two even without his consent. . . . Would Souvanna be really
> upset if we did?''[24]

Available records do not indicate when or how Unger conveyed Washington's wishes to Souvanna, but U.S. Air Force RF-101 and U.S. Navy
RF-8A and RA-3B jet reconnaissance flights, code-named "Yankee Team,"
first flew over southern Laos on May 19 and began flights over the Plain of
Jars two days later. According to a State Department account submitted to
a U.S. congressional committee in 1969, Souvanna approved the flights on
May 18 and issued a communique on May 28 endorsing the flights as
"necessary to observe Communist violations of the accords."[25]

The facts do not support this account of early approval by the prime
minister. First, it was on May 18 that Ambassador Unger reported Souvanna's opposition to the reconnaissance flights. If the Congressional testimony
is correct, Souvanna was persuaded in a matter of hours to reverse his
negative position on the reconnaissance flights.[26] Such a rapid change of
heart is improbable. Moreover, Ambassador Unger recalls showing Souvanna the first photographs taken by the Yankee Team. In Unger's words,
"Souvanna was very stressed and upset, *but still did not want to give his
approval for the flights. He condoned it [by not objecting] . . . but never
really supported the flights. He never said you must not do this*" (emphasis

added). Souvanna's great fear, according to Unger, was that Laos would again be dragged into the greater battle for Indochina.[27]

Air America's T-28 Strike Force

The May 18 Washington-Vientiane teleconference also revealed another major change in U.S. policy toward Laos: the decision to use American civilians to fly T-28 combat missions over Laos. Unger observed in his May 18 cable that the United States, if willing to authorize American low-level reconnaissance flights over Laos, should also find acceptable the use of American-piloted T-28s in Laos. The Washington group responded:

> On T-28's we still not rpt not prepared to authorize US military personnel to fly these in PDJ [Plain of Jars] combat. Instead we now repeat now propose turn over the four now rpt now [deleted] at once to Lao, fly them up to Vientiane with bombs . . . and let them be operated by US civilian pilots.[28]

CIA and Air America officials in Vientiane quickly and secretly recruited American civilian pilots to the fly the T-28s. Thomas G. Jenny, a former U.S. Marine Corps pilot now flying U-10 Helio-Couriers for Air America, recalled that he and four other Air America pilots were called by a supervisor to a meeting at the Air America station manager's office. A CIA official asked the pilots if they were willing to fly RLAF-marked T-28s on specified, CIA controlled, attack missions. All agreed and were told by the CIA officer they would soon receive familiarization training at Udorn.[29]

On May 20 Unger requested formal State Department authority to use Air America-piloted T-28s. The ambassador also advised that Souvanna had agreed to the use of the American civilians and discussions were underway to

> issue papers to these pilots and [adjust] personnel records to "terminate" employment with Air America or Bird so that pilots would have status of civilian technicians hired individually by RLG [Royal Lao Government].[30]

Unger's request was approved by the Department of State on the same day.[31]

Meanwhile, the JCS had ordered CINCPAC to transfer immediately five

T-28s and five RT-28s from U.S. Military Assistance Command Vietnam (MACV) to the Waterpump unit. The JCS message noted that the T-28s would be "immediately painted with RLAF markings" and "picked up . . . by civilian pilots or RLAF pilots as indicated by Ambassador Unger."[32]

Two days after Unger received formal State Department authority to use the civilian pilots, the Waterpump unit began T-28 refresher training for the six Air America volunteers. The group, all former military pilots with T-28 experience, spent two days on strafing and bombing practice (dropping napalm and five-hundred-pound bombs) and were judged by the Waterpump instructors to be highly qualified for combat.[33]

On May 25 and 26 the Air America strike force, more commonly called the A Team, attacked targets on the Plain of Jars.[34] Reportedly, during this time Major Drexel B. Cochran, Waterpump commander, also flew at least one authorized strike mission against targets on the Plain of Jars.[35] Ambassador Unger, acutely aware of the international implications should one of the Americans be shot down, remained in the Air America operations building during all of these strike missions.[36] The State Department, with Ambassador Unger as the on-scene commander, now exercised control over an American- and Thai-piloted combat aircraft squadron.

Expanding the Air War in Laos

On June 6, 1964, a U.S. Navy RF-8A Yankee Team reconnaissance jet flown by Lieutenant Charles F. Klusmann was downed by communist gunfire while on a mission over the northeastern corner of the Plain of Jars. Within an hour Air America transport planes had located the pilot and called for a rescue pick-up by Air America H-34s. As the helicopters descended they were hit by gunfire, and an observer was killed. Four Thai-piloted T-28s were then dispatched from Vientiane to provide cover for the rescue. The Thai's were unable to find their target, and a decision was made to send in the A Team T-28s. By the time the Americans reached the scene, however, the Pathet Lao had removed Klusmann from the area.[37] The next day, while flying in the same area, another Navy aircraft was hit. The pilot parachuted safely to the ground and was picked up the following day by an Air America H-34 helicopter.[38]

The loss of the two reconnaissance aircraft resulted in immediate American action. Air America strike force T-28s, directed by CIA case officers in an orbiting transport aircraft, struck communist positions all over the northeastern corner of the plain. The T-28s, according to one of the American pilots, were "officially" flying in support of the search for the downed Navy flyers. In reality the CIA was ordering them to destroy previously identified targets.[39] A more forceful display of U.S. anger and resolve occurred on June 9 when eight U.S. Air Force F-100s attacked a communist antiaircraft position at Xieng Khouang on the Plain of Jars.[40]

For Air America the June 8 rescue of the Navy pilot was a proud accomplishment and the first of many military "saves" to come. Nonetheless, CINCPAC's initial reaction to the shoot-downs was to propose the deployment to Udorn of U.S. Marine Corps rescue helicopters. The idea was shelved when it was recognized that U.S.-marked military aircraft could not be prepositioned legally in Laos, and that the reaction time from Udorn would be too slow. Consequently, COMUSMACV recommended to JCS that Air America be provided with five additional H-34s, and that the contract between DEPCHIEF and Air America be changed to include military rescue work.[41] After some resistance from Admiral Felt at CINCPAC, the Secretary of Defense ordered four H-34s delivered to Air America.[42] It was a wise investment.

The Chinese Connection

Two days after the F-100 air strikes, and apparently without the authority of the United States, Thai-piloted RLAF T-28s attacked the Pathet Lao headquarters at Khang Khay and damaged the Chinese Economic Mission building, killing a civilian.[43] These raids were not publicized, and the United States did not comment on the matter until it was revealed by the PRC's New China News Agency. The Chinese blamed the United States and called the act a "new debt of blood."[44] Prince Souphanouvong also charged that the strikes were conducted by American-flown T-28s "with jets flying cover overhead."[45] The United States denied any involvement in the raids, and the U.S. Air Force air attaché in Vientiane, Colonel Robert L. F. Tyrrell, recalled that "we suspected that they [the Thai pilots] were getting instructions maybe from their own government to hit other than briefed targets."[46]

The attack on Khang Khay exacerbated an existing tense situation between Vientiane and Beijing. On June 9 the *People's Daily* had declared, "The Geneva Agreements are in danger of being completely wrecked."

Shortly thereafter the PRC began to attack Souvanna personally. In turn, Souvanna challenged the (long-standing) presence of two Chinese organizations in Laos: the PRC Economic and Cultural Mission in Khang Khay and the Chinese "road builders" in northern Laos. The Chinese responded by asserting that Souvanna had asked for the establishment of the Khang Khay mission in 1961, and that all road-building efforts had ceased in 1963. They rebuked Souvanna for his "absurd and incredible . . . lack of good faith." This flurry of accusations was an important turning point in PRC-RLG relations: from this time forward the PRC refused to recognize Souvanna's administration as the legitimate government of Laos.[47]

It was not surprising that Souvanna had finally called attention to the Chinese activities at Khang Khay. In 1962 the Royal Lao government had agreed to China's "economic and cultural" presence. At that time the Lao also agreed to Chinese assistance in building a "goodwill" road connecting the northern Lao town of Phong Saly with the village of Mengla in China's Yunnan province. In the intervening years, however, it had become increasingly apparent the Chinese were using the mission and the "road builders" for more than strictly cultural and humanitarian purposes.[48]

According to the testimony of William Sullivan before the U.S. Congress, the Chinese Mission at Khang Khay was headed by a People's Liberation Army general officer. The Chinese were suspected by U.S. intelligence sources of having other PLA officers present in Khang Khay to teach "training and tactics" as well as to facilitate the logistics of the movement of Chinese military aid to the Pathet Lao and North Vietnamese armed forces in Laos.[49]

However, the most extensive Chinese activities in Laos, by far, were the road-building operations of the PLA engineering units. Initially, the Chinese worked on the Phong Saly to Mengla road. This fifty-mile "Laotian-Chinese Friendship Highway" was officially dedicated and handed over to the Pathet Lao on May 25, 1963. Without Lao government consultation the Chinese then began to conduct numerous road surveys and built a series of "feeder roads" near the Yunnan border. Moreover, there were growing indications that the Chinese intended to extend their "friendship" roads toward the south and Thailand. The presence of the Chinese, variously estimated at between three and ten thousand men, and their roads was a legitimate concern to the Vientiane government.[50]

The FAR as a "Tripwire"

In early May 1964 the State Department queried the American embassy in Vientiane on the merits of reintroducing a U.S. Military Assistance Advisory Group into Laos "as a means of demonstrating U.S. intent." Ambassador Unger's opening response reflects the thin facade of U.S. activity in Laos.

> Overt changeover over three years ago of PEO into MAAG seemed not to have greatly impressed communists. Since they are no doubt assuming U.S. already deeply involved in advising Lao and supervising delivery and use of MAP, surfacing of any advisory teams would only serve to put U.S. publicly on record as violating Geneva Accords.

Unger then continued with a frank and somber assessment of the Royal Lao armed forces.

> MAAG and White Star teams did a highly commendable job under difficult circumstances, but their experience demonstrated that it is almost impossible to put any real spine into FAR. U.S. prestige was tarnished since one FAR disaster after another inevitably tended to rub off onto U.S. advisors. As stated many times before, do not believe we could ever make fighting force out of FAR such as able to withstand determined Viet Minh-backed PL drive. We should regard FAR as no more than tripwire, all while of course trying to strengthen it wherever possible by appropriate deliveries necessary MAP equipment, advice from ARMA and AIRA [U.S. Army and Air Force attaches], support by T-28's, etc.

Ambassador Unger ended his assessment "I recommend U.S. not unnecessarily involve itself in open violation Geneva Accords and that U.S. prestige not repeat not be publicly linked with such an inept and uninspired army as are the FAR/Neutralists today." [51]

Operation "Triangle"

In mid-July 1964 ten battalions of FAR and neutralist troops launched an attack on Pathet Lao positions west of the Plain of Jars near the junction of Routes 7 and 13. The campaign, code-named "Triangle," was conceived by the Lao government and designed to relieve pressure on neutralist forces located at Muong Soui on the Plain of Jars. The United States, responding to Prime Minister Souvanna's request, was heavily involved in Triangle. Air America transports airlifted troops and supplies, U.S. jets and Thai-piloted T-28s flew reconnaissance and strike missions, and U.S. Forward Air Controllers (FACs) were brought into Laos to direct the air attacks. Air America T-28s, however, were specifically excluded from the operation.[52] A State Department cable advised Ambassador Unger that the U.S. "public and third-country position would be that the operation is mercenary Air America and not US Government . . . and relates directly to the defense of Neutralist forces."[53] Triangle continued for more than ten weeks and met with considerable success on the ground.[54] The intense communist antiaircraft fire directed at the Lao, Thai, and U.S. pilots, however, took its toll.

Action Without Authority

On August 14 an RT-28 was forced down and an F-105 damaged.[55] Four days later the "roof fell in." A Thai-piloted RT-28 was shot down along with an Air America H-34 responding to the scene. Another T-28 flying to the area in bad weather also crashed. Fortunately, three Air America T-28s and a number of U.S. Air Force F-100s and F-105s were able to provide cover fire while an Air America H-34 successfully rescued the wounded and badly burned American pilot. The Thai pilots were never recovered.[56]

Notwithstanding this success, the point remains that in an immediate effort to rescue the downed flyers, Ambassador Unger had disobeyed State Department guidelines. Without prior Washington approval Unger had dispatched Thai and Air America T-28s with permission "to use napalm in effort rescue crew T-28 . . . and any surviving members of helicopter with Air America crew."[57] Air America General Manager David Hickler, who was in the Air America operations center when Unger was briefed on the emergency, remembers that the ambassador was acutely aware his decision could have major ramifications for U.S. interests in Southeast Asia. According to Hickler,

> the Ambassador listened attentively . . . asking the proper questions, and was the center of a quiet but earnest crowd of about ten very concerned individuals. Finally, after a quiet moment of reflection, he said, "OK, let's go. Napalm if it must be but no, repeat no villages or houses are to be hit." Later the Ambassador individually briefed each pilot.

Further, Hickler reported that, while awaiting developments Unger told him that "he [Unger] had acted without proper authorization . . . [but] was well aware of our pilots' concern for a fellow pilot. But he also expressed his duties and obligations . . . to abide by the Geneva accord.'' It was a very difficult time for Ambassador Unger, but he had not hesitated in making his decision.[58]

In a ''Flash'' [highest priority] cable to the State Department Unger explained his action and recommended a cover story.

Regret need for immediate decision prevented me from obtaining prior authorization for use of AA pilots in FAR operation. If any AA piloted T-28 downed and captured we should if queried deny any T-28's piloted by Americans. Instead recommend our reply should state Americans were . . . serving as crew members of helicopter that went to rescue Lao pilots of downed T-28.[59]

The incident raised considerable concern in Washington. White House advisor McGeorge Bundy wrote President Johnson on August 18 that while Unger ''was acting in an emergency situation, and it may well be that we have held him on too tight a guideline here . . . a direct issue of action without authority does exist.'' Bundy further advised the president that the White House staff had already undertaken an ''intense and immediate review'' of the American T-28 program.[60]

The same day Secretary of State Dean Rusk sent a personal ''NODIS'' [No distribution] message to Unger.[61] In an August 19 ''Eyes Only for the Secretary'' response, Unger replied,

Eye fully appreciate and will be closely guided by your message. Situation at time Eye authorized use American pilots in my judgment did not permit of even brief delay entailed in exchange of Flash messages; However, Eye believe our procedures here can be tuned up to assure that we have more time for such decisions in future.[62]

In an August 19 State Department message the American embassy in Vientiane was told ''Yesterday's loss of two T-28's and AA helicopter, together with serious political and military risks involved in rescue operations, raises anew questions of utility and risk factors involved in present . . . T-28 strikes.'' Unger was asked to provide ''suggestions as to how T-28 operations during weeks ahead could best be used so as to maintain above advantages while at same time minimizing possible calls upon U.S. planes and personnel.''[63] Unger responded on August 20, ''I do not see much prospect of reducing calls on US planes and personnel for SAR [search and rescue] operations if we hope to exploit the advantages of our T-28 strike force in present military situation.'' The ambassador ended his cable, showing the strain and frustration of his duties in Vientiane, by saying,

> We are deeply preoccupied with problem of control of military operations in this very difficult political and military situation and constantly attempt keep risks at minimum consistent with objectives which we have set for ourselves in Laos.[64]

In a companion message Ambassador Unger requested greater authority in conducting search and rescue missions.

> Believe Eye require advance authorization for use Air America pilots in T-28 SAR operations if they are to have reasonable chance of success. Eye am confident there would be sharp reduction of effectiveness all air operations if pilots were not persuaded we were prepared to take all reasonable measures to rescue them once they were down. Eye hope Department will grant me discretionary authority to use Air America pilots in T-28s for SAR operations when Eye consider this indispensable to success of operation and with understanding that whenever situation permitted Eye would seek specific authorization from Washington.[65]

As revealed in *The Pentagon Papers,* on August 26 Secretary Rusk agreed to Unger's request.[66]

Despite flying hundreds of search-and-rescue support missions and a handful of ground attack sorties over the next few years, the A Team suffered no casualties and just two lost aircraft.[67] Thus, to the vast relief of the U.S. government, the communists were never able to prove the existence of this State Department/CIA "air force."[68]

America's Yankee Team reconnaissance missions were primarily a reaction to the North Vietnamese penetration of South Vietnam. For the most part, the movement of communist soldiers and supplies across the Plain of Jars and south along the eastern Lao corridor threatened Saigon, not Vientiane. Washington's interest in Laos was now, therefore, merely an adjunct to the expanding war in South Vietnam.

From this point forward the United States would become involved in two distinct, yet interrelated wars in Laos. First, the aerial bombardment of supplies and men traversing Laos destined for South Vietnam. Second—the primary focus of this study—a continuing American effort conducted mostly beyond the confines of the Geneva Accords to protect the Royal Lao government against the North Vietnamese-backed Pathet Lao. America's war in Laos would now move into the shadow of the much larger struggle for South Vietnam.

Chapter Six

WILLIAM SULLIVAN'S WAR

Direction of this war effort was a tremendously absorbing and enervating task. I eventually carried in my head, just short of my subconscious, a working knowledge of our deployments, the terrain, the roads and trails, the enemy dispositions, and our aircraft availability. Many a night I . . . had to decide whether to order the evacuation of an outpost under attack, to hold on, to reinforce, to call for air support, or to mount a diversionary action. . . . It was a far cry from the normal pursuits of the striped-pants set.[1]
    —William H. Sullivan, U.S. ambassador to Laos, 1964–69.

Charles Stevenson appropriately called the conflict in Laos "William Sullivan's war."[2] Indeed, during his tenure in Laos Sullivan presided over a considerable air and ground campaign. More important, however, was Sullivan's ability to manage the conflict in such a way as to preserve the facade of American adherence to the Geneva agreements. For nearly five years he ensured the concealment of American military aid to Laos and, thereby, provided Souvanna Phouma and the Soviet Union with the political "cover" necessary to ignore U.S. violations of the Geneva agreements.[3]

The Field Marshall

Considered brilliant by most and tyrannical by many, in November 1964 William H. Sullivan succeeded Leonard Unger as U.S. ambassador to Laos.[4] Sullivan, who had been Averell Harriman's principal deputy in Geneva, was especially well informed regarding U.S. foreign policy objectives in Southeast Asia. He was also completely comfortable with the power invested in him by the May 1961 "Kennedy Letter." When questioned about this authority by a U.S. Senate committee in 1969 Sullivan said

> This letter provides the Ambassador with Presidential authority to direct the actions of the various representatives of the agencies present in his mission and requires coordination by them with him in the execution of their functions. Laos [has] no organic [U.S.] military command present and functioning on Lao soil . . . many functions that would ordinarily in a circumstance such as we face in Laos [would] be a direct responsibility of the military chain of command. By virtue of the 1962 agreements and by virtue of the circumstances prevailing in Laos, these are matters that fall within the province of the Ambassador and of his policy directions.[5]

According to former CIA official Douglas Blaufarb, Sullivan's specific authority was required for all U.S. activities originating in Laos, for some Lao military operations, and for air and ground actions that, although planned elsewhere, would occur inside the country. This power included:

> Permanent and temporary assignment in Laos of all personnel concerned with military activity. Budget requests for MAP. Ground rules governing movements of U.S. advisory personnel within Laos. Construction of U.S. military facilities. Sizable movements of Lao military . . . by U.S.-controlled aircraft. Advance approval of preplanned [U.S.] air attacks against targets in Laos. Approval of rules of engagement and ground rules for other types of [U.S.] activity.[6]

Sullivan's authority in Laos was well known to U.S. military officials from Southeast Asia to Washington. Admiral U.S. Grant Sharp, CINCPAC from 1964 to 1968, recalls excellent relations with Sullivan, even though the ambassador would often bypass CINCPAC and communicate directly with the JCS. "Sullivan had presidential authority in Laos and that was OK with me. I was convinced the fight was in Vietnam."[7]

This view of Sullivan's role was not shared by General William C. Westmoreland, commander, U.S. Military Assistance Command, Vietnam (COMUSMACV): "Sullivan was often involved in purely military matters . . . but the key to the matter was Washington's interpretation of the Geneva Agreements of 1962. Sullivan had marching orders from the White House and made no secret of his clout."[8] Sullivan later remarked

> By the time I went to Laos as Ambassador, I had been working here [Washington] very closely with Mac Bundy, Bob McNamara, Bus Wheeler,

and John McCone, and all the other bosses of the individual members of the team out there, all of whom I could get in touch with directly.[9]

As a result, although Westmoreland chafed at the ambassador's involvement in COMUSMACV's Laotian operations, Sullivan's authority over U.S. military activity in Laos went largely unquestioned.[10] Admiral Sharp and General Westmoreland were soon referring to Sullivan as "the field marshall."[11]

These myriad responsibilities, as well as the performance of normal diplomatic functions, called for innovative embassy management techniques. Ambassador Sullivan continued Leonard Unger's policy of a daily staff meeting but began the practice, "unprecedented in the Foreign Service," of attending the gathering. Sullivan·said

> I [took] steps as Ambassador there to have a daily meeting with all the chiefs of various elements of the mission, all of the representatives of the other agencies, to make sure not only that I was informed of all their problems and interests and intentions, but that there was cross-fertilization [between the elements and agencies]. In this way there was no excuse for anyone being out of step through ignorance of the facts.[12]

It was during these meetings and in private sessions with the CIA Station Chief and the embassy's military attaches that Sullivan shaped and administered his multifaceted war.

The Vang Pao Army

In early 1962 the CIA and Vang Pao established two large bases for what was now commonly called *L'Armée Clandestine:* one at Long Tieng, the new Military Region Two headquarters for the "secret army," and another at Sam Thong, a USAID-operated hill tribe refugee center and, in effect, the civil headquarters for the Hmong. Both complexes were located a few miles southwest of the Plain of Jars and possessed modern communications equipment, medical facilities, and all-weather, laterite-surfaced airfields. Supported by CIA and U.S. military advisors—who seemed to possess an unlimited supply of airplanes, equipment, and supplies—and confident of USAID-administered care for those Hmong displaced by the fighting, Vang Pao pressed his guerilla war against the North Vietnamese and Pathet Lao.[13]

By 1964 *L'Armée Clandestine* had taken a form and strategic posture

which would remain largely unchanged for the next five years. Vang Pao
had reorganized his army into

> two categories of units, regional platoons and companies assigned local
> tasks, and a species of strike force called a Special Guerilla Unit, or
> SGU. The SGU's were directly under Vang Pao's headquarters and were
> used for major offensive or defensive purposes. In time they numbered
> over ten thousand out of a total irregular force of about thirty thousand.[14]

Vang Pao and his advisors concentrated on simple, weather-driven tactics. During the June-to-October rainy season the SGUs could be transported by U.S. military and U.S.–contracted aircraft, or both, into communist-controlled areas where they could harass enemy positions and supply lines. The North Vietnamese and Pathet Lao forces, which had become
"road-bound . . . dependent upon wheeled vehicles to move their heavy
weapons and to bring up their rice and ammunition", were forced to remain
in defensive posts until the weather cleared; thus, the war in northeastern
Laos took on a seasonal routine where the Hmong scored military gains
during the rainy months and then retreated in the face of communist offen-
sives in the dry season.[15]

During early 1964, for example, the North Vietnamese deployed an
estimated four battalions (twelve hundred men) to the area of Nong Het,
near the Lao-Vietnamese border, to counter Hmong guerilla operations.
The Hmong, practicing good tactics, avoided contact with the numerically
superior enemy. But then, on February 25, the Vietnamese launched a
massive artillery and mortar barrage against the Hmong stronghold at Phou
Khe, a seven thousand-foot-high mountain southwest of the Plain of Jars.
In a fifteen-hour battle the communists were able to capture the base and
disperse the Hmong defenders.[16]

On February 19, 1966, a combined Pathet Lao–North Vietnamese force
staged an intensive attack on Na Khang, also known as Lima site 36. Na
Khang, located northeast of the Plain of Jars, was an important forward
operating area and served as a CIA "sector" headquarters. It was also a
base from which U.S. search-and-rescue helicopters could be dispatched to
pick up downed pilots in Laos and North Vietnam.

During the engagement Vang Pao arrived by helicopter at a small village
near Na Khang. As the general was stepping from the aircraft he was shot
in the right arm and chest.[17] Vang Pao was immediately evacuated to Korat,
Thailand, for treatment at a U.S. Air Force hospital. Although Vang Pao
was not critically wounded, the Pathet Lao immediately began to propagan-

dize the Hmong leader's death. One American reported that a "pall fell over the Hmong upon hearing the news." Vang Pao soon made a tape recording refuting his demise in Hmong, Lao, and French. The tape was played for three days over a government radio station and convinced the Hmong field units of Vang Pao's survival. Vang Pao was later flown to Tripler Army Medical Center in Honolulu, Hawaii for further medical treatment and a short vacation.[18]

When the general returned to Laos he ordered Battalion 201, the Hmong unit operating closest to him at Na Khang, to assemble at Long Tieng. Apparently Vang Pao, upon checking with his unit commanders, had been told that evidence suggested that it was not a communist soldier who shot the general. The entire unit was asked to drink a "special water" which, according to Hmong beliefs, would kill anyone who did not possess a "true heart."[19]

This incident accurately reflects Vang Pao's "two worlds." On one hand the general could call upon the full range of advanced American weaponry and matériel support. At the same time, Vang Pao and his people remained quite superstitious and, in a Western sense, wholly unsophisticated. While Vang Pao was hospitalized in Thailand, Ambassador Sullivan intervened personally to convince the general to have a steel pin placed in his arm. The general agreed to the operation only after the ambassador explained that "the steel would eventually melt as it was warmed by the body, and would eventually depart from the system just like bad spirits."[20] This spirit belief, which the Hmong call *Tlan,* brings into question Vang Pao's full understanding of modern military technology.

Vang Pao was unquestionably a brave and charismatic leader who possessed an unparalleled understanding of the North Vietnamese mind-set.[21] He was a "soldier's soldier" who quickly impressed many senior U.S. military and civilian officials. In the spring of 1972 General Creighton W. Abrams, General Westmoreland's successor as COMUSMACV, met Vang Pao at Long Tieng and later remarked to CIA Chief of Station B. Hugh Tovar that the Hmong commander was "a major general by anybody's standards."[22] There seems little basis, however, for Ambassador Sullivan's claim that Vang Pao was "a military genius," who planned and controlled the war in northeastern Laos.[23] The Hmong general provided tremendous inspiration to his people. But, as the war progressed and involved greater levels of modern technology, it was CIA and U.S. military expertise that controlled the planning and direction (with the ambassador's approval) of the secret war in Laos.

Watching the Enemy

Because aerial reconnaissance alone was insufficient to determine the full
extent of enemy operations, Hmong and Thai PARU also engaged in "Road
Watch" (RWT) and commando operations along the border and inside
North Vietnam. These teams became essential to intelligence collection and
to what William Colby has termed "the perfect marriage of the guerilla and
the airplane."[24] According to a USAF pilot who worked with the Vang Pao
army,

> The Road Watch teams . . . were well trained, used their binoculars,
> counted trucks, counted troops, determined where they were moving, and
> got hard intelligence. They were effective. The difficult thing about Road
> Watch teams was trying to recruit because the mortality rate was pretty
> high. It wasn't so difficult inserting them; you could take them in by
> chopper and put them down fairly near the target area and have them go
> in over the ground. But then getting them out [was often very difficult].[25]

A typical RWT mission is described in a December 17, 1966, USAF
document: "[Road Watch team] now being readied for 5 day operation with
observation post . . . overlooking Route 912. Position . . . presents very
good vantage point . . . [S]egment contains numerous truck parks . . .
supporting considerable vehicular and foot traffic."[26] The RWT were routinely flown into enemy territory aboard USAF CH-3, and later CH-53,
"Jolly Green Giant" helicopters. These missions, designated "Pony Express," were often augmented by Air America H-34s and supported by
USAF ground attack aircraft.[27]

RWT observations were reported in a variety of ways. Still and movie
cameras were used by some of the teams to provide intelligence officials
with photographs of enemy activity. The CIA also provided the RWTs with
picture cards showing communist vehicles and weapons. Each piece of
equipment was assigned a code name, thereby allowing the infiltrators to
radio simple messages to circling aircraft and to intelligence centers in Laos
and Thailand.[28] More common, after 1967, was the use of "counting
devices" that allowed the RWT "to press picture-coded keys as many times
as they saw a particular piece of equipment pass by on the trail. This
information would then be gathered by an orbiting aircraft."[29] Theodore
Shackley, CIA station chief in Laos during Ambassador Sullivan's tenure,
says that lightweight communications beepers were sometimes implanted in
the stocks of assault rifles provided to Hmong agents. This allowed the CIA
to track the locations of their operatives.[30]

Commando operations inside North Vietnam and along the border included tapping Vietnamese telephone lines and ambushing and destroying
enemy trucks, ammunition, and fuel supplies. One of the most daring,
albeit least effective, commando actions occurred in July 1970 when a team
of twenty-two Hmong raiders infiltrated North Vietnam. Their mission was
to attack the town of Hoa Binh, an important logistical point located half-
way between Hanoi and the Vietnamese-Lao border. The Hmong succeeded
in firing eight mortar rounds at a supply depot before being detected by
Vietnamese soldiers with tracking dogs. In a prolonged firefight twenty-one
of the commandos were killed, and the lone survivor was captured and
imprisoned.[31]

Refugee Relief

This alternating, offensive/defensive war had a tragic effect on the Laotian
hill tribes and their traditional mountain lifestyles. In addition to the misery
over their dead and wounded, the tribesmen were buffeted constantly by the
maneuvering of Vang Pao and communist forces. Villagers were unable to
plant and harvest crops, tend their livestock, or take any other actions other
than those required for their day-to-day existence. Refugee assistance,
therefore, became a very important component of U.S. military assistance
to the Royal Lao government. As one U.S. military officer who served with
the Hmong has said, "The Hmong cast their lot with us. We said that we
would take care of them."[32]

USAID, by presidential decision, was given responsibility for refugee
care. In April 1972 a senior USAID official stated

> The AID organization in Laos has been providing the care and feeding as
> well as health services for many tens of thousands of refugees for more
> than 10 years. Some of these refugees are the dependents of paramilitary
> forces who have long since been forced out of their native hills by the
> North Vietnamese Army. Some of the sick and wounded are paramilitary
> soldiers. . . . Some are civilians: men, women, and children unconnected
> with the armed forces.[33]

The Sam Thong–based USAID refugee headquarters was the nerve
center for these services and for the coordination of daily movements of
people and supplies throughout northeastern Laos. Heading the USAID
effort was Edgar "Pop" Buell, a retired Indiana farmer who first came to
Laos in 1960 as a volunteer with the pacifist International Voluntary Ser-

vices organization.[34] Buell was a profane, hard-working widower who dedicated his life to the Hmong. In turn, he was revered by the highlanders and praised by everybody in the American Mission in Laos.[35]

Using Air America and the other civilian air carriers, Buell provided the dislocated tribespeople with food, building materials, and medical attention. Sam Thong and Long Tieng rapidly grew into large, bustling towns, populated by refugees and the families of Vang Pao's soldiers. USAID workers at Sam Thong also monitored the needs of those who remained in the mountains. Contract aircraft constantly delivered supplies to remote mountaintops and valleys and also provided a tribal shuttle service to the markets of Long Tieng and Sam Thong.[36]

Bookkeeping

The tempo of Vang Pao's military operations and the associated refugee support programs required hundreds of contracted airlift sorties per week. Helicopter and fixed wing crews were very busy, mostly in the daytime, handling refugee assistance, troop movements, and unit resupply.[37] These intertwined military and refugee support activities posed unique scheduling and accountability problems.

Although the civilian air carriers in Laos operated under separate USAID, CIA, and USAID/RO (DOD) contracts, aircraft crews often performed work where the contracts were "mixed." It was not unusual for a single pilot to fly a variety of missions, both military and civilian related, over the course of a day. For example, morning duty at a Lima site could involve the movement of food supplies, while the afternoon assignment might entail the movement of FAR or SGU troops.

This complex system was managed by an "Air Support Branch" (ASB) within the USAID/RO. The ASB, in close coordination with the contract air carriers and the "customers", would publish at Udorn and Vientiane a daily flight operations schedule. However, with the aircraft often operating at the direction of on-scene USAID, CIA, and USAID/RO officials, success was largely dependent upon responsive and flexible air crews.[38]

The "secret" nature of the war notwithstanding, U.S. and contractor regulations required strict accountability for every aircraft sortie. Pilots-in-command were responsible for recording the actual flying hours devoted to each contract, and these flight logs were submitted to company supervisors. The records then became the basis for U.S. government compensation to the contractors.[39] U.S. congressional inquiries into the mixing of these contracts, and the appropriateness of USAID's involvement in military-related activity, would eventually result in revised accounting procedures. These changes will be discussed in the following chapter.

The Military Aid Pipeline

The United States employed two clandestine logistical systems to channel military aid into Laos; one, Department of Defense, directed at the Lao military regulars and the other Central Intelligence Agency designed to support the Laotian paramilitary forces. DEPCHIEF and the USAID/RO, designed to sidestep the Geneva accords, acted in the place of the prohibited U.S. Military Assistance Advisory Group.

> [DEPCHIEF] wrote the programs, established the training arrangements, and provided technical assistance. USAID/RO worked with the Ambassador, the Attaches, and the RLG [Royal Lao Government] General Staff and forces in determining support requirements. To a very limited extent USAID/RO personnel performed advisory functions in field units. USAID/RO did little monitoring of MAP material use and maintenance.[40]

The CIA operation, of which little information has been declassified, was managed and directed by the agency from its 4802d Joint Liaison Detachment at Udorn, Thailand. Unlike the DOD system, where most of the Laos-destined matériel was delivered by merchant ships to Thai ports and then trucked up to the border and transported across the Mekong River, all CIA supplies were air-shipped from Udorn into Laos.[41]

The CIA program, by its very nature, operated with limited bureaucratic oversight. On the other hand, the DEPCHIEF-administered Military Assistance Program was subject to strict guidelines. Nevertheless, the limited ability of Requirements Office personnel to inspect the Lao use and maintenance of U.S.-supplied military equipment invited corruption and misuse of the matériel. While the United States was determined to minimize violations of the Geneva agreements, it became clear that the military aid program required the presence of additional U.S. military personnel.

"Project 404"

In 1966, the Department of Defense began "Project 404", a covert augmentation of DEPCHIEF and the U.S. military attachés in Laos. Under the program about 120 U.S. Air Force and Army personnel and some 5 civilians were administratively assigned to DEPCHIEF in Thailand but served in Laos.

> Included were [radio] communicators, intelligence, and operation specialists in about a 70/30 army/air force mix. They were stationed at RLAF bases and Army Military Region Headquarters to advise, assist in the targeting effort, and to effect coordination of regional air support requirements.[42]

Project 404 substantially improved the U.S. military aid program to Laos. For the first time DEPCHIEF and the U.S. attachés in Laos had active-duty U.S. military personnel submitting regular status reports on the condition of U.S. supplied matériel and the performance of the Lao military. This feedback was essential to the proper management of the aid program and allowed planners to determine more effectively future Lao military needs.[43]

Apart from placing additional active-duty military personnel in the kingdom, Project 404 also signaled an important change in the U.S. military's involvement in the Laotian war. Although many acted as legitimate trainers for the Lao, a good number of the 404 personnel assumed technical duties related to the burgeoning Southeast Asian air war. In particular, the men filled an important need for skilled coordination between the Lao Air Operations Centers and Laotian and American military aircraft.

The "Ravens"

Similarly, faced with a lack of qualified indigenous air controllers, the United States in late 1966 began to station in Laos nearly two dozen USAF Forward Air Controllers (FACs), nicknamed "Ravens." Apparently this was a unilateral decision; according to 1969 Congressional testimony, "The RLG did not ask for FACs per se; however, in the RLG request for US assistance, the Country team determined they were necessary to provide proper control for air operations."[44]

The Ravens, all volunteers with previous FAC experience in Vietnam, were given six-month temporary duty orders and administratively assigned to the Waterpump detachment at Udorn, Thailand. In practice, the men lived and worked at one of the five Lao Air Operations Centers (Luang Prabang, Vientiane, Long Tieng, Savannakhet, and Pakse). The group wore civilian clothes, carried USAID identification cards, flew Royal Lao Air Force 0-1, U-17, and T-28 aircraft, and operated under the direction of the American ambassador in Vientiane.[45] Flying with English-speaking indigenous observers and Forward Air Guides who possessed the authority under the Lao "rules of engagement" to validate targets, the Ravens provided indispensable targeting assistance for U.S. and Laotian aircraft.[46]

Not surprisingly, Long Tieng was one of the busiest and most demanding FAC assignments in Laos. Nearly a dozen Ravens flew in support of Vang Pao's operations, and the elite pilots meshed well with the Hmong irregulars and their CIA case officers. For many of the Ravens, however, the assignment at Long Tieng was bittersweet. Isolation from the regular U.S. Air Force, combined with a feeling that their highly dangerous work was unappreciated by senior American military officers, produced dissension and morale problems. One outspoken Raven told an Air Force interviewer,

> We felt our duty was to Vang Pao and CIA, and the Air Force came in way last. The Air Force paid us, and that was about all they did. We got no support from Vientiane [or higher headquarters]. Our loyalties lay with Vang Pao and the CIA.[47]

The Raven perception of their Vientiane- and Thailand-bound leaders was well known within the U.S. embassy in Laos. Nonetheless, the Ravens performed a critical function and their superiors mostly ignored the irreverent behavior. It was, after all, U.S. policy which required the FACs to operate as "civilians" outside of normal military control. A certain degree of independence and grousing was accepted. Thus, Colonel Tyrrell, a long-term air attaché in Laos, praised the Ravens as "a great bunch . . . a few oddballs along the line, but for the most part . . . they did a fantastic job."[48]

The Raven program in Laos was viewed quite differently by a number of senior U.S. Air Force officers. Major General James F. Kirkendall, who served as a senior air force commander in Vietnam and Thailand, recognized the importance of the Raven FACs. But General Kirkendall believed that some of the Ravens exhibited a contempt for authority that extended to their flying. "This kind of thing is human nature but I can only regretfully note that their lack of discipline both in the air and on the ground resulted in the unnecessary deaths of far too many of these fine young men."[49]

General Kirkendall's comments also reflected a larger U.S. military concern that the American embassy in Vientiane was improperly employing air power in Laos.

Managing the Air War in Laos

On December 8, 1964, Ambassador Sullivan received a joint State–Defense Department message "to seek approval for American airstrikes on hostile communications in Laos."[50] In a December 10 response Sullivan advised Washington that the prime minister was ready to "cooperate in full measure with our proposals." Still, Souvanna Phouma was opposed to any public acknowledgement of the attacks, by either the Lao or the U.S. governments. Sullivan reported:

> He [Souvanna] fully supports the US program of pressures against North Vietnam and believes they should be carried out with deliberate "*Sang-Froid* [coolness]." He reviewed his familiar contention that actions speak louder than words and believes we should . . . let the actions speak for themselves.[51]

Secretary of Defense Robert McNamara quickly authorized the air attacks and on December 14 four U.S. Air Force F-105 jets, accompanied by eleven reconnaissance and combat air patrol aircraft, struck at a bridge near the town of Nape in eastern Laos. A navigational error caused the F-105s to miss their target, but the bombing of eastern Laos, called "Barrel Roll," was under way.[52] Additional U.S. bombing programs in southern Laos, code-named "Steel Tiger" and "Tiger Hound," began, respectively, in April and December of 1965.[53]

Ambassador Sullivan possessed considerable faith in his own military judgments and rarely sought counsel outside his embassy. Sullivan has written, "Washington gave me a free hand to run it as best I could without interference. I can remember only two direct military instructions that I received in the four-and-a-half years in Laos."[54] When Sullivan did require military advice it came from the CIA chief of station and the U.S. military attachés. In the particular case of air power, Colonel Robert Tyrrell has said:

> I report to the Ambassador proposals for air strikes that come to us from the Laotian military forces and the American military commands and in turn, I submit to U.S. commands the requirements for air strikes approved by the Ambassador, which supplements the RLAF [Royal Lao Air Force] capability.[55]

This procedure caused a great deal of resentment within U.S. military circles in Udorn and Saigon. Aside from the galling presumption that a diplomat knew more about the employment of air power than trained airmen, the presence of Road Watch teams sometimes prevented COMUS-MACV from striking areas along communist infiltration routes in southern Laos.[56]

Also, under this system, an embassy-based air force colonel was acting in the place of a senior air commander. U.S. Air Force general officers in Thailand and South Vietnam had no choice but to endure a situation where their planes were being ordered into battle by a military subordinate. Moreover, air force officers in Udorn and Saigon widely believed that the CIA station chief in Laos was actually the ambassador's primary military advisor, and that the attaché merely carried out the instructions of the CIA, as approved by the ambassador.[57]

Nevertheless, because of the Kennedy letter's authority and the attaché's chain of command, the U.S. military had little recourse but to accept Sullivan's decisions. The ambassador wrote the attaché's efficiency report and sent it directly to Washington. Therefore, what the generals at Udorn and Saigon thought of the attaché was far less important than what the ambassador observed in the embassy.

As discussed above, Ambassador Sullivan's authority created unique command and control problems for the U.S. military and, in particular, the U.S. Air Force. In response to the peculiar situation in Laos and the growing presence of U.S. aircraft and airmen in Thailand, the Department of Defense decided in November 1965 to establish a new air headquarters at Udorn Royal Thai Air Force Base. This new command, initially called Deputy Commander, 2d Air Division/Thirteenth Air Force, was redesignated in April 1966 as Deputy Commander, 7th/13th Air Force (7/13th AF). The Air Force major general in charge of the 7/13th AF had greatly varied responsibilities.

> He reported to the American ambassadors in Thailand and Laos on military matters in their respective areas; to the Commander, Thirteenth Air Force [located in the Philippines] for administrative and logistic matters involving USAF units in Thailand; and to the Commander, Second Air Division [later Seventh Air Force] in Saigon for the combat operations of those units.[58]

Nevertheless, Ambassador Sullivan looked to the general at the 7/13th AF and COMUSMACV for support, not advice. The first deputy commander, 7/13th AF has said, "In spite of my key position in the command chain . . . I was not privy to all that went on. About the only time I really got in the "know" was on those occasions when they [the CIA] got in a bind with the enemy."[59] His successor reports that "Deputy Commander 7th/13th was primarily a political position rather than an active participant in the conflict."[60]

Thus, even though the air war in Laos and Vietnam had become increasingly complex—the very reason the 7/13th AF was established—Sullivan relegated the general and his staff officers at Udorn to the status of clerks hired to carry out his air power decisions. This procedure lasted throughout Sullivan's tour in Vientiane and into the term of his successor, G. McMurtrie Godley.

By 1971 the unconventional system had bred considerable frustration at 7/13th AF headquarters. Major General Andrew J. Evans, Jr., deputy commander of the 7/13th AF, expressed concern and a lack of optimism in his end-of-tour report.

> There are no checks on the Air Attache except those which can be exercised by the Deputy Commander 7/13AF through his personal relationship with the U.S. Ambassador. As long as the U.S. Ambassador has overall responsibility for military actions in Laos there seems little likelihood that significant improvements can be made.[61]

Military Assistance Advisory Group in Exile

DEPCHIEF was the Department of Defense organization that, because of the extraordinary political situation which existed in Laos, came under the scrutiny and demands of the U.S. ambassador to Laos. Headquartered in Bangkok to avoid an outright violation of the Geneva accords, the organization was, nevertheless, intended as a Military Assistance Advisory Group for Laos—*intended,* because under Ambassador Sullivan's leadership DEPCHIEF was only a Military Assistance Group. To reiterate, military supplies and equipment provided to the Royal Lao military were delivered through the cooperative efforts of DEPCHIEF and the USAID Requirements Office. But, as in his relationship with the air force commander at Udorn, Sullivan desired no military counsel from the U.S. Army officer who commanded DEPCHIEF. Further, the USAID/RO and the Project 404 augmentees were the only U.S. "advisory" personnel allowed in Laos. In the eyes of the ambassador, DEPCHIEF's role was to "supply rice and bullets." There was no advisory function within this "exiled" Military Assistance Advisory Group.[62]

Once again, presidential authority permitted Ambassador Sullivan to manage a U.S. military organization. The DEPCHIEF commander, who in any normal MAAG position would have been required to oversee the ordering, delivery, and use of all U.S.-supplied military materials, was kept at arm's length in Thailand. Called to testify before a U.S. congressional committee in 1969, DEPCHIEF commander Colonel Peter T. Russell explained:

> I am a nonresident member of the U.S. country team in Vientiane. Unlike other MAAG's, Deputy Chief receives all requests and calls for support, services, and training through the Requirements Office of USAID Laos. My authority ends on the Thai side of the Mekong. We have no functions in Laos proper.[63]

Occasionally DEPCHIEF personnel would travel to Vientiane for meetings, but "much to their chagrin . . . [they] were always viewed as outsiders."[64]

When Ambassador Sullivan was asked directly about the limited role of DEPCHIEF in Laos he responded,

> I would say that, in the beginning, it was a meticulous respect for the Accords that dictated the distance between Vientiane and Udorn [and Bangkok]. The arrangements set in place by Ambassador Unger were, as a consequence, still in position during my 4½ year tenure.[65]

Ambassador Sullivan is much too modest. He was intimately involved in all facets of the war in Laos and, as Assistant Secretary of State William Bundy has said, "There wasn't a bag of rice dropped in Laos that he [Sullivan] didn't know about."[66] Ambassador Sullivan was a man with a mission: strict U.S. adherence to the Geneva accords when possible, and total secrecy when violations were necessary for the defense of Laos and the furtherance of America's Southeast Asia policy. Excluding large numbers of U.S. military personnel, and particularly senior officers, was an important part of the ambassador's strategy. No one should doubt that William Sullivan fashioned American policy in Laos. He was a very self-assured leader, and it is disingenuous for him to suggest he merely followed the practice of his predecessor.

By the time Ambassador Sullivan arrived in Laos CINCPAC had reduced the DEPCHIEF command position from that of a major general to a colonel. The position continued to be filled by U.S. Army colonels until upgraded to the rank of brigadier general in February 1972.[67] The political and military reasons for this rank structure, and why it was ultimately changed, will be reviewed in the following chapter.

The Primitive War

In line with his tight control of DEPCHIEF and air operations, Ambassador Sullivan paid close attention to the ground war in Laos. Sullivan felt the CIA and the USAID Requirements Office were handling the land campaign quite well by themselves.

> Our ground activity was really quite primitive and consisted of an "ebb and flow" operation, responsive to the monsoon and the actions of the DRV [North Vietnam]. The tactics in that repetitive strategy were actually managed by . . . General Vang Pao. We did, of course, add certain refinements such as helicopter airlift; but they were never on such a level that our CAS [CIA] and RO guys were over their heads. Moreover, much of what we did was "seat-of-the-pants" stuff in which nobody had accumulated much experience. Therefore, on balance, our people were probably as well—or better qualified—than the DEPCHIEF group for the things they did.[68]

Ambassador Sullivan's contention—that DEPCHIEF assistance was unnecessary due to the limited sophistication of Vang Pao's ground operations and the experience of CIA and RO personnel—was justifiable only during the early stages of the ground war. When the CIA began to support Vang Pao's SGU movements with large numbers of helicopters and fixed wing aircraft, the war had progressed well beyond a "seat-of-the-pants" operation. And military records contradict Sullivan's recollection that there were no "complex military campaigns . . . except for air operations" during his tenure in Laos.[69] The "helicopter airlift" referred to by the ambassador included USAF Pony Express infiltration and exfiltration missions. As discussed above, Pony Express was in full operation during Ambassador Sullivan's term in Vientiane.

"Operation Duck," conducted in late March 1969, is an excellent example of a highly complicated air/ground mission.[70] According to a 7/13th AF report on Operation Duck the following forces and aircraft were committed in this SGU attack against an enemy cave complex in southern Laos:

> Two SGU companies (115 men each Co) assault force. USAF fragged [directed] resources included: seven CH-3's three UH-1's plus eight (Air America) H-34's for airlift of SGU companies, six A-1E's for escort of helicopters, two O-2's for FAC, eight F-105's and four A-1E's to kill and

disperse enemy between HLZ [helicopter landing zone] and objective caves.

The operation met unexpected enemy resistance, however, and the helicopters attempted an immediate withdrawal. Air America was able to evacuate a large number of troops, but five of the USAF helicopters suffered battle damage and had to return to base. The following day, under cover of A-1E strike aircraft, USAF and Air America crews completed the extraction.[71] Considering the number of U.S. aircraft involved, and the amount of coordination and expertise required for the success of missions like Operation Duck, William Sullivan's war cannot be described as "primitive."

There is, however, some question as to whether Sullivan actually approved the operation. The ambassador's recollection is that he "declined to sanction" the mission and that "Duck" was "conceived and executed from across the river in Udorn" immediately after his final departure from Laos. To support his position, Sullivan says he was summoned to Washington every six months by President Lyndon B. Johnson and told to keep U.S. military operations to a minimum. Sullivan further recalls that

> President Johnson became increasingly disillusioned with the military as the war in Vietnam dragged on. He felt he had been dragged into an unending conflict after being assured that victory would be quick and relatively easy. He did not want to be similarly dragged into bigger and bigger adventures in Laos.

Sullivan says, in addition, that Operation Duck was "the sort of escalation that Johnson wished to avoid and that he feared would happen if the U.S. military took over."[72]

Ambassador Sullivan's charge that Operation Duck was ordered by U.S. military officials in Thailand and delayed until his departure is impossible to substantiate. Sullivan clearly had a mandate from the president to hold the line on U.S. military activity in Laos. Still, by 1969 the war was escalating and, as it moved from guerilla operations to a more conventional conflict, the U.S. military likely yearned to counter the communists with more sophisticated weapons and tactics. It is certain, however, that this expansion could not have occurred without CIA approval. The exit of Sullivan, who was not immediately replaced by a new ambassador, offered the U.S. military and the CIA the opportunity to introduce a different strategy. While Sullivan perceived that the U.S. military was anxious to expand the war in Laos, it appears the CIA was also culpable.

The Loss of Phu Pha Thi

Through 1967 and into 1968, Hmong military units continued their harassment of communist forces. During this period attack missions by U.S. aircraft against targets in North Vietnam and Laos increased substantially. In 1967 and 1968 U.S. fighter-bomber and bomber aircraft reportedly dropped more than 350,000 tons of bombs throughout Laos. During the same time period approximately 500,000 tons of ordnance were released on targets in North Vietnam.[73]

The efficient bombing of North Vietnam and Laos depended partially upon a Hmong/Thai-defended U.S. outpost located on the ridge of a 5,800-foot-high mountain in northeastern Laos. The ever-changing weather conditions in Southeast Asia posed serious navigation problems for American pilots. In 1966 the United States responded by establishing a Tactical Air Navigation System (TACAN) on the ridge at Phu Pha Thi,[74] also known as Lima site 85. The TACAN was thereafter referred to as "Channel 97." More important, in mid-1967, the United States installed a TSQ 81 radar bomb facility at Pha Thi.[75]

Located less than 20 miles from the North Vietnamese border and only 160 miles from Hanoi, Pha Thi was an ideal location for the radar system. Regardless of weather conditions, USAF technicians could safely guide strike aircraft to targets within 60 miles of Hanoi. The code name for this operation was "Commando Club."[76] Pha Thi was also used by the CIA as a staging area for commando missions and as a refueling station for USAF rescue helicopters.[77]

Pha Thi thus became a tempting target for the North Vietnamese and on January 12, 1968, in an air action without precedent in the Vietnam War, two Soviet-built AN-2 biplanes attacked the site! Air America helicopter pilot Captain Theodore H. Moore, who was flying artillery ammunition to Pha Thi, recalled,

> On 11 January 1968 a MIG [Soviet-built jet aircraft] flew over Site 85 and I presume took photographs. The next day it looked like World War I as I witnessed two biplanes attempting to destroy the electronic gear at Site 85. One of the airplanes dropped explosives and the other, which appeared to carry rockets and machine guns, fired at the site.[78]

The radar equipment was not damaged but two soldiers and two female civilians were killed and two soldiers wounded.[79]

Captain Moore, flying a UH-1 helicopter, chased the two communist aircraft while his flight engineer, Glenn Woods, began firing an AK-47 rifle at the fleeing biplanes. Woods' gunfire caused one of the AN-2's to crash and burn; the other biplane flew underneath the helicopter and crashed into the side of a mountain.[80] According to an official U.S. Air Force report, a Hmong patrol found three bodies, believed to be Vietnamese, in the wreckage of one of the aircraft.

> Investigations at the site and of the aircraft wreckage by a 7AF Intelligence team revealed that 120 mm mortar rounds had been converted to "bombs." Dropped through tubes in the floor of the AN-2, the "bombs" became armed in the slip stream and detonated on impact. The rockets were 57 mm, and were carried in rocket pods under the wing of the AN-2.[81]

Immediately following the episode Air America fired Captain Moore for "causing an international incident." However, after being lauded during a debriefing in Vientiane by "ten to twelve" CIA agents, Moore received the Agency's support and was rehired. He was, however, reassigned to southern Laos.[82]

The North Vietnamese did not give up their attempt to destroy the radar installation at Pha Thi. The security of Pha Thi was maintained by a Hmong military unit based at the foot of the mountain at a location that controlled the only open path to the top. The other accessible routes to the radar site were seeded with antipersonnel mines. One hundred Hmong and two hundred Thai irregulars were stationed at the site. In addition, the CIA and Air Force technicians had radio communications that enabled them to summon rescue helicopters and direct air strikes on any approaching enemy forces.

On March 11, 1968, the radar complex came under a combined artillery and ground attack. North Vietnamese soldiers, reportedly using, for the first time, light-weight mine detectors, successfully climbed to the top of Pha Thi. At the time there were eighteen Americans at the site: sixteen USAF technicians, one CIA case officer, and one enlisted USAF Forward Air Controller from the attaché office in Vientiane. A number of the technicians reacted to the assault by using pre-positioned rope slings to lower themselves down the side of the mountain and into a cave. The communists were able to grenade and machine-gun many of these men.

U.S. Air Force and Air America helicopters were called to the scene and rescued five of the technicians, the CIA officer, the FAC, and a small number of the indigenous defenders. This left eleven Americans at the site, eight known to be dead and three presumed dead. In an effort to "destroy the technical and personal equipment left behind,'' over a two week period the U.S. Air Force repeatedly bombed the site.[83]

The loss of lives at Pha Thi greatly distressed the U.S. military. Beyond that, the incident created a potential diplomatic problem for the United States and the Souvanna government. The existence of the facility was an obvious violation of the Geneva agreements, and when Ambassador Sullivan told the Lao prime minister that some of the bodies had not been recovered, ''Souvanna winced . . . and said they increased the risks that [the] enemy could be able, if he chose, to make some pretty damaging disclosures.''[84] The Vietnamese, however, perhaps realizing a protest would reveal their own illegal presence in Laos, did not make an issue of the site.

The circumstances surrounding the communist attack on Phu Pha Thi remain a controversial issue. Many have criticized Ambassador Sullivan for not ordering the Americans evacuated earlier.[85] However, intelligence information available at the time indicated the site was safe. Vang Pao has said that no one suspected the communists possessed mine detectors and would be able to make their way up the mined side of the mountain. Further, he has related that those killed ''were technicians who really were not well-trained soldiers.''[86]

During an August 21, 1990, interview in Vientiane, General Singkapo Sikhotchounamaly, former commander of all Pathet Lao forces, said, regarding the attack on Phu Pha Thi, ''About one hundred Pathet Lao and more than two hundred North Vietnamese were involved in the attack. They used mine detectors. Some injured Americans were captured at the site and sent to North Vietnam.'' This was the first instance of any informed Lao communist official discussing the Pha Thi battle and revealing that some Americans had survived. General Singkapo's remarks also included the first official Pathet Lao admission that the Lao communists, as a matter of policy, turned over captured Americans to the North Vietnamese.[87] To date, the United States lists eleven Americans who were stationed at Phu Pha Thi in the ''presumptive status of dead, body not recovered.'' U.S. officials are currently seeking permission from the Lao government to search for the remains of American dead that might exist at the former radar site.[88]

Despite General Singkapo's declaration on August 21, 1991, of willingness to discuss his knowledge of the captured Americans with U.S. MIA/ POW experts, the Lao government consistently blocked access to the general. Senior officials in the Lao government told U.S. representatives that Singkapo was senile. Finally, a year later, General Singkapo was interviewed by William R. Gadoury of the U.S. Joint Casualty Resolution Center, and claimed that he had been "misunderstood." [89]

During my interview with the general he was consistently clear and precise in his recollections of specific wartime events. Indeed, Singkapo took great pleasure in recounting his contributions to the revolution. I believe General Singkapo perceived our talk as an opportunity to place his personal history in an American study of the war. He was quite open and, doubtless, did not consider the ramifications of his remarks. It remains to be seen if there will ever be a complete account of the attack on Phu Pha Thi.

The secret war in Laos was, indeed, William Sullivan's war. Ironically, having successfully concealed for more than four and one-half years the true degree of American involvement in Laos, Ambassador Sullivan returned to Washington and quickly found himself compelled to describe publicly America's "quiet war."

Chapter Seven

CHANGING WAR; CHANGING RULES

Former CIA Director William E. Colby has said that the intelligence agency had a major role in Laos because it was important to conduct a "non-attributable war." [1] Commencing in 1962 this presidentially directed strategy of "quiet" American involvement in the Lao war was handled jointly by the Department of Defense, the United States Agency for International Development, the Central Intelligence Agency, and, with predominate authority, the Department of State. In late 1969, however, growing criticism of the country's role in the Vietnam War and unconfirmed press reports of American paramilitary activity in Laos led Missouri Senator Stuart Symington to conduct formal congressional hearings on U.S. involvement in the Far East. Hearings transcripts, albeit heavily censored, provided the first detailed official information on American activities in the kingdom of Laos. Nevertheless, the program of covert American military assistance to Laos continued and, with greater participation by U.S.-paid Thai ground forces and American air power, took on the characteristics of a more conventional military struggle.

The Secret War Goes Public

On October 20, 1969, a subcommittee of the Senate Committee on Foreign Relations began closed hearings on the relationship between the United States and the kingdom of Laos.[2] The witnesses called to testify included senior Defense, State, and USAID officials, as well as the director of the CIA. Particularly noteworthy were the appearances of William Sullivan, then serving as deputy assistant secretary of state (Bureau of East Asian and Pacific Affairs), the U.S. Army and Air Force attachés from Vientiane, and the commander of DEPCHIEF.

Senator Symington began the hearings with a political declaration that would characterize the often contentious exchanges between the witnesses and the subcommittee.

> Today the Subcommittee . . . begins hearings on Laos. . . . In past years, high government officials have wrapped activity there in a cloak of secrecy, keeping details not only of policy but also of implementation of that policy hidden from those of us in the legislative branch with responsibilities in the foreign policy and military fields.[3]

Over a period of four days the committee and its well-prepared staff conducted a spirited and rigorous examination of some very circumspect witnesses. Issues covered included U.S. commitments and military assistance to Laos, U.S. and North Vietnamese adherence to the Geneva Accords, Lao and American air operations, the capabilities of the Lao military, and the unique roles in Laos of the American ambassador and USAID. Once the hearings were completed the White House insisted that the committee transcripts be subjected to a thorough security review. In April 1970 the heavily censored transcripts were released to the public.[4]

A month earlier, on March 6, responding to congressional pressure and military events in Laos, the White House issued a detailed statement by President Richard M. Nixon on the American-Laotian relationship. It was revealed that there were 1,040 Americans working on behalf of the U.S. government in Laos—616 directly employed by the U.S. government and 424 working under American contracts. "The total number [of personnel], military and civilian, engaged in a military advisory or military training capacity . . . [is] 320. Logistics personnel number 323." By comparison, the president said, "there are 67,000 North Vietnamese troops in this small country." Nixon stressed his point:

This is the picture of our current aid to Laos. It is limited. It is requested. It is supportive and defensive. It continues the purposes and operations of two previous administrations. It has been necessary to protect American lives in Vietnam and to preserve a precarious but important balance in Laos.

The statement went on to say, "No American stationed in Laos has ever been killed in ground combat operations."[5]

The press immediately began to report "leaked" stories to the contrary, causing the White House to issue a modified statement on March 8, 1970, admitting that, since the beginning of 1969, six American civilians and a U.S. Army captain had been killed in Laos. Total American "hostile deaths" in Laos since 1964 were put at one military advisor and twenty-six civilians.[6]

These official declarations were clearly erroneous. Winston Lord, special assistant to National Security Advisor Henry Kissinger, was responsible for drafting the March 6 statement. In his memoirs Kissinger says the mistakes in the account were "the result of a series of misunderstandings and a failure of communication." He also reports that "Nixon was furious . . . for a week I could not get an appointment to see him." Kissinger does not, however, address the fact that the second statement was also inaccurate.[7]

Nixon's reported anger would seem to suggest that the president was truly surprised at the number of U.S. casualties and had not intentionally attempted to deceive the American public. Nevertheless, since so many senior officials in the State Department, the CIA, and the Pentagon were aware of the losses at Phu Pha Thi and the full extent of U.S. activities in Laos, it seems unlikely that Kissinger's staff was unable to compile an accurate version of America's Laotian involvement.

Predictably, given the controversy generated by the initial statement, President Nixon's effort to avert future criticism and inquiry into U.S. military activity in Laos was largely unsuccessful. The press corps continued to demand information on the "secret war" and congressional investigators began yearly visits to Laos. However, the president's acknowledgement that Americans were providing military assistance to the Lao did not, as feared by previous U.S. administrations and the Souvanna government, bring about any strong Kremlin reaction.[8] For nearly six years, the Soviets had mostly accepted the fiction of American and North Vietnamese compliance with the Geneva accords. Further, according to Lao specialist Arthur Dommen, by 1970 Moscow believed the American antiwar movement would soon force the United States out of Indochina.[9] America's war in Laos would continue another three years, but ultimately the Kremlin's judgment turned out to be correct.

The "Congo Club"

In June 1969 G. McMurtrie Godley became U.S. ambassador to Laos. Godley was well versed in paramilitary operations, having served from 1964 to 1966 as ambassador to the Congo, a post known for its involvement in nontraditional diplomatic activity.[10] In Laos Godley surrounded himself with people who had previously served with him in the Congo, including the CIA station chief, the deputy chief of the U.S. mission, and the head of the embassy's political section. According to Charles Stevenson, Godley had an affinity for military operations and was particularly agreeable to military requests.[11]

Unfortunately—from the U.S. military perspective—Godley continued in the Sullivan tradition, relying on the CIA's military judgments. Unlike Sullivan, however, Godley did not enjoy an affable working relationship with Colonel Robert Tyrrell, the embassy's air attaché. Tyrrell had a unique vantage point, having at various times worked in Laos for Ambassadors Unger, Sullivan, and Godley. Tyrrell has praised Unger and Sullivan, but has said "I didn't get along with . . . Ambassador Godley. I don't know why because I certainly was loyal to him. . . . But you can't get along with everybody no matter what you do." Colonel Tyrrell also believed that his official, and supposedly "Eyes Only", communications with USAF headquarters in Saigon, were being read by the CIA.[12] In fairness, it should be said that former CIA official B. Hugh Tovar strongly denies that the CIA was reading Tyrrell's messages, or anyone else's.[13] In any case, Tyrrell's difficulties were symptomatic of the strain between the American embassy in Vientiane and the U.S. military commanders at DEPCHIEF and the 7/13th AF.

Just Rice and Bullets

One of those called back to Washington to present testimony before the Senate Foreign Relations Committee was the DEPCHIEF commander, Colonel Peter T. Russell, U.S. Army. Under questioning Colonel Russell had disclosed that DEPCHIEF did not operate in an advisory manner, but rather reacted to requests from USAID/RO.[14] This was a politic way of saying that DEPCHIEF was operating outside standard military regulations. This nonprofessional approach to military assistance was a problem that caused great concern to Russell and to senior CINCPAC and JCS military officers.

As a combat veteran who had worked extensively with paramilitary forces in South Vietnam, Russell arrived in Thailand prepared to lend his expertise to the Lao land campaign. He was quickly initiated into the "ambassador's war." Upon assuming command of DEPCHIEF, Colonel Russell requested and received permission to attend a Country Team meeting in Vientiane. Although the colonel's initial visit went well, his return the following week was met by the Country Team with surprise and faintly disguised irritation. The presence in Laos of the DEPCHIEF commander was clearly unwelcome. Colonel Russell's place was not at the table in Vientiane where decisions on the war were made; it was in Bangkok where he was expected to carry out, swiftly and efficiently, the embassy's wishes.[15]

Colonel Russell's experience is instructive. By choice, the U.S. ambassador to Laos decided to accept counsel from only two senior military officers, the U.S. Army and Air Force attachés.[16] In view of the growing level of U.S. military aid to Laos and the spiraling air war, the ambassador's reliance on two colonels who were also responsible for many other diplomatic and representational duties seems wrong-headed. But, as noted since 1962 the CIA had readily assumed major responsibilities for military operations in Laos. The ambassador believed the CIA and his military attachés possessed the skills necessary to successfully manage the war. Change, however, was on the way.

Easing the Ambassador's Grip

By 1969, if not before, the Joint Chiefs of Staff had become convinced that DEPCHIEF's responsibilities in Thailand and Laos required the attention of an army general. According to recently declassified CINCPAC records, the JCS proposed on December 18, 1969, that the secretary of defense approve the "assignment in Laos of a general officer who would serve as Defense Attache/CINCPACREP [CINCPAC representative] Laos." "Political implications" prevented prompt adoption of the recommendation, but the JCS and CINCPAC continued to press for the change.[17]

The military's rationale for requesting senior supervision was cogently explained by Colonel Russell in his 1971 end-of-tour report. Having served in the DEPCHIEF position for three years, Russell felt strongly that the American military aid program to Laos was both inefficient and poorly managed.

> On the Lao Country Team . . . ostensibly all are equals; however, some are more equal than others and DEPCHIEF is least equal of all. RO is a USAID organization, not responsible to or responsive to DOD direction. Neither DEPCHIEF nor CINCPAC can guide, inspect or request reports of RO, although RO can commit DOD to enormous expenditures of money, effort or equipment. Thus, with hundreds of millions of dollars involved annually in military affairs only; no one is really in charge.[18]

In mid-1971 the JCS won a partial victory in its quest to bring greater control and coordination to the Lao military aid program. On June 8 the secretary of defense directed the relocation of DEPCHIEF from Bangkok to Udorn, Thailand. The four most important components of the American military aid program to Laos—DEPCHIEF, the CIA's 4802d Joint Liaison Detachment, the Air America headquarters, and the deputy commander of the 7/13th AF—were now located in one place. Moreover, plans were underway to assign a U.S. Army brigadier general as DEPCHIEF commander.

A General Joins the Country Team

Brigadier General John W. Vessey, Jr., who enlisted in the U.S. Army in 1939 and rose through the ranks to become chairman of the Joints Chiefs of Staff from 1982 to 1985, took command of DEPCHIEF in February 1972. The result of General Vessey's initial meeting with Ambassador Godley, upon his arrival in Laos, was predictable. According to Vessey, "Ambassador Godley was not going to talk to me. When he finally did, he made it very clear to me that he did not ask for, did not want, and did not need a general on his staff. We later became good friends." [19] Ambassador Godley remembers that Vessey "was not given the warmest welcome imaginable, but shortly his straightforwardness, common sense in military matters, intelligence, charm and sense of humor won the day." [20]

General Vessey's persuasive powers and hard work soon won an unprecedented concession from the ambassador. Travel to Laos by DEPCHIEF personnel had always been limited, and required the ambassador's personal approval. Meetings involving DEPCHIEF, therefore, were often held in Thailand. In a memorandum to Ambassador Godley on September 30, 1972 the general pointed out the inefficiency of the system and suggested that the ambassador allow Vessey to control the DEPCHIEF visits to Laos.[21] Ambassador Godley quickly approved Vessey's request. The general had not only successfully joined the embassy's Country Team, he soon was Ambassador Godley's primary military advisor.[22]

Over the next five months General Vessey conducted a comprehensive inspection of the field and training units of the Royal Lao Army, of Vang Pao's irregular forces, and of the American-paid Thai "volunteer" troops in Laos. Traveling extensively throughout the kingdom, Vessey brought a no-nonsense approach to military discipline and preparedness. What he found was often disappointing; it seemed clear that the Royal Lao Army and the Hmong irregulars, left to their own devices, were woefully unprepared to meet any North Vietnamese threat.[23] In contrast, the Thai SGUs "had some very good leaders and there were some soldiers who fought very well. Nevertheless, most of the battalions were only marginally effective and that only when provided continuous liberal air support."[24]

Paying for the Lao War

Paying for America's military assistance program to the kingdom of Laos was a complex undertaking involving funds from the Defense Department, the United States Agency for International Development, and the Central Intelligence Agency. Following the extensive Senate Foreign Relations Subcommittee hearings on Laos in 1969, congressional critics of U.S. involvement in Laos increased their scrutiny of America's role in the Lao war. The Senate Foreign Relations Committee dispatched investigators to Laos, and the Senate Committee on Armed Services began a close review of all DOD funding requests. Senator Stuart Symington expressed his concern over monies spent in Laos:

> It is apparent the Executive Branch considers itself free to draw upon first one appropriation and then another, or to shift programs back and forth between as many as three departments or agencies. In some instances activities which were once considered appropriate for funding by AID were then shifted to the Defense Department and later to the CIA.[25]

This congressional scrutiny led to a number of important changes in U.S. funding of the Lao military assistance program. In 1970 USAID costs for food and delivery expenses for Lao "military and paramilitary forces, and paramilitary dependents" was transferred to the Defense Department. The same year the CIA accepted funding responsibility for USAID-provided medical services and supplies to paramilitary forces.[26]

Beginning in fiscal year 1968 (July 1, 1967), the White House shifted the source of monies for Laos from the Military Assistance Program (MAP) funding to the Military Assistance Service Funded (MASF). According to administration officials this change, which also affected South Vietnam and Thailand, was made "to provide the flexibility needed to respond to combat conditions in Southeast Asia."[27] However, the switch placed the funding within the Defense Department's *overall* budget and, therefore, precluded the country-by-country review conducted under MAP procedures.[28] Critics, like Senator Symington, charged that the change from MAP to MASF allowed the White House to hide the actual costs of U.S. activity in Laos. As a result, in 1971 Symington succeeded in gaining the passage of legislation that placed a $350 million limit on all U.S. aid to Laos.[29]

The "Symington Ceiling" was a watershed in U.S. involvement in Laos. For the first time there was serious congressional oversight of the vast amounts of money and material provided the Lao kingdom.

During this same period the costs of air support in the Lao war— exclusive of the U.S. military air campaigns over Laos—were mostly consolidated and transferred to the Department of Defense. However, because many CIA and USAID programs continued to utilize aircraft that were now under DOD contracts, representatives of the CIA, USAID, and DEPCHIEF formed a "Joint Agency Cost Sharing Team" to determine cost allocations. In February 1973 the team negotiated a cost-sharing agreement that called for the three agencies to send a consolidated monthly electrical message to the Department of Defense. The DOD could then direct the transfer of appropriate amounts of CIA, USAID, and DEPCHIEF funds.

According to a U.S. Air Force contracting officer, the establishment of the joint team also allowed DOD officials to more closely monitor the billings of contractors. This added scrutiny uncovered a number of questionable cost-accounting practices that were quickly modified.[30]

Expanding the War

In the fall of 1969, at the urging of his CIA advisors, Vang Pao planned a daring campaign to retake the communist-controlled Plain of Jars. Operation "About Face" was designed to be, mostly, a hit-and-run assault against the battle-hardened North Vietnamese 316th Division. The decision to use the Hmong against such a large, conventional force was controversial, and several CIA veterans openly questioned the wisdom and morality of such an undertaking.[31] Nevertheless, the operation went forward and, supported by some two hundred daily USAF sorties, on September 12, 1969, Vang Pao's forces captured the Pathet Lao "provincial capital" at Xieng Khouang. According to a U.S. Air Force history, enormous amounts of supplies and equipment were captured, "including more than 3 million rounds of ammunition, 150,000 gallons of gasoline, 12 tanks, 30 trucks, and 13 jeeps."[32] Vang Pao recalls that his men also seized over a thousand new AK-47s, six 85-mm howitzers, a number of 12.7-mm and 37-mm antiaircraft artillery pieces, and seven tons of canned food.[33] Two weeks later Vang Pao's men captured the key town of Muong Soui. Operation About Face had caught the North Vietnamese totally off-guard.

Vang Pao's success was brief, however. The North Vietnamese launched a tank-led counterattack in January of 1970 and recaptured Xieng Khouang the following month. To stem the offensive B-52s were, for the first time, ordered to strike targets in northern Laos. On February 17 and 18 the bombers flew thirty-six sorties, dropping almost eleven hundred tons of munitions on the Plain of Jars.[34] One author has reported that these air attacks caused the disappearance of the Plain of Jars "after a recorded history of 700 years."[35] It should also be noted, however, that for many years the communist forces had bombarded the plain with substantial amounts of artillery and mortar fire.

Over twenty years later, visitors are still startled by the cratered landscape, and by the munitions remnants that continue to maim and kill those living on the plain. In September 1990, flying above the plain in the early morning, I thought the water-filled craters resembled thousands of shiny coins. On the ground it seemed incongruous that such a quiet, cool, green plain could have been subjected to such a massive assault. But the steady stream of Vietnamese trucks that I saw headed down Route 7 were a quick reminder of why the area had been such an important target.

Despite the B-52 attacks, the North Vietnamese captured Muong Soui and in early March 1970 laid siege to Long Tieng. Vang Pao was forced to deploy his troops around the southwest corner of the plain, and the CIA increased the number of defenders by moving in irregular forces from southern Laos. Over the next two weeks, Lao and U.S. aircraft flew hundreds of sorties against the Vietnamese positions. Particularly effective were night missions flown against NVA resupply activities by AC-47, AC-119, and AC-130 gunships. Faced with additional troops and relentless air power, on March 26 the North Vietnamese withdrew to the Plain of Jars.[36] Casualty figures from this offensive are not available, but an estimated 110,000 refugees, who had settled near Long Tieng and the adjacent USAID headquarters at Sam Thong, were forced to flee into the surrounding area.[37] The Lao government, and Vang Pao and his American advisors, had suffered a major setback.

Over the next two years the momentum in war continued to swing back and forth. In May 1971 Vang Pao launched another operation, this one called "About Face II," and retook the Plain of Jars. Predictably, six months later the communists pushed the government forces back and were once again in control of the mountains surrounding Long Tieng. According to the U.S. embassy in Vientiane, the troop strength of the North Vietnamese and Pathet Lao in the immediate area was about 12,000, while Vang Pao's forces comprised nineteen battalions of hill-tribe irregulars (5,100), ten battalions of Thai irregulars (3,100), and four battalions of FAR infantry (645).[38]

The battle became a contest between North Vietnamese long-range artillery and American and Lao air power. While the Vietnamese used their 130-mm guns to pound government positions, U.S. and Laotian pilots flew thousands of strike sorties. Despite the use by U.S. aircraft of precision-guided "smart bombs," the communists did not withdraw from the Long Tieng area until the onset of the monsoon rains in mid-April.[39]

While Vang Pao's Military Region II forces were struggling to prevent the North Vietnamese army from controlling northeastern Laos, CIA-directed irregular forces in southern Laos (MR III and IV) were attempting to frustrate the flow of men and arms moving down the labyrinth known as the Ho Chi Minh Trail. Since as early as 1964 small teams of irregulars, mostly Lao Theung tribesmen, had infiltrated areas along the trail in order to collect intelligence and conduct harassment raids. By mid-1967 the irregulars were being formed into Special Guerilla Unit (SGU) battalions and had scored a number of battlefield successes against NVA forces. Many of these SGUs became some of the most combat-proficient troops in Laos and, in times of crisis, they were often used to bolster the defenses of other military regions.[40] However, the SGU battalions were never expected to challenge aggressively the NVA strong points that dotted the Laotian panhandle. That was a monumental task attempted in February 1971 by the South Vietnamese Army and its American allies.

Attacking the Ho Chi Minh Trail

In mid-January 1971, the Nixon administration decided to strike at the heart resupply network of the North Vietnamese in southern Laos near the town of Tchepone. Faced with strong domestic pressure to withdraw U.S. forces from South Vietnam, Washington decided on a massive blow against the communists, hoping to bolster the Saigon government's confidence and speed the departure of American troops. A U.S.–South Vietnamese incursion of Cambodia in May 1970 had successfully destroyed North Vietnamese base camps that supplied and supported communist forces in central and southern South Vietnam. Coupled with Cambodia's closure of its ports to communist-bloc country cargo ships, the attack into Cambodia had created serious supply problems for the North Vietnamese and Viet Cong. The Ho Chi Minh trail through Laos, always important to communist operations, had become the lifeline of Hanoi's efforts to topple the South Vietnamese government.

The raid into Laos, designated "Lam Son 719," proved to be far more problematic than the Cambodian operation. In late December 1970 the United States Congress, outraged at what it perceived to be a widening of the war, passed the Cooper-Church Amendment. Thereafter U.S. military forces were prohibited from "operating on the ground inside Cambodia or Laos."[41] Lam Son 719, therefore, became the litmus test for the South Vietnamese military. Could the ARVN successfully manage a complex airborne assault into Laos against veteran North Vietnamese soldiers?

On February 8, 1971, seventeen thousand South Vietnamese troops began their push into Laos along National Route 9 toward communist-controlled Tchepone. They faced an estimated NVA force of thirty thousand combat and twenty thousand logistics troops. The ARVN were, however, bolstered by some ten thousand U.S. forces located just inside South Vietnam. For the next six weeks U.S. artillery and air strikes bombarded suspected communist positions, while more than six hundred U.S. Army helicopters carried the South Vietnamese into and out of the fray.[42]

Regrettably, the ARVN forces were not up to the task. Indecisive and incompetent leadership, inspired North Vietnamese resistance, and the absence of U.S. advisers turned an anticipated victory into a rout of the South Vietnamese. Fighter-bombers and B-52s pounded the area as U.S. helicopter crews braved communist artillery to evacuate their dispirited allies.

The costs of Lam Son 719, in men and matériel, were staggering. A senior U.S. officer reports nearly 10,000 American and South Vietnamese casualties—1,402 Americans (215 dead) and 7,683 South Vietnamese (1,764 dead). On the communist side, an estimated twenty thousand NVA were killed, mostly by air strikes. Including both ARVN and NVA losses of equipment, the operation claimed thousands of trucks, armored vehicles, artillery pieces, and tanks. Over 100 U.S. helicopters were destroyed and 618 were damaged.[43] And so disaster befell America's only effort to use significant numbers of conventional ground forces against communist troops in Laos.

Lao military forces were not involved in Lam Son 719; indeed, the operation was launched without any notification or prior coordination with any senior Lao generals. According to General Soutchay Vongsavanh, who was stationed in southern Laos at the time,

> The most significant thing about Lam Son 719, as far as the Lao were concerned, was that it confirmed their belief that the North Vietnamese trail structure was an American/South Vietnamese/North Vietnamese problem and that the principals involved did not regard the RLG position as germane to the issue.[44]

When asked by Ambassador Godley to approve the assault into his country, Prime Minister Souvanna Phouma's response was typically equivocal. Souvanna was not opposed to the operation, but insisted on maintaining the facade of neutrality.[45] Officially, he knew nothing. The prime minister's decision not to inform his military of Lam Son 719 reflected Vientiane's historic attitude toward southern Laos. According to General Soutchay, the Lao government was much more concerned "with developments in MR II [northeastern Laos] and the threats to life in Vientiane." The southern Lao felt like "country cousins to the Lao elite in Vientiane who saw the threat in MR II as more directly affecting them."[46]

The Souvanna government had, for the most part, been willing to ignore communist activity in southern Laos. But after Lam Son 719 the North Vietnamese expanded their presence in the Laotian panhandle. Increasingly, Royal Lao regular and irregular units clashed with numerically superior, and often better-armed, North Vietnamese forces. As in the war in northeastern Laos, the CIA used Air America and Thai irregulars to bolster the Lao forces. U.S. Air Force helicopters provided additional airlift, while fighter-bombers and B-52s battered the region with air strikes. By the end of 1972, however, the NVA was in firm control of their critical network from southern Laos into South Vietnam and Cambodia.[47] Eventually, these Lao base camps would provide the means to topple the Saigon government; Vientiane would soon follow.

In December 1990, I received permission from the Lao government to cross southern Laos on Route 9, from the Mekong River to the Vietnamese border at Lao Bao. Villages along this pot-holed main artery are now known for their shiny boats, constructed from the drop-tanks of aircraft. Rusting tanks and aircraft wreckage litter the surrounding jungle. Tchepone is now little more than a small truckstop. When I asked what had happened to the town, a resident explained that in 1975 the people who had loyally supported the revolution were moved to the larger cities along the Mekong River, "inheriting" the homes and possessions of former Royal Lao government officials.

Reaching the Lao-Vietnamese border, only a short distance from the former U.S. enclave at Khe Sanh, was both a thrill and a disappointment to me. Border guards forbade me from taking photographs. Standing in a cold rain driven by a strong wind, I quickly realized that they were not interested in negotiating this matter. Nevertheless, I gazed at the rising jungle, and found that it was not hard to ignore the present-day sputter of Soviet-made trucks and shut out the cackle of Vietnamese hawkers and prostitutes. It was, in fact, all too easy to imagine the violent battles that had shaken the area and, finally, had resulted in the destruction of any hope that the ARVN forces could stand alone against the NVA.

The Breakdown of the Hmong Army

Since early 1968 the Hmong army of Vang Pao had shouldered the majority of Royal Lao government responsibility for offensive ground operations in northeastern Laos. Conceived originally as a guerilla force, the Hmong were reorganized into three-hundred-man "Guerilla Battalions" (three companies of a hundred men each), and "Mobile Groups" of three to six battalions. As the years passed the Hmong were increasingly involved in conventional actions against sizable North Vietnamese forces.

According to Douglas Blaufarb, the Hmong were devastated. "The years of war had taken such a toll that the Meo [Hmong] resistance had exceeded the limits of its strength and was flagging. The steady drain of casualties had forced Vang Pao to call up thirteen- or fourteen-year olds."[48]

By 1969, or perhaps earlier, some Hmong elders were pleading with

Vang Pao to move the mountain people from the northeast to western Laos, or even to the mountains of northern Thailand. Before the beginning of the 1971–72 "dry season" campaign the U.S. embassy in Vientiane declared:

> If the Meo [Hmong] suffer severe losses in the PDJ [Plain of Jars] campaign this year . . . massive refugee movements will be generated . . . and impetus behind the Meo [Hmong] desire to pull out of the war completely will grow significantly. If the civilians begin to leave . . . it would be difficult if not impossible for Vang Pao to prevent his troops from joining their dependents in a mass exodus from MR [Military Region] II.[49]

No longer a functioning army, the Hmong soldiers of northeastern Laos had become merely a dispirited throng of war-weary people urgently seeking safety for their families.

The declining Hmong military capability was a serious concern to the U.S. government. In September 1969 the American embassy in Vientiane had warned CINCPAC:

> Despite our current efforts, when the next dry season arrives, the enemy will find himself much further forward than ever before at this time of year. Unless we can increase our strength, we shall be only capable of employing . . . the spoiling attack . . . and hope that with adequate air support we can hang on. The Meo [Hmong] are nearing the bottom of their manpower barrel. The RLG must get more mileage from its regular forces.[50]

Sadly for the Hmong, after more than fourteen years of American military aid the Royal Lao Army remained incapable or unwilling to fight the North Vietnamese. Hundreds of millions of dollars had failed to offset poor leadership and motivation and, even with the assistance of U.S. air power, the men of the FAR would not stand and defend their country. Thus, after employing the Hmong for a decade as surrogate soldiers while "building" a lowland Lao army, the United States was still unable to depend upon the FAR. Instead, America increased the Thai involvement in the Lao war.

Brother Races

Since 1962 the CIA's 4802d Joint Liaison Detachment had worked closely with Headquarters 333, a covert Royal Thai military unit. Initially, Headquarters 333 managed the Lao operations of PARU teams, a Royal Thai army artillery battalion, and CIA-directed intelligence collection activities.[51] As Hmong casualties soared HQ 333 and the 4802d JLD began to recruit Thai "volunteers" for duty in Laos. According to an official U.S. Air Force study,

> Arrangements for the actual recruiting of Thais were made at the Ambassadorial level in Bangkok. These arrangements were then translated into quotas which were assigned to the various RTA [Royal Thai Army] units. It was then up to the unit commander to fill the quota. Most frequently, squads, platoons, or whole companies volunteered as a unit. These volunteers were then sent to a CAS [CIA] training center.

The Thai soldiers were given Lao names and identity cards, but continued to receive "regular pay, benefits, longevity, [and] promotions."[52] The United States funded all of these costs, plus a substantial pay supplement.[53] By April 1971 at least twelve Thai "volunteer" SGU battalions had served in Laos.[54]

Although a Thai general, Vithoon Yasawasdi, served as the principal link between the CIA and the Royal Thai government, Bangkok officially denied any formal involvement in the volunteer program.[55] Pressed in March 1970 to comment on the subject, Deputy Prime Minister Prapass Charusathiara said, "We are brother races. A Laotian living in Korat [Thailand] goes home to fight. He is not a Thai Army soldier sent to fight there."[56]

Despite this obfuscation of the facts it was clear the program provided the Thais a number of important benefits. Bangkok, as discussed earlier, was anxious to see the communists stopped on the Lao side of the Mekong River. Moreover, the generals who ruled Thailand were delighted with the excellent equipment, training, and valuable combat experience their men received at U.S. expense. Of course, these advantages did not come without considerable risk to the fighting men. During the 1971 defense of Long Tieng one Thai battalion suffered more than 60 percent casualties.[57]

The Final Save

Communist offensive military operations in Laos characteristically ceased with the start of the rainy season, and the North Vietnamese and Pathet Lao moved to heavily defended base camps. This strategy was changed in

April 1972 when the communists decided to withdraw only a day's march from Long Tieng. As a consequence, Vang Pao's annual assault on the Plain of Jars met immediate resistance. According to one account, the government offensive went no farther than the southern edge of the plain before it encountered a tank-supported North Vietnamese infantry force.[58]

Fortunately for Vang Pao and his threatened headquarters, the U.S. Air Force was also revising its tactics. After a November 1972 Laos visit General John W. Vogt, commander of 7th AF, ordered the 7/13th AF to develop an F-111 bombing program for northern Laos. The communist forces had previously been able to resupply and maneuver during periods of darkness and bad weather. The F-111's night and all-weather capability would allow uninterrupted strikes against communist targets. Moreover, the Air Force had developed a ground beacon that provided the F-111 with an "easily identifiable and accurate offset air point for radar bombing."[59]

Although Ambassador Godley was initially skeptical of the system, fearing it would reduce the fulfillment of his requests for B-52 air strikes, Major General James D. Hughes, deputy commander of the 7/13th AF, ordered the beacons located in Laos. By mid-November four beacons were in place and the F-111s were regularly striking targets in the Long Tieng area. Combined with daylight attacks by F-4s and B-52s, the F-111s "broke the . . . attack on Long Tieng even before it could be launched." Godley was soon claiming the beacons were his own idea.[60]

In anticipation of a cease-fire, in late December the remaining communist forces near Long Tieng withdrew and took up positions on and around the Plain of Jars.[61] The U.S. Air Force had once again saved the headquarters of the "secret war." But, after nearly nine years, American air power was about to end its participation in the Lao war.

Years of ambassadorial control over military operations in Laos had, however, left many American officers puzzled and annoyed. General Hughes, notwithstanding a good personal relationship with Ambassador Godley, shared the professional frustrations of his predecessors at the 7/13th AF. The successful introduction of the F-111/beacon program in Laos brought about a major improvement in U.S. bombing operations. But it did not convince Godley that the 7/13th AF should have the principal role in directing air operations in Laos. Ambassador Godley continued to delegate the control of air resources to his CIA station chief.[62]

In his 1973 end-of-tour Report General Hughes was quite blunt in his assessment of this policy.

The spontaneity with which the CIA approached planning may have been workable in the Congo where it had the convenience of a relatively simple force of B-26s and T-28s flown by mercenaries on its own payroll, but it was hardly suitable to the requirements of an organization as complex as the U.S. Air Force in Southeast Asia.[63]

Reflecting on America's military experience in Laos and anticipating the possibility of future wars, General Hughes advised:

It is essential that we not forget the lessons we have learned in Laos. In any future similar conflict, we must ensure that the Ambassador has, and uses, a senior, tactically experienced air advisor. It is interesting to speculate on the results that could have been achieved by an . . . air effort, directed and guided by experts with professional experience and judgement, and supporting competently led ground forces with the spirit and will to fight.[64]

In the spring of 1973 the U.S. military aid program to the Royal Lao government was about to enter a new, and final, phase.

Chapter Eight

THE DENOUEMENT OF U.S. MILITARY AID TO THE ROYAL LAO GOVERNMENT

P athet Lao declarations notwithstanding, the war in Laos only marginally involved the political aspirations of the Lao people. A purely Lao solution to the kingdom's political problems would have been achieved with ample compromise and minimal bloodshed. The carnage visited upon Laos was the result of Ho Chi Minh's military and political struggle to reunite Vietnam, and the United States' concomitant effort to halt the spread of communism in Southeast Asia. Thus, there had never been any doubt in Vientiane or Washington that an agreement ending the war in Vietnam would also bring about a Laos settlement.

The Third and Final Agreement

On September 22, 1972, as negotiators from the United States and the Democratic Republic of Vietnam in Paris moved toward apparent concordance, the Pathet Lao announced their willingness to begin peace talks with the Lao government. The communists' offer, made without preconditions, was promptly accepted by the Souvanna government, and on October 17 the two sides commenced formal discussions in Vientiane. The debate centered immediately on two concerns: the American, Thai, and Vietnamese presence in Laos and the development of a new, truly representative Laotian government. After more than twenty years of war, the basic issues of foreign intervention and Communist party participation in the Lao political process were unchanged.[1]

There was, however, one critical difference between the 1954 and 1962 Geneva Agreements on Laos and any forthcoming political settlement. Permeating the 1972 peace talks was Souvanna's certainty that the Nixon administration was determined to extricate the United States from war in Indochina. There was little indication that America would ever again commit its military power and national prestige to protect the Lao kingdom's avowed quest for neutrality.

Reacting to the fitful Paris negotiations, the Vientiane talks made little progress until mid-December 1972. Following a week-long strategy session at their Sam Neua headquarters, on December 12 the Pathet Lao delegation presented Souvanna with a draft agreement. Although the Lao government countered with its own proposal, the two sides were not far apart. Still, a Lao settlement awaited a final outcome in Paris.[2]

On January 27, 1973, DRV Politburo Member Le Duc Tho and U.S. National Security Advisor Henry A. Kissinger signed the Paris Agreement on Ending the War and Restoring Peace in Vietnam. Article Twenty of the agreement specifically addressed the security concerns of the Lao government.

> The parties participating in the Paris Conference on Vietnam shall strictly respect the . . . 1962 Geneva Agreements on Laos. Foreign countries shall put an end to all military activities in Cambodia and Laos, totally withdraw from and refrain from reintroducing into these two countries troops, military advisors and military personnel, armaments, munitions and war material.[3]

In a written pledge, which was not part of the final Paris peace agreement, Le Duc Tho assured Kissinger that within fifteen days the PAVN would initiate a cease-fire in Laos.[4]

On February 9, en route to Hanoi, Kissinger stopped in Vientiane for talks with Souvanna.[5] What happened next is a matter of some dispute. Kissinger has written that he was emotionally moved by Souvanna's plea that the United States ensure North Vietnamese compliance with the Paris

Agreements. Kissinger told Souvanna, "We have gone through great difficulties, and we did not come all this way in order to betray our friends."[6] In contrast, Arthur Dommen has claimed that Kissinger came to Vientiane "to inform the Laotians that U.S. military support was approaching its end and that, unless they soon accepted whatever settlement was being offered by the . . . [Pathet Lao] in return for a cease-fire, they stood to lose everything."[7]

Recently available evidence indicates that at this critical juncture U.S. policy toward Laos was ill-defined and somewhat in disarray. While Kissinger was, likely pressuring Souvanna to come to agreement quickly with the Pathet Lao and, in effect, undercutting the Royal Lao bargaining position, the U.S. embassy in Vientiane was being ordered by the State Department to plan for continued conflict in Laos. As will be expanded on later, this was a curious circumstance that brought puzzlement and consternation to both the Lao government and those American planners attempting to comply with the provisions of the Lao peace settlement.

When Kissinger reached Hanoi on February 10 he was confronted with some adroit diplomatic gamesmanship. Prime Minister Pham Van Dong told Kissinger that a Vietnamese withdrawal from Cambodia and Laos would not take place upon imposition of a cease-fire, as Kissinger believed, but only upon the conclusion of a political settlement in the two countries. Although Kissinger has called the Vietnamese action an "outrageous interpretation" of Article Twenty of the Paris agreements,[8] he took no action that would have interfered with the ongoing American prisoner-of-war release. Dommen believes that the Vietnamese communists were told by their Vientiane embassy of Kissinger's ultimatum to Souvanna and felt they had the leverage to present the American diplomat "with a fait accompli in Hanoi."[9] This scenario seems to ring true.

Shortly after Kissinger's Hanoi visit the Pathet Lao and the Royal Lao government came to terms, and on February 21, 1973, the Agreement on the Restoration of Peace and Reconciliation in Laos was signed in Vientiane. A cease-fire took effect the next day.

The Vientiane Agreement

Articles Two, Three, and Four of the Vientiane Agreement had an impact on the U.S. military aid program to the Royal Lao government. Article Two declared that foreign countries would cease the bombing of Lao territory, and that all foreign armed forces would completely and permanently cease all military activities in Laos. Article Three included a prohibition against "espionage by air and ground means." Article Four required:

> Within a period no longer than 60 days, counting from the date of the establishment of the Provisional Government of National Union . . . the withdrawal of foreign military personnel, regular and irregular, from Laos, and the dismantling of foreign military and paramilitary organizations must be totally completed. "Special Forces"—organized, trained, equipped and controlled by foreigners—must be disbanded; all bases, military installations and positions of these forces must be liquidated.[10]

The Royal Lao government, which the agreement called the "Vientiane government side," and the Pathet Lao, or "Patriot Forces side," were required to hold general elections to elect a new National Assembly and form a "Government of National Union." The immediate requirement, to be implemented within thirty days of signing the agreement, was the establishment of a Provisional Government of National Union (PGNU) and a National Political Consultative Council (NPCC). These two entities would administer the country's affairs until the formation of a permanent government. Stalling on both sides delayed the signing of a protocol on the formation of the PGNU and the NPCC until September 14, 1973, and the new government was not promulgated until April 5, 1974.[11]

Outwardly, the Vientiane Agreement and the creation of the PGNU seemed to hold great promise for the Lao kingdom. The inclusion of the Pathet Lao in the governmental process seemed to set the stage for resolution of the country's internal political problems. Moreover, the Democratic Republic of Vietnam had pledged—albeit obliquely—to remove its army from Laos, thereby solving the kingdom's only serious external security threat. After nearly two decades of demonstrating that American money alone could not produce a good army, the Royal Lao government could scarcely have expected much more.

America immediately undertook efforts to comply with the Vientiane Agreement. A halt to all U.S. bombing of Laos went into effect with the February 21 cease-fire. This included the activities of the Raven Forward Air Controllers and the Laos-based Waterpump personnel.[12] With two brief exceptions, the United States had ended some nine years of combat air operations over Laos. On February 23, at the request of the Souvanna government, B-52s attacked encroaching PAVN forces on the Bolovens plateau in southern Laos. The heavy bombers also returned in April 1973 to strike communist forces attempting to overrun a Vang Pao position on the Plain of Jars.[13] A complete ban on American air reconnaissance missions, which would have severely reduced the capability to detect communist cease-fire violations, was not consistently followed.

The United States also began planning for the reduction or elimination of the other components of the Lao military aid program: civilian contract air services, the Thai SGUs, Vang Pao's irregular army, Project 404, the USAID Requirements Office, and DEPCHIEF.

The Demise of Air America in Laos and Thailand

The cease-fire in Laos signaled the end of Air America's long association with the American aid program to Laos. A longtime target of Pathet Lao propaganda, the communists justifiably considered the airline part of the CIA's paramilitary operations, and there was little possibility that a new Lao government would allow the company a continued presence in Laos. Moreover, although the Air America air maintenance facility at Udorn was considered by the U.S. military one of the finest in Asia, and would have been a logical source of postwar repair and upkeep for Lao Air Force transports, the Thai government opposed the continued presence in Thailand of the high-profile foreign contractor.

In addition to political problems, the airline also suffered from a sharp reduction in USAID and DOD air support missions after the cease-fire. By June 1973 the Air America fleet had been cut by half, and by year's end another 25 percent was eliminated. The contracts of other, smaller air carriers were similarly affected. In mid-1974 Air America sold its Udorn facility and turned the complex over to the Thai government-affiliated Thai-Am corporation.[14] Nonetheless, Air America continued reduced operations in Laos well into 1975 and played a key role in the evacuation to Thailand of General Vang Pao and many of his followers.[15]

For more than a decade Air America was synonymous with U.S. activity in Laos. This study has discussed only briefly the airline's everyday resupply missions and its extraordinary involvement in special operations and search-and-rescue missions in Vietnam and Laos. Much of what the Air America pilots and crews accomplished in Southeast Asia will never be completely revealed or appreciated. But without Air America, or a similar civilian air carrier, the United States could never have supported a military aid program in Laos. It is also important to note that during their service in

Laos many Air America pilots and crews, at considerable risk to themselves, were responsible for saving the lives of dozens of downed American, Thai, and Lao military aviators.[16]

Withdrawing the Thai SGUs

Since 1969 the Thai SGUs had played a critical role in the defense of northeastern Laos. When the cease-fire took effect on February 21 the CIA and Thai Headquarters 333 had twenty-seven infantry and three artillery battalions (about seventeen thousand Thai soldiers) serving in Laos.[17] In accordance with Article Four of the Vientiane Agreement the Thais were required to leave Laos within sixty days of the formation of a provisional government.[18] However, the scope of the Thai involvement, and the political and military reasons for their presence made the SGU withdrawal from Laos a very complex process.

As the Lao conflict approached an apparent political conclusion there was considerable doubt in Washington, Bangkok, and Vientiane as to whether the Vietnamese communists would withdraw completely from Laos. The continuation of the Thai SGUs in Laos, therefore, was envisioned as a possible guarantee against DRV noncompliance. Vice President Spiro T. Agnew, on the eve of an early February 1973 visit to Thailand, was informed by the U.S. embassy in Bangkok that the Thai SGUs could "serve as a deterrent to violations of the cease-fire and leverage to bring about the withdrawal from Laos of [the] North Vietnamese."[19]

Moreover, even after the Thai SGUs returned home, there were plans to maintain at least part of the force along the Thai-Lao border as a "hedge against [the] resumption of hostilities."[20] On January 19, 1973, in Bangkok this position was reviewed and affirmed by Thai Prime Minister Thanom Kittikachorn in a meeting with White House Chief of Staff Alexander M. Haig, Jr.[21] A month later, in a meeting with then Assistant Secretary of State William H. Sullivan, Prime Minister Souvanna Phouma agreed that the Thai SGUs should be kept ready in Thailand for a possible reintroduction into Laos.[22]

By April 1973 however, with a relatively successful cease-fire in effect and no progress in the formation of a new Lao government, the United States reevaluated the cost and usefulness of the SGU program.[23] The maintenance of a single Thai infantry battalion for one noncombat year in Laos was calculated at $1.15 million dollars, while a fifteen battalion force, based in Thailand for six months, was estimated to cost nearly $13 million dollars.[24] When the SGU expenses were added to the other planned Lao military and economic aid programs the total was expected to exceed the "Symington Ceiling" on allowable U.S. aid to Laos.

There was also growing doubt in the U.S. embassy in Vientiane that the SGUs, whether in Laos or Thailand, would indeed act as a deterrent to DRV violations of the Paris Agreement.[25] Past performance demonstrated that the irregulars were effective in Laos only when backed by American air power and logistical support. The SGUs were a political statement, but without U.S. backing they were not a significant military threat. Having just managed to disengage American combat forces from South Vietnam and in the throes of the Watergate revelations, the Nixon administration was understandably uneasy about the continuation of a program that conceivably could draw the United States back into war in Indochina.

On July 1, 1973, the U.S., in concert with the Thai and Lao governments, began eliminating the Thai SGU program. The Thai force in Laos was immediately reduced to seventeen battalions (two artillery and fifteen infantry) and Headquarters 333 was told the SGUs would be cut to ten battalions (one artillery and nine infantry) by January 1, 1974. Termination of the program was planned for June 30, 1974, "irrespective of whether the units are deployed in Laos or garrisoned in Thailand."[26]

The End of Vang Pao's Army

In anticipation of the imminent cease-fire, on February 20, 1973, the Lao government ordered the integration into the Royal Lao Army of eighteen thousand Lao irregulars funded and directed by the CIA. This action prevented the Pathet Lao from demanding the dissolution of what essentially were prohibited "paramilitary forces." Even after assimilation into the Lao Army the former irregulars maintained their unit integrity and were paid supplemental bonuses by the CIA.[27]

Vang Pao remained in command of Military Region II (northeastern Laos) and, along with his CIA advisers, awaited the coming provisional government. But, in the opinion of the new DEPCHIEF commander, Brigadier General Richard G. Trefry, U.S. Army, neither the Hmong general nor his advisers seemed to understand that American largesse was about to end. Repeated suggestions to improve roads in the region, and thereby prepare for the complete withdrawal of contract air support, were mostly ignored. Similarly, Vang Pao was in no hurry to incorporate his command into the Royal Lao Army logistics system. The Lao supply line was admittedly slow and bumbling, but it would soon be the sole source for Vang Pao's forces.[28]

The inescapable truth was that Vang Pao knew the Pathet Lao had marked the Hmong army for elimination. Since 1962 the Hmong had suffered over ten thousand killed; more than one hundred thousand Hmong were now refugees dependent upon government support. Vang Pao felt he could do little more than await the formation of the PGNU and the certain coming of communist retribution.[29]

Reorganizing the U.S. Military Presence in Laos

By mid-February 1973, planning was well underway for a U.S. military assistance program for the Lao kingdom after the cease-fire. In contrast to past U.S. covert policies, DEPCHIEF recommended the creation of a uniformed thirty-man Defense Attaché Office (DAO) within the U.S. embassy in Vientiane. The DAO would assume all responsibilities previously assigned to the USAID Requirements Office, Project 404, and DEPCHIEF. Under the plan, the DAO would be commanded by a defense attaché who would act as the ambassador's senior military advisor and would oversee all U.S. military assistance programs. A small staff in Udorn, Thailand, would assist with logistical matters.[30]

The presence in Vientiane of a defense attaché would finally establish a single U.S. manager for Lao military assistance. Douglas S. Blaufarb has argued that after the 1962 Geneva Agreements the U.S. ambassadors to Laos, and in particular Ambassador Sullivan, acted as the "single manager" for the Lao war.[31] The ambassadors exercised tremendous control over all aspects of U.S. activity in Laos, but they were not military managers. To a great extent their judgments were influenced by CIA officials, like Blaufarb, and military attachés with no operational responsibilities. As General Vessey stated in a final memorandum to Ambassador Godley, the proposed Defense Attaché Office would allow the "U.S. Mission in Laos . . . [to] more closely conform to the general pattern of [other] U.S. Missions."[32]

When General Trefry explained the reorganization proposal at the Vientiane Country Team meeting on February 20, 1973, Ambassador Godley's only comment related to the proposed DAO rank structure. Under the plan the defense attaché would be an army brigadier general, supported by two assistant attachés—an army colonel and an air force lieutenant colonel. Godley, who a year earlier had snubbed General Vessey upon his arrival, wanted a general and two full colonels.[33] The winds of change were certainly blowing in Vientiane.

In April 1973 Brigadier General Trefry took operational control of the Requirements Office and merged its duties with the Project 404 and DEP-CHIEF responsibilities. The general concentrated his personnel on building a workable logistics system for the Royal Lao military. The task was made difficult by years of Lao dependency on foreign technicians, like the Filipino ECCOIL employees, and a misguided belief that everything would somehow work out. After all, twice before the United States had helped the Lao government out of its troubles.[34]

There was, nonetheless, reason to believe that the United States was not totally committed to a significant military withdrawal from Laos. On March 31, 1973, the State Department directed the U.S. embassy in Vientiane to "take no steps which might impair existing U.S. or RLG military operational capabilities until further notice." This restriction placed the Vientiane Country Team, and particularly the U.S. military aid officials, in a very awkward position. DEPCHIEF, as mentioned earlier, was struggling to make the Lao self-sufficient. At the same time, the State Department was directing that there be no degradation in U.S. support of the Lao military. This directive was also in conflict with the reduced availability of aid funds for Laos. Although General Trefry attempted on numerous occasions to gain "relief" from the order, the State Department never officially rescinded its edict.[35]

Despite the ambiguous directions, the number of Americans involved in the Lao military aid program was significantly reduced. At the time of the cease-fire there were about 180 U.S. military and civilian employees working with the Lao military. By late August 1973 this number had been reduced by nearly half.[36]

Although Charles S. Whitehouse, the newly arrived U.S. ambassador to Laos, and his staff recognized the possibility that the impending provisional government could ban the introduction of any military equipment into the kingdom, the U.S. went ahead with the establishment of a Defense Attaché Office.[37] On September 5, 1973, with the approval of Prime Minister Souvanna Phouma, General Trefry moved from Udorn to Vientiane with a fourteen-man support team and became the U.S. defense attaché to Laos.

DEPCHIEF was then officially placed under the control of the Defense Attaché Office.[38] The United States was now prepared to administer a continued, albeit much reduced, military assistance program in Laos.

Formation of the PGNU

The Provisional Government of National Union was finally promulgated by royal decree on April 5, 1974. In a foreboding act, two days earlier Prince Souphanouvong had entered Vientiane to celebrations and excitement unseen in the capital for many years.[39] Souvanna Phouma was selected as the new prime minister and president of the Council of Ministers. Prince Souphanouvong took charge of the newly formed National Political Consultative Council, which immediately became the most powerful political force in the new government. Souphanouvong's royal charm and political savvy were soon winning support from all levels of Lao society.[40] Moreover, Souvanna suffered a heart attack on July 11, 1974, opening the way for his brother to gain even more influence.[41]

The provisional government declared Vientiane and Luang Prabang neutral cities and the Pathet Lao quickly shared in the administration and policing of these two capitals. Yet the communists refused to allow outside representatives to visit the Pathet Lao "capital" at Sam Neua or to travel in any of their "liberated zones." A statement attributed to the Pathet Lao and often repeated in Vientiane was "What is ours is ours, and what is yours is half ours."[42] The Pathet Lao, although never a dominant military force, were certainly winning the political war in Laos.

Closing Out U.S. Military Aid to Laos

With the establishment of the PGNU on April 5, 1974, all foreign military personnel not assigned diplomatic status were required to leave the kingdom within sixty days. Over the previous six months the Thai SGUs in Laos had been slowly reduced in strength and the remaining few battalions left the kingdom on May 22, 1974.[43] On the June 5 deadline the U.S. military presence in Laos stood at thirty military personnel and fifteen civilians, all duly registered with the new government.[44]

For the next seven months the DAO did what it could to resupply the Royal Lao army, without also providing assistance to the Pathet Lao forces.

However, on February 15, 1975, General Khamouan Boupha, the Pathet Lao secretary of state for defense, formally asked the United States to begin providing all military assistance directly to the PGNU. Khamouan's request was turned aside. But, with steadily increasing Pathet Lao control of the Lao government, continued U.S. military aid to the FAR was soon to become a very contentious issue between the PGNU and the United States.

Laos Becomes the Third Domino

Following the formation of the PGNU the Pathet Lao and their North Vietnamese allies moved against the FAR military positions. Vang Pao, defiant at his Long Tieng headquarters, attempted to fight the communist encroachments. But the Hmong no longer enjoyed American or Thai assistance, and Souvanna had decided the Hmong general had outlived his usefulness. On May 6, 1975, Vang Pao and the prime minister had a very angry confrontation; the general resigned his commission.[45] Vang Pao then requested and quickly received U.S. air support to ferry several thousand Hmong and Lao Theung from Long Tieng to the safety of Udorn, Thailand. The exodus included those most likely to bear the immediate brunt of communist retribution: military officers and civil servants and their families from the provinces of Sam Neua and Xieng Khouang. On May 14, Vang Pao, his immediate family, and a number of senior Hmong officers were flown by the CIA to exile in Thailand. In the following days and months tens of thousands of Hmong followed Vang Pao across the Mekong.[46]

In the wake of the April 1975 communist victories in South Vietnam and Cambodia, and the collapse of the Vang Pao army, five noncommunist members of the PGNU cabinet resigned and fled to Thailand. They were soon joined by thousands of panicked Royal Lao government military and civilian officials. Prime Minister Souvanna Phouma responded on June 7, 1975, by appointing a Pathet Lao collaborator, Peng Phongsavan, as minister of defense and Pathet Lao General Khamouan Boupha as commander of the Lao armed forces.[47]

The Defense Ministry then announced that DAO personnel would require special permission to visit any military installations. Not surprisingly, requests for access by the U.S. defense attaché, Brigadier General Roswell E. Round, Jr., U.S. Army, were ignored.[48] Moreover, Khamouan Boupha sent word to General Round that the DAO should immediately transfer to his ministry all U.S. Military Assistance Program funds designated for the

Royal Lao military. Round recalls that the Pathet Lao general backed up his demand with a thinly veiled threat that he would "make sure you [Round] provide us this money." General Round reported the situation to CINCPAC and was ordered by the headquarters to temporarily move to Udorn, Thailand.[49]

By the end of April, Ambassador Whitehouse and the director of USAID had both departed Laos; there were no announced plans for replacements. On May 10 the State Department approved plans for a quiet withdrawal from Laos of nonessential U.S. personnel and their families. "This was to be done as inconspicuously as possible . . . so as to avoid giving a wrong signal to our friends and creating the impression that we are pulling out of Laos." Four days later, Pathet Lao-controlled student mobs seized equipment and ransacked the USAID facility in Savannakhet and confiscated USAID supplies in Luang Prabang.[50] On May 21 the USAID headquarters in Vientiane was occupied by 150 students and Lao employees. A week long stand-off between the demonstrators and two U.S. Marine guards and an American civilian, who had barricaded themselves in one of the buildings, was settled with a U.S. promise to end the USAID program.[51] As a result, the American presence in Laos was quickly reduced from more than twelve hundred, including dependents, to about seventy-five people.[52]

In one last effort at reaching an accommodation with the new Lao government, on June 2, 1975, Assistant Secretary of State Philip C. Habib arrived in Vientiane for talks with Souvanna Phouma. According to the U.S. Embassy in Vientiane the prime minister told Habib

> The press says the Pathet Lao are taking over. It's not true. Perhaps in five or six years Laos will be communist, but they are reasonable and nationalists. They respect our monarchy and there will be no dictatorship.[53]

The Pathet Lao, however, intensified their harassment of Americans and in late June communist supporters seized five more U.S. facilities. The would be no further negotiation; Washington formally closed the USAID mission to Laos on June 30, 1975. General Round returned to oversee the evacuation of American personnel and, on July 5, carried sensitive embassy communications equipment to a waiting U.S. aircraft. The last U.S. defense attaché to Laos and the remnants of his staff flew off just minutes before the arrival of Pathet Lao policemen.[54] On July 31 the American Embassy, now staffed by just twenty-two personnel, announced the termination of the military aid program for the Royal Lao government. Two weeks later

DEPCHIEF operations in Thailand were discontinued.[55] Twenty years of U.S. military assistance to Laos had come to an end.

Following a Congress of People's Representatives held in Vientiane on December 1 and 2, 1975, the Pathet Lao declared an end to the Lao monarchy and the establishment of the Lao People's Democratic Republic.[56]

Chapter Nine

CONCLUSIONS ON A
"NONATTRIBUTABLE" WAR

The American military aid program in Laos began as an adjunct to other U.S. security initiatives in the region. Rejecting the 1954 Geneva settlement as inadequate to preclude communist aggression in Southeast Asia, the Eisenhower administration orchestrated the creation of the Southeast Asia Treaty Organization. When the United States succeeded France in training the South Vietnamese armed forces, it also began providing military assistance to the French Military Mission in Laos. America's "can do" spirit was, however, inconsistent with the lax French colonial work ethic and the United States moved immediately to take charge of Lao military training.

Initial U.S. efforts at Lao military assistance, which began in 1955, fell miserably short. The Program Evaluations Office was encumbered by a staff of military retirees and former or would-be military personnel; it lacked direction, experienced great difficulty with the French military, and was hampered by the convoluted Lao political situation. Nevertheless, Washington allowed the PEO to muddle along for more than three years before deciding that the program required the attention of a senior active-duty military officer. The arrival of Brigadier General Heintges in February

1959 signaled Washington's decision to begin a full-fledged military aid program and, therefore, an even greater departure from the 1954 agreements.

Although it was not planned, General Heintges' assignment coincided with Prime Minister Phoui Sananikone's announcement that the Royal Lao government viewed the 1954 Geneva Agreements as fully implemented. This declaration, and the recent replacement of Pathet Lao cabinet members by right-wing army officers, touched off increased military contact between the Pathet Lao and the Lao army. The Royal Lao Army acquitted itself in its usual desultory fashion, evidence that the PEO had accomplished little, and the Phoui government publicly requested greater U.S. military aid.

Washington responded quickly to the Lao request and Heintges soon had several hundred U.S. Army Special Forces trainers and Filipino contract technicians assigned to the PEO. The arrival of these additional personnel and an increased budget still did not markedly improve the fighting capabilities of the Royal Lao Army. The Green Berets were frustrated by the short length of their tours in Laos and the refusal of Lao officers to take part in any training programs. And, while the integration of Filipino technicians into the Lao military seemed expedient at the time, it inculcated a reliance on foreigners that stifled later efforts to make the Lao armed forces more self-sufficient.

The expanded American presence in Laos provided opportunities for enormous graft and malfeasance within the royal government. Pathet Lao propagandists rightly pointed to suddenly wealthy civil servants, while the Lao people waited futilely for promised roads, schools, and clinics. The Lao army's enlisted force was exploited by their officers, who often shortchanged the men in their pay and food rations and sold newly arrived U.S. military equipment. A sincere, but naive attempt by Captain Kong Le to redress these injustices and end foreign influence in his country elevated the Laotian civil war into a confrontation of superpowers.

Kong Le's 1960 coup and the installation of Souvanna Phouma as prime minister were immediately and firmly opposed by the United States and Thailand. Since the 1954 signing of the Manila Pact, Washington and Bangkok had been united in their efforts to oppose the inclusion of the Pathet Lao in any Lao coalition government. This anticommunist fervor caused the United States and Thailand to overlook the copious shortcomings of General Phoumi's military leadership and his financial misdeeds, while precipitously dismissing anyone who considered involving the Pathet Lao in a political settlement.

The Thai blockade of Vientiane, the suspension of American military aid to Souvanna's government, and blatant PEO assistance to General Phoumi's forces only exacerbated the situation. For five years the U.S. had enjoyed the advantage of resupplying the Lao military through Thailand by air transport and highway shipment. In contrast, support for the Pathet Lao from China and North Vietnam had to make its way into Laos via time-consuming truck convoys. When Souvanna countered these actions by accepting Soviet military aid he dramatically balanced the military assistance scales. Suddenly, the United States and its new president were faced with an unprecedented Soviet airlift and the realization that the Russians had decided to test America's resolve in Southeast Asia.

The Laotian crisis, escalating in the first days and months of the Kennedy administration, threatened to undercut the young president's international credibility, his foreign policy agenda, and force the United States into a war with the Soviets. Kennedy insisted that he would not be "humiliated" by the Soviets, but the president and his advisors knew enough about the land and people of Laos to decide that the United States should avoid, if possible, a conventional war in Laos. The White House decided to pursue a strategy of tough military "signaling" to the Soviets, while expanding the Lao military assistance program and ordering the development of a secret and unconventional military force in Laos.

Earlier U.S. military assistance efforts in Laos were covert in deference to the 1954 Geneva Accords and mostly focused on the training and support of a conventional army. The Kennedy administration, beginning in 1961, greatly expanded America's involvement in Laos. Since the Royal Lao Army had repeatedly shown its ineptitude, the United States simply recruited a group that would fight. Emphasizing the dangers the communists posed to the Hmong way of life, the CIA was able to develop a surrogate army for the lowland Lao. Determined to make Laos a bastion of freedom, Washington chose to ignore the consequences of supporting a government that was often reluctant to shed blood in its own defense. Although diplomatic maneuvering would prompt a brief respite in U.S. military activity, America's covert Lao war policy was set.

The 1962 Geneva Agreements allowed the United States and the Soviet Union to back away from military confrontation, but the diplomats did little to solve the Lao kingdom's security concerns. President Kennedy, despite the knowledge that North Vietnamese forces remained in Laos, complied with the Geneva terms and ordered a complete withdrawal from Laos of the U.S. Military Assistance Advisory Group. The president acted at the urging of Ambassador W. Averell Harriman, who firmly believed the Soviets could ensure North Vietnamese adherence to the accords. Harriman's faith was misplaced, and perhaps the Kremlin truly misjudged its sway over Hanoi. In any case, Ho Chi Minh never had any intention of abandoning his Laotian highway to South Vietnam.

In addition to Harriman's Soviet "guarantee," there was also a State Department judgment that Hanoi's forces would be circumspect in their violations of Laotian neutrality. This is a critical point in understanding America's Lao policy.

Because the North Vietnamese were transiting Laos en route to make war in South Vietnam, the White House was now conceding that American intervention, if necessary, should occur in South Vietnam and not Laos. In addition, the administration believed that as long as the North Vietnamese denied their presence in Laos, the U.S. could also undertake "nonattributable" military action in the kingdom without fear of international condemnation. Accordingly, Washington could then move its focus to Vietnam where, administration experts predicted, the U.S. could more easily defend the region against communist expansion.

The CIA experienced little difficulty in implementing this covert war policy. Vang Pao and his Hmong clans, driven off their mountains by continuing communist pressure and facing hostility in the lowlands, had little choice but to fight. Air America's experienced pilots and unparalleled repair facilities promised professional and durable air support. Once USAID was directed by the president to assist the CIA with refugee relief and "cover" for agency operatives, the team was complete. The training of the lowland Lao army was left to DEPCHIEF, the U.S. military attachés in Laos, and the USAID Requirements Office.

Without Thai air bases and Thai manpower the United States could not have supported a meaningful covert war in Laos. Bangkok, anxious to see the United States stem communism on the far side of the Mekong, allowed the basing of hundreds of American aircraft—which flew missions over Laos, Cambodia, and the Vietnams—and established "Headquarters 333" to work in concert with the CIA. At no financial cost the astute Thais were able to gain increased border security and hundreds of millions of dollars in military and economic aid. Moreover, the American presence guaranteed the Thai a powerful and immediate buffer against any large-scale communist aggression.

The political implications of the United States conducting a secret war in a neutral country left no doubt that the American ambassador to Laos would have to have strict control over the operation. Even though the "Kennedy letter" enunciated the ambassador's authority over the embassy's "Country Team," the State Department was quite judicious in the selection of its senior Vientiane diplomat. Leonard Unger became the first ambassador to undertake the extraordinarily difficult job of publicly proclaiming American adherence to Lao neutrality, while secretly directing a prohibited military assistance program. Ambassador Unger was more than equal to the task and was subsequently posted to Bangkok where he continued to be an active participant in arranging Thai support for the Lao war.

Ambassador William Sullivan was the most important and influential man in the twenty-year history of America's military assistance program in Laos. For more than four years Sullivan ran the Vientiane Country Team and the Lao war with virtual impunity. His experience in Geneva and support in Washington provided Sullivan with formidable foreign policy insight and political clout. Ambassador Sullivan established himself as the supreme and unquestioned arbiter of all U.S. activities in Laos. His personal attention and involvement in every aspect of the American Mission insured its smooth and professional operation; Sullivan's flaw was an undisguised distrust of the American military.

Ambassador Sullivan believed that U.S. policy objectives in Laos dictated that the U.S. military presence there be minimal. As the war in Vietnam intensified, Sullivan was under increasing pressure from the U.S. military command in Saigon to ease these restrictions. The ambassador was correct in refusing to delegate all of his military authority to COMUS-MACV. America's announced respect for the 1962 Geneva Accords would have looked foolish, indeed, if Laos had been designated a part of COMUS-MACV's theater of operations. Nonetheless, Sullivan could have allowed COMUSMACV, through the 7/13th Air Force, a much greater role in the direction of the air war. Professional military advice on aerial operations would not have exposed America's true military involvement in Laos and it might have improved the air campaign.

Sullivan's decision to exclude COMUSMACV and the 7/13th Air Force from almost all decision making elevated the military role of the CIA. In particular, through the ambassador, the CIA exercised considerable control over American military air power. As evidenced by the recollections and writings of many senior U.S. Air Force officers, CIA officers were mostly untrained in the employment of sophisticated bomber aircraft. Also questionable was the Agency's direction of Air America and U.S. Air Force helicopters in the insertion and extraction of large numbers of troops. In defense of the CIA role, William Sullivan and William Colby have both pointed to the Agency's long experience in Laos as compared to the usual one-year U.S. military tour of duty. Still, Sullivan could have directed a closer association between the CIA and the 7/13th AF that might have capitalized on the expertise of both organizations. It is obvious the CIA wanted air power on demand, with no outside interference.

Ambassador Sullivan also insisted that DEPCHIEF play a minor role in Lao operations. The USAID Requirements Office was staffed by dedicated people, mostly former military men. But the RO, even with the addition of Project 404 personnel, was able neither to gauge the effectiveness of the Lao military nor adequately supervise Lao use of American aid. The results were sloppy training, abuse of military equipment, opportunities for whole-sale malfeasance, and an ineffective army. If the DEPCHIEF commander had been given a responsible place on the embassy Country Team, the RO workers and their colleagues in Thailand might well have developed more effective training programs. Such a collaboration offered the chance of some real improvement in the Lao military.

The military situation in Laos began to change in the late 1960s. America's covert paramilitary war in Laos was fast escalating into a conventional conflict with enormous human and financial costs. The increased aggressiveness of the North Vietnamese dry-season campaigns, a new administration in Washington, and a growing antiwar feeling in the American Congress brought change, albeit slowly, to America's Lao policy.

Ambassador G. McMurtrie Godley, who enjoyed close associations within the CIA, initially retained most of William Sullivan's management policies. The CIA station chief continued to serve as the ambassador's principal military advisor and DEPCHIEF and the 7/13th AF were largely ignored. As the war in Laos accelerated, Godley and his Country Team found themselves increasingly involved in large-scale military operations. The Hmong, who for years had effectively served as guerilla fighters, were now regularly employed against sizable North Vietnamese forces. Marginally equipped and poorly suited for conventional combat, the Hmong suffered horrific casualties. The kingdom's defense began to depend almost entirely on massive aerial bombing and the infusion of additional Thai artillery and infantry units. Nevertheless, Godley clung to the policies of the past and allowed his staff to dictate military requirements to a wholly exasperated 7/13th AF and COMUSMACV.

After years of effort, in 1972 the Pentagon convinced the State Department that DEPCHIEF required the attention of a general officer. Brigadier

General Vessey's performance quickly won Godley's confidence, and, for the first time since the departure of Major General Tucker in October 1961, there was a professional military leader in Laos. Vessey's expertise and recommendations led the way for much improved relations between the U.S. Embassy in Vientiane and senior U.S. military officials in Thailand and South Vietnam. Visits to Laos by U.S. general officers, unthinkable in the past, began to occur with some frequency. Increased understanding, on both sides of the Mekong, measurably improved cooperation on military matters.

However, public revelations about the true extent of America's involvement in the kingdom brought about stiff reductions, mandated by the U.S. Congress, in Lao military aid. By late 1972 there was little question that the United States would soon disengage from the war in Vietnam. The U.S. military had "joined" the Vientiane Country Team a little late.

The war in Laos was always fought in the shadow of Vietnam, so when Hanoi and Washington concluded a settlement there was no doubt that the Lao conflict would soon end. Dr. Kissinger's recollections notwithstanding, the Royal Lao government had no choice but to complete a cease-fire agreement with the Pathet Lao. Nevertheless, Prince Souvanna Phouma was hardly an unwitting victim of American foreign policy. By late 1964 the prince was fully aware of America's covert Lao ground and air campaigns. For more than eight years Souvanna had accepted, and often requested, U.S. military activity in Laos. During much of this period, the prince also maintained close contact with his brother, Prince Souphanouvong. The prime minister and Henry Kissinger might well have enjoyed a mutual discussion on Metternich.

The February 1973 Vientiane Agreement stopped U.S. bombing in Laos and, once a new Lao coalition government was formed, mandated the expulsion of Air America and the Thai SGUs. Although some in Washington hoped that the new Lao government would allow the retention of a small U.S. military assistance program, America's covert war in Laos was at an end.

Over the next year, as the Pathet Lao and the royalists attempted to form a new government, the United States continued to supply the Royal Lao Army with military aid. It was a wasted effort. For too many years, with U.S. acquiescence, the Lao military had been content to sit out the war and allow the Americans to pay the Hmong and Thais to defend the kingdom. Now, even with the imminent cancellation of the U.S. military aid program, there was no sense of urgency. Some senior Lao military officers believed

Souvanna and Souphanouvong would come to a compromise and, as before, the communists would only be part of a new government. Others,
reflecting a traditional Lao perspective, were resigned to their fate. The Lao
were not, and could never be, "Turks."

The formation of the Lao Provisional Government of National Union
resulted in the complete withdrawal by late May 1974 of the remaining Thai
SGUs and the departure of all nonaccredited U.S. military personnel from
Laos. The United States had fully complied with the Vientiane Agreement,
even though President Nixon, like President Kennedy in 1962, knew that
the North Vietnamese remained in Laos. Unlike Kennedy, however, Nixon
was not thinking about a future U.S. covert return to Laos. On May 9,
1974, the U.S. House Judiciary Committee had opened impeachment hearings on the president of the United States. Regardless of North Vietnamese
duplicity, U.S. military involvement in Laos and the rest of Indochina had
come to an end.

When the North Vietnamese forces entered Saigon on April 30, 1975,
the Pathet Lao knew their victory was also near. Plans for any future U.S.
military aid program in Laos completely evaporated, and the U.S. embassy
in Vientiane was drawn down to a skeleton staff. The military assistance
program in Laos was ended.

This study began with a basic question: Why was Laos of importance to
the United States? The answer inheres in the geopolitical foundation of the
containment strategy. The engine that drove America's overall post–World
War II involvement in Southeast Asia was its determination to halt communist expansion before it consumed the entire continent. Laos, which
uniquely bordered all the region's other states, was a key component of any
successful communist movement in South Vietnam, Thailand, and Cambodia. The preservation of a truly neutral Laos, which would deny communist trespass of the kingdom, therefore figured prominently in the U.S.
containment strategy. This examination has shown, however, that Laotian
neutrality was never achieved. Communist violations of the 1954 and 1962
Geneva Agreements were countered by the establishment of a covert U.S.
military assistance program for Laos, also a clear violation of Laotian
neutrality.

Was American policy toward Laos, therefore, a failure? The answer
depends upon one's criteria. State Department official Roger Hilsman, in
To Move a Nation, has called President Kennedy's containment stratagem
of neutralizing Laos a "triumph of statecraft." Hilsman and successive
White House advisors discerned the political, military, and physical tangle

of Laos; the chaotic, land-locked country was no place to fight another Asian ground war. To this end, America's objective of shifting the conventional military confrontation with the communists to Vietnam was both pragmatic and adept. For more than a decade the United States successfully maintained the facade of Laotian neutrality and focused its armed forces on winning the public war in Vietnam.

The geographic imperative of Laos nevertheless remained. Official neutrality notwithstanding, Laos was essential to the spread of communism in Southeast Asia. The kingdom's eastern provinces were Hanoi's critical avenues to the south. In response, U.S.-controlled Hmong and Thai ground forces worked hard to disrupt these resupply activities. Increasingly, American bombers rained the Ho Chi Minh Trail with tons of bombs. Yet, both sides wisely avoided a full-scale war in Laos. The North Vietnamese army and their Pathet Lao allies could have struck at many of the important Laotian river cities, including Luang Prabang. Washington could have ordered American troops inserted into Laos and placed along the Trail. In either case the result would have been an immediate and bloody escalation of the war. Both countries refrained from direct confrontation and precipitous military action, so this "nonattributable war" exacted relatively few American casualties.

By avoiding direct military intervention in Laos, America also relinquished an opportunity to sever Hanoi's pipeline to South Vietnam. Despite harrassment by the "secret army" and massive American bombing, the North Vietnamese continued to make their way south. The United States, unwilling to commit American ground forces to Laos, constrained by a war-weary and disillusioned public, and allied with an ineffective South Vietnamese military, could not defeat the North Vietnamese. Ultimately, Laotian "neutrality" worked to the advantage of Hanoi and doomed U.S. objectives.

Washington could take some solace in the fact that relatively few American lives were lost in Laos, and the majority of the Lao Lum and their cities escaped the fighting, but one Laotian group suffered greatly. For the Hmong of northeastern Laos there was no neutrality. Their horrific casualties were payment in advance for the promise of a better life, free of communist or lowland Lao controls. Americans solicited these highland guerilla fighters; still, U.S. policymakers cannot be held completely responsible for the Hmong losses. The elite of Vientiane and Luang Prabang, who openly viewed the mountain people as little more than savages, were quite willing to sit back and allow their Hmong surrogates to fight the communist trespassers. After all, the lowland Lao army rarely possessed the determination to stand and fight effectively against the North Vietnamese. Moreover, communist proscriptions were anathema to the Hmong way of life. U.S. involvement increased the level of violence, but even without American assistance most of Vang Pao's Hmong clans would have resisted the North Vietnamese.

A final legacy of America's Laotian policy is that it cemented Thai–U.S. relations. A major confrontation in Laos would have quickly spread across the long and porous Thai-Lao border. Anxious to assist in the containment of communism, Bangkok permitted the United States to build critical air facilities and to recruit manpower for the "secret army." As the war expanded these nominally Royal Thai Air Force bases became the cornerstone of the American bombing campaigns in Laos, Cambodia, and North Vietnam. The U.S.–paid Thai forces increasingly took the place of the decimated Hmong guerrillas. Thailand acquired enormous economic and military benefits from the American presence, and the United States obtained what some observers have termed an "unsinkable aircraft carrier."

America's war in Laos, hidden from public view for so long, deserves greater study. The unique relationships, among the Departments of State, Defense, and the Central Intelligence Agency, along with the cooperation of the Royal Thai government, and the sacrifices of the Hmong people, all merit further examination. America's longest war cast a long shadow and, nearly twenty years later, there is still much to be learned.

NOTES

Preface

1. A sortie is a single air support mission.

2. See Castle thesis "Alliance in a Secret War."

3. See Castle dissertation, "At War in the Shadow of Vietnam."

4. Goldstein, *American Policy Toward Laos,* and Stevenson, *The End of Nowhere.* There are, however, a number of books that provide excellent surveys of post–World War II Laos. See Brown and Zasloff, *Apprentice Revolutionaries;* Dommen, *Conflict in Laos;* Dommen, *Laos: Keystone of Indochina;* Fall, *Anatomy of a Crisis;* Sisouk Na Champassak, *Storm Over Laos;* Thee, *Notes of a Witness;* and Toye, *Laos: Buffer State or Battleground.*

5. Goldstein, *American Policy,* 13.

6. Unfortunately, a substantial amount of the U.S. military's Vietnam-era holdings have been destroyed. It is my personal observation that this destruction has resulted from a combination of ignorance, indifference, and efforts to reduce the amount of stored classified materials.

7. U.S. Central Intelligence Agency, letter to the author, of April 20, 1989.

8. U.S. Department of Defense letter from General Robert J. Wood, to Major

General C. V. Clifton, military aide to the president, September 12, 1962, in the possession of the author (hereafter cited as Wood letter).

9. Two of these men went on to very senior positions in the U.S. government. John W. Vessey, Jr., a brigadier general during his assignment to the organization, rose to four-star rank and served as chairman of the Joint Chiefs of Staff. At this writing he is the president's special representative on MIA/POW matters. His successor at DEPCHIEF, Brigadier General Richard G. Trefry, went on to become a lieutenant general and, from 1990 to 1992, the military assistant to the president of the United States.

10. U.S. Agency for International Development, *Facts on Foreign Aid to Laos,* Embassy of the United States, Vientiane, Laos, April 1971, 26–27 (hereafter cited as USAID, *Facts*).

1. Introduction

1. My telephone interview with Colonel Peter T. Russell, U.S. Army, retired. Colonel Russell commanded DEPCHIEF from 1968 to 1971.

2. The term used for overseas CIA offices and case officers was often *CAS* (Controlled American Sources). In Southeast Asia U.S. military personnel almost always used *CAS,* not *CIA.* The terms are interchangeable, but I shall use *CIA.*

3. While Udorn Royal Thai Air Force Base was the headquarters for Air America operations in Laos and Thailand, the company had other offices and contractual obligations throughout the Far East. The story of Air America's predecessor, Civil Air Transport, as well as early details on Air America can be found in Leary, *Perilous Missions.* See also Leary and Stueck, "The Chennault Plan to Save China," 349–64. Detailed information regarding the CIA's ownership of Air America can be found in the final report of the Senate Select Committee to Study Governmental Operations with Respect to Intelligence Activities, *Foreign and Military Intelligence,* Senate Report 94-755, Books 1 and 4, 94th Cong., 2d sess., 1976 (hereafter cited as Church Committee Report).

4. Although Air America was the first and largest civilian air carrier working in Laos, it is important to note that there were other air transport companies working within the kingdom. Details on these other organizations will be provided in later chapters.

5. Official accounts of U.S. bombing activities in Southeast Asia may be found in Momyer, *Airpower in Three Wars,* and in Berger, ed., *The United States Air Force in Southeast Asia.*

6. Fall, *Anatomy,* 23. Arthur M. Schlesinger, Jr., refers to Laos as "a state by diplomatic courtesy" in *A Thousand Days,* 323.

7. Indochina was a creation of nineteenth-century French imperialism. It comprised five separate Southeast Asian administrative regions; Cochinchina (southern Vietnam), Annam (central Vietnam), Tonkin (northern Vietnam), Cambodia, and Laos. Cochinchina was, technically, a colony, while Annam, Tonkin, Cambodia,

and Laos were protectorates. See Steinberg, ed., *In Search of Southeast Asia*, 179–80.

8. Department of the Army, Donald P. Whitaker et al., *Laos: A Country Study*, 11, 19.

9. The plain takes its name from the presence of more than a hundred stone receptacles. They are believed to be the artifacts of a Chinese culture existing some two thousand years ago. Dommen, *Conflict*, 2–3.

10. For an impassioned review of the bombing of the Plain of Jars see Fredric R. Branfman, *Voices from the Plain*.

11. Dommen, *Conflict*, 6. The proper transliteration of lowland and highland Lao names, both of people and places, has long been subject to various interpretations. This lack of consistency was compounded after December 1975, when the new Communist regime instituted a number of changes in the written Lao language. I have attempted to use the spellings most often found in scholarly works about Laos. I use the terms *Laos* and *Royal Lao government* interchangeably when referring to the recognized government operating from the administrative capital at Vientiane.

12. Whitaker, *Country Study*, 149–54. See also USAID, *Facts*, 35–71.

13. Whitaker, *Country Study*, 20–21. According to United Nations statistics, the population of Laos in March 1985 was just over 3.5 million. Currently, the population is estimated at about 4 million. United Nations, "Salient Features of Lao PDR" (document in my possession).

14. Whitaker, *Country Study*, 268. The provinces were: Phong Saly, Houa Khong, Luang Prabang, Houa Phan (Sam Neua), Xieng Khouang, Sayaboury, Vientiane, Borikhane, Khammouane, Savannakhet, Saravane, Sedone, Champassak, Vapikamthong, Attopeu, and Sithandone. The military regions were: Military Region I, comprising Phong Saly, Houa Khong, Sayaboury, and Luang Prabang; Military Region II, Houa Phan and Xieng Khouang; Military Region III, Khammouane and Savannakhet; Military Region IV, Saravane, Attopeu, Champassak, Sedone, Vapikamthong, and Sithandone; Military Region V, Vientiane and Borikhane. See Soutchay Vongsavanh, *RLG Military Operations*, 23–25.

15. According to the United Nations, the Lao People's Democratic Republic has officially proclaimed sixty-eight distinct ethnolinguistic groups in Laos (United Nations, "Salient Features of Lao PDR"). For an excellent summary of communist policy toward the various Lao hill tribes see Gary D. Wekkin, "The Rewards of Revolution: Pathet Lao Policy Towards the Hill Tribes Since 1975" and Gary Y. Lee, "Minority Policies and the Hmong", both in *Contemporary Laos*, ed. Stuart-Fox. 181–219.

16. In 1970 it was estimated that there were eight times as many Lao living in Thailand as in Laos. Whitaker, *Country Study*, 41.

17. Westermeyer dissertation, "The Use of Alcohol and Opium Among Two Ethnic Groups in Laos," 15; Whitaker, *Country Study*, 41–45.

18. Whitaker, *Country Study*, 50–51.

19. Ibid., 107, 124. Animism, the belief that natural objects, natural phenom-

ena, and the universe itself possess souls or consciousness, is a pervading influence in the lives of most Lao. A strong belief in *phi* is quite common among both Lao Buddhists and non-Buddhists.

20. Ibid., 50–51.

21. Ibid., 52–53.

22. LeBar, Hickey, and Musgrave, *Ethnic Groups,* 73. For additional information on Hmong migration into northern Southeast Asia see Wiens, *China's March* and Geddes, *Migrants of the Mountains.* For a detailed study of the Hmong see Yang Dao, *Les Hmong du Laos.*

23. Whitaker, *Country Study,* 54–55.

24. Westermeyer, *Use of Alcohol and Opium,* 19.

25. Ibid., 16–17.

26. Kunstadter, ed., *Southeast Asian Tribes* 287–88. See also Scott's dissertation, ''Migrants Without Mountains, 98–106.

27. Whitaker, *Country Study,* 55. Additional information on the Hmong language may be found in Heimbach, *White Meo-English Dictionary,* and in Hendricks, Downing, and Deinard, eds., *The Hmong in Transition.*

28. ''On the evening of 9 March, the Japanese ambassador to French Indochina presented Governor-General Admiral Jean Decoux with an ultimatum demanding that direct control of the government, police, and armed forces of the colony be turned over to the Japanese. Two hours later Japanese forces moved against French forts and garrisons all over Indochina. . . . The Japanese coup . . . marked a turning point in the history of Indochina. It signalled the end of the painful French pretense to sovereignty and provided new opportunities for . . . opponents of the French.'' Spector, *Advice and Support,* 30.

29. For a detailed review of French rule in Laos see Toye, *Buffer State or Battleground,* 23–49. A well-documented study of the early Lao nationalist and communist movements is found in Geoffrey C. Gunn, *Political Struggles in Laos.* A lengthy review of Prince Phetsarath's life, believed by several experts to be an autobiography, is *Iron Man of Laos,* by ''3349'' [cited in bibliography by title].

30. Dommen, *Conflict,* 22. Souvanna Phouma and Phetsarath shared the same father (Viceroy Boun Khong) and mother. Souphanouvong had the same father, but was born to the viceroy's eleventh wife. All three men were educated in Europe, and Phetsarath and Souvanna Phouma returned home to prominent positions. In contrast, Souphanouvong, a brilliant student with enormous promise, was posted by the French to a low-paying position at Nha Trang, Vietnam. The young prince remained in Vietnam for seven years and, clearly, was influenced by this experience. See Brown and Zasloff, *Apprentice Revolutionaries,* 29.

31. A lengthy review of the Lao Issara government in exile can be found in Gunn, *Political Struggles,* 187–214.

32. Sisouk, *Storm Over Laos,* 14–15.

33. Souphanouvong traveled to Hanoi in July 1946 and met with Ho Chi Minh. The prince was impressed with Ho's aggressive tactics and sought to emulate them See Fall, *Anatomy,* 40–41. Souphanouvong's ''resentment of French colonialism,

compounded by personal rebuffs; his exposure to socialist ideas in France during the Popular Front; his receptivity to Vietnamese vitality, represented by his Vietnamese wife; and his princely ambitions to assume leadership made him ready and willing to join the anticolonial cause of the Viet Minh.'' Brown and Zasloff, *Apprentice Revolutionaries,* 29.

34. Dommen, *Conflict,* 28, 34.

35. Ibid., 34.

36. Fall, *Anatomy,* 43–44. Souphanouvong's predilection toward Ho and the Viet Minh would result in the establishment in 1955 of the Lao Communist party. Brown and Zasloff, *Apprentice Revolutionaries,* 29, 47. A complete review of this relationship is found in Langer and Zasloff, *North Vietnam and the Pathet Lao.* See also monograph by Edwin T. McKeithen, ''The Role of North Vietnamese Cadres in the Pathet Lao Administration of Xieng Khouang Province,'' and Zasloff, *The Pathet Lao.*

37. George C. Herring, ''The Truman Administration and the Restoration of French Sovereignty in Indochina,'' *Diplomatic History* (1977), 1:101, and 104–5. Professor Herring goes on to say, that ''neither Truman nor the top State Department officials to whom he turned for guidance shared Roosevelt's appreciation of the significance of Asian nationalism or his profound distrust of France. The Truman administration never considered making France accountable to some international authority. It quickly acquiesced in the restoration of French sovereignty and refused to use its influence to get France to make some accommodation with Indochinese nationalism.'' Ibid., 115–16.

38. For example, ''Ho Chi Minh made a number of efforts to bring the Vietnamese cause to the attention of the U.S. Government, but his letters to Truman and Secretary of State James F. Byrnes . . . were officially ignored.'' Gibbons, *The U.S. Government and the Vietnam War, Part I,* 22. See also Herring, ''Truman Administration,'' 112, and Patti, *Why Viet Nam?* 231, 350, and 380–81.

39. Spector, *The Early Years,* 96. For a review of the Franco-Viet Minh war see Fall, *Street Without Joy,* 22–310 and Davidson, *Vietnam at War,* 31–252.

40. As quoted in Goldstein, *American Policy,* 47.

41. *Pentagon Papers: Gravel Edition,* I:64–65.

42. Cited in Schaller, *The American Occupation of Japan,* 232.

43. Professor Gibbons points out that some observers have mistakenly assumed the Korean War prompted the decision to establish the missions. U.S. military assistance to Indochina was, as indicated, part of an NSC strategy approved months earlier. Gibbons, *U.S. and the Vietnam War, Part I,* 73.

44. Spector, *The Early Years,* 116.

45. Herring, *America's Longest War,* 20.

46. Ibid., 23.

47. In 1954 the U.S. Foreign Operations Administration estimated that from 1950 to 1954 the United States provided France with about $1.2 billion for the war in Indochina. In March 1954 a French politician reported that the United States was ''carrying 78 percent of the cost of the Indochina war.'' Goldstein, *American*

60. Dommen, *Conflict*, 53.

61. In contrast, "the reaction of the American public to the Geneva settlements was largely one of indifference. Opinion had been alerted in April by the administration's warnings of possible intervention in Indochina. . . . Rumors of intervention continued to circulate about Washington in May and June but, invariably, other news stories, such as the Army-McCarthy hearings and the Guatemalan insurrection, were given greater prominence in the American press. By mid-July the American people were little concerned with the vagaries of the Geneva negotiations." Randle, *Geneva 1954*, 350.

62. Goldstein, *American Policy*, 89, and Cameron, ed., *Vietnam Crisis*, I:321.

63. Spector, *The Early Years*, 228.

64. This policy recognized the fundamental post–World War II change in Thailand's traditional diplomatic stance of "bending with the wind." Randolph, *The United States and Thailand*, 10–11, 19.

65. U.S. Department of Defense, 12 books. *United States–Vietnam Relations, 1945–67* 10:738 (hereafter cited as DOD, *U.S. Vietnam Relations.*).

66. U.S. covert operations in Thailand were not unprecedented. The CIA had been involved in secret paramilitary training in Thailand since at least 1951. This secret U.S.–Thai project will be explored in greater detail in chapter three.

67. SEATO was dissolved in 1977.

68. Modelski, ed., *SEATO: Six Crises*, 292. See also Herring, *America's Longest War*, 44–45.

69. Randolph, *The U.S. and Thailand*, 10–11. See also Wiwat Mungkandi, "Thai-American Relations in Historical Perspective," *United States–Thailand Relations* (Berkeley: Institute of East Asian Studies, University of California, 1986), 14–15.

70. Muscat, *Thailand and the United States*, 11. For a Thai perspective of U.S. foreign aid to Thailand see Nongnuth Kimanonth, "The U.S. Foreign Aid Factor in Thai Development, 1950–1975," *Thai-American Relations in Contemporary Affairs*, (Singapore: Executive Publications, 1982), 138–47. See also Caldwell, *American Economic Aid to Thailand*, 38–41.

71. Muscat, *Thailand and the U.S.*, 20.

72. Randolph, *The U.S. and Thailand*, 14–15. "Technical and economic assistance made available through the USOM totalled up to approximately $440.1 million for the period from September 1950 to June 1965. Of this, a sum of $365.9 was given in the form of grants; and the rest [$74.2] was made up of loans." Jha, *Foreign Policy of Thailand*, 39. USOM was the country-level office of the International Cooperation Agency (ICA), which later became the Agency for International Development (AID).

73. Randolph, *The U.S. and Thailand*, 15.

74. As cited in Jha, *Foreign Policy of Thailand*, 46.

2. Neutrality That Doesn't Work

1. Randle, *Geneva*, 609.

2. In 1954 the Pathet Lao had an army of between fifteen hundred and three thousand men. Brown and Zasloff, *Apprentice Revolutionaries*, 57. As mentioned earlier, during the Franco-Vietminh War the Vietnamese committed some forty thousand troops to Laos. For a review of the origins of the Royal Lao Army by a former Royal Lao army general see Sananikone, *The Royal Lao Army and U.S. Army*, 14–30. Prior to fleeing his country General Sananikone was chief of staff of the Royal Lao Army and the last under secretary of defense.

3. Brown and Zasloff, *Apprentice Revolutionaries*, 56.

4. Goldstein, *American Policy*, 110.

5. Ibid, 111.

6. As a result, Souvanna resigned his post in May. He was reinstated in August when the politicians were unable to form a government without him. Ibid, 114.

7. Souphanouvong became head of the Ministry of Plans, Reconstruction, and Urbanism. Phoumi Vongvichit was made head of the Ministry of Cults and Fine Arts. Goldstein, *American Policy*, 117. Phoumi, the son of a provincial governor and a former civil servant under the French, would become one of the most important members of the Pathet Lao. Dommen, *Conflict*, 76.

8. Prior to Yost's arrival the "U.S. diplomatic presence in Laos consisted of a single Foreign Service Officer, who did his own typing." Stevenson, *The End of Nowhere*, 27–28.

9. U.S. assistance was made possible under the terms of the December 1950 Pentalateral defense pact and a September 1951 U.S.–Lao economic assistance agreement. Wing, et al., "Case Study of US Counterinsurgency Operations in Laos, 1955–1962" (hereafter cited as Wing, *Case Study*), E4. The size of the U.S. mission in Laos increased from a "dozen or so at the end of 1954 to forty-five in the autumn of 1955 to eighty-two in August 1956 to over one hundred in December 1957." Stevenson, *The End of Nowhere*, 29.

10. Wing, *Case Study*, E6. U.S. economic aid was to increase substantially. In fiscal years 1956 and 1957, the U.S. provided $48.7 million and $44.5 million, respectively. Goldstein, *American Policy*, 134. See also House, Committee on Government Operations, *U.S. Aid Operations in Laos*, 6–9 (hereafter cited as U.S., *Aid Operations*).

11. The U.S. government believed military assistance to Laos was permitted under the ninth article of the Geneva settlement. It stated, "Upon the entry into force of the present Agreement and in accordance with the declaration made at the Geneva Conference by the Royal Government of Laos on July 20, 1954, the introduction into Laos of armaments, munitions and military equipment of all kinds is prohibited with the exception of a specified quantity of armaments in categories specified as necessary for the defence of Laos." Randle, *Geneva 1954*, 584.

12. This ratio is based on U.S. expenditures from 1955–62. Wing, *Case Study*, E5–E6.

13. A French training mission to the *Force Armée Royale* (FAR) and two French military bases were exempted. French forces were directed not to exceed fifty-five hundred troops. Randle, *Geneva 1954*, 583–84.

14. Goldstein, *American Policy*, 166.

15. My interview with Hansel, October 27, 1990. Mr. Hansel was a PEO employee. PEO manning "consisted of six persons during the first year and an average of 22 during the second and third years." Wing, *Case Study*, A10.

16. Wing, *Case Study*, A10. MAP funds were made available to foreign governments on a nonreimbursable (grant) basis under the provisions of the Mutual Security Acts of 1949, 1951, 1954, and later the Foreign Assistance Act of 1961. The aid was designed "to help strengthen the forces of freedom by aiding peoples of less developed friendly countries." St. Jean, McClain, and Hartwig, "Twenty-Three Years of Military Assistance to Laos." 5–6.

17. Wing, *Case Study*, A14, B6, and *Pentagon Papers: Gravel Edition*, V:252. The frustrated PEO felt compelled to undertake some activities without the consent of the American ambassador to Laos. On at least two occasions in 1957–58 the PEO arranged for the training of small numbers of Lao army personnel in Thailand. This instruction, under Project ERAWAN, was carried out with the full cooperation of the U.S. MAAG to Thailand and the Royal Thai army. Wing, *Case Study*, B9. There were problems with some of the Lao students. According to Arthur Dommen, "Lao officers sent for training to Thailand did not even bother to show up for classes." Dommen, *Conflict*, 139.

18. Toye, *Buffer State or Battleground*, 112.

19. One of the embassy's efforts was a preelection crash project called "Operation Booster Shot." Intended to boost the image of the Royal Lao government in rural areas, the program included "well-digging, irrigation projects, repair of schools, temples, and roads; altogether more than ninety work projects." The U.S. ambassador to Laos later testified to Congress that he had "struggled for sixteen months to prevent a coalition government." Cited in *Pentagon Papers: Gravel Edition*, V:253, 255. See also Brown and Zasloff, *Apprentice Revolutionaries*, 61–64.

20. Brown and Zasloff, *Apprentice Revolutionaries*, 64.

21. Stevenson, *The End of Nowhere*, 66. Goldstein describes *les Jeunes* (the Young Ones) as "students just returned from abroad, junior officials, and young army officers." Goldstein, *American Policy*, 143. The CIA was instrumental in the creation of the CDNI. See Hilsman, *To Move a Nation*, 114–15.

22. Dommen, *Conflict*, 111.

23. Toye, *Buffer State or Battleground*, 118–19.

24. Some U.S. newspapers viewed this statement as a prelude to sending additional military aid to the Royal Lao government. Fall, *Anatomy*, 97. By this time the International Control Commission (ICC)—the supervisory and inspection body established by the Geneva agreements to oversee implementation of the settlement—

had halted their operations in Laos. Dommen, *Conflict,* 110. See also Randle, *Geneva 1954,* 522–23.

25. As noted, the integration was part of the December 1956 settlement between Souvanna and Souphanouvong.

26. Brown and Zasloff, *Apprentice Revolutionaries,* 67. One of the Pathet Lao battalions awaiting integration had been placed under guard at a government base on the Plain of Jars. On May 18, 1959 the Pathet Lao unit escaped and successfully reached the safety of the Vietnamese border near Sam Neua. "That the Pathet Lao did so [escaped] with 700 men, their families, chickens, pigs, weapons, and household articles is testimony to the military skill which the Royal Army was to display in many subsequent encounters with the Pathet Lao." Stevenson, *The End of Nowhere,* 71.

27. Goldstein, *American Policy,* 152.

28. During an interview, Sisana Sisane, formerly Pathet Lao minister of Information and presently chairman of the LPDR Social Science Research Committee, called the Vientiane purge the "worst mistake of the Royal Lao government." The Pathet Lao "could not have achieved victory otherwise. It placed the people on the side of the Pathet Lao. Without the arrests of the senior leadership there would have been no issues. This created the hatred of the people." Sisana was one of those interned with Souphanouvong. He described their jail as a "horse stable." My interview with Sisane, August 20, 1990. This point of view is also expressed in official LPDR histories of the war. See Vongvichit, *Laos and the Victorious Struggle,* 118.

29. The decision to send General Heintges, an active officer, was made by the Defense Department's Office of International Affairs (ISA) in consultation with the commander in chief, Pacific (CINCPAC). Wing, *Case Study,* B11. Admiral Harry D. Felt, (CINCPAC, 1958–64), recalled later that the early PEO "was a terrible organization and there was scandal coming out about this. It was . . . composed mostly of retired military people who hadn't any experience in that part of the world but needed a job, I guess. We replaced all these worthless people." Admiral Felt thought very highly of General Heintges, remarking that he was a "wonderful guy . . . [who] was fluent in French." "Reminiscences of Admiral Harry Donald Felt, vol 2, 510, and my interview with Admiral Felt, March 1, 1990. Admiral Felt has graciously allowed me to quote from his oral history. In 1959, corruption within the U.S. mission to Laos was the subject of an extensive congressional investigation. U.S., *Aid Operations,* 1–5. See also Goldstein, *American Policy,* 181–93.

30. Wing, *Case Study,* B11–B12, C10. For the official version see U.S. Department of State, *The Situation in Laos,* 23. In the midst of the negotiations between France, Laos, and the United States, the American ambassador to Thailand recommended that an all-Asian military advisory group be organized. He suggested a unit comprising of Filipinos, Vietnamese, Thais, Pakistanis, and Koreans, commanded by a Filipino retired general. Wing, *Case Study,* A15. There is no further information on the ambassador's plan, or whether it was ever seriously considered.

31. Wing, *Case Study,* B12. A detailed account of the Heintges plan is found at C79–C80.

32. Ibid., B13–B14. See also Rod Paschall, "White Star in Laos," in *Pawns of War: Cambodia and Laos,* ed., Arnold R. Isaacs, et al. (Boston: Boston Publishing, 1987), 64.

33. *Pentagon Papers: Gravel Edition,* II:647, and Wing, *Case Study,* 29.

34. Wing, *Case Study,* C9, C17.

35. Sanchez, letter of January 6, 1989. Mr. Sanchez was a Special Forces medic in Laos. See also Department of Defense, "Final Report of Military Assistance and Advisory Group, Laos," 7 (document in my possession).

36. Phoumi, a southern Lao related to Prime Minister Sarit Thanarat of Thailand, had once been chief of staff to Prince Souphanouvong. He received an army commission in 1950 and served as a military advisor at the Geneva Conference. A 1957 graduate of the French War College, he was bright, ambitious, and aggressive. Phoumi was just the sort of person the U.S. military and the CIA favored to lead the Lao army and, perhaps, the country. However, many in the U.S. embassy, including the ambassador, believed Phoumi was simply an opportunist. Dommen, *Conflict,* 127–28.

37. Ibid., 129.

38. Ibid., 133.

39. Ibid., 133–34. Hilsman also describes this CIA activity, but adds "the Communist agents also distributed money, but they added terrorism, too, including assassination." Hilsman, *To Move A Nation,* 122.

40. Stevenson, *The End of Nowhere,* 88.

41. My interview with Sisane on August 20, 1990. See also Toye, *Buffer State or Battleground,* 135–36, Brown and Zasloff, *Apprentice Revolutionaries,* 73–74, and Vongvichit, *Laos and the Victorious Struggle,* 126.

42. Sananikone, *The Royal Lao Army,* 60. General Sananikone was a member of the CDNI.

43. Brown and Zasloff, *Apprentice Revolutionaries,* 73.

44. Stevenson, *The End of Nowhere,* 14. During an interview Kong Le told me that the families squabbled interminably over control of the kingdom's commerce and armed forces. The introduction of massive amounts of U.S. aid intensified the competition and corruption became endemic. All the while little attention was paid to the severe problems facing the common folk. Not surprisingly, the country's mostly illiterate and poor minorities became increasingly disaffected. See my April 1989 interview in Honolulu with Major General Kong Le, coup leader and former commander of the Lao Neutralist Army. Of note, Kong Le was in Hawaii to raise money for his "resistance army in Laos." The army, according to a Kong Le associate, numbered forty-seven thousand armed men. During his 1989 visit, and another in September 1990, Kong Le attempted to convince the local Lao community to fund armed resistance efforts against the LPDR government. Reaction from the Lao in Hawaii ranged from indifference to unqualified support. It was my

personal observation that, during his visits, Kong Le was always surrounded by sycophants, many of whom resided on the United States mainland and slept and ate in the homes of Lao families. Kong Le resides in Paris. The figure of forty-seven thousand men was substantially inflated. In my confidential interview in Bangkok on September 17, 1990, an informed source told me Kong Le's forces numbered less than a thousand.

45. Kong Le is a Phu Tai, a sub-group of the Lao Tai.

46. Kong Le's unit, the "2d Parachute Battalion was an elite, hard-fighting unit. Kong Le . . . had led it on many successful operations in Sam Neua as well as in southern Laos." Sananikone, *The Royal Lao Army*, 61. Kong Le received U.S. "Ranger" training at Fort McKinley, Philippines. Toye, *Buffer State or Battleground*, 139–42. A former U.S. Army Special Forces medic who worked with Kong Le's unit had high praise for the officer's "determination and sincerity," but believed him to be "politically naive." He believes Kong Le tired of his unit, the "fire brigade," being placed in the toughest combat situations while senior Royal Army officers lived in safety and luxury. My interview in Bangkok on August 16, 1990, with Michael H. Sherwood.

47. My interview with Kong Le, April 18, 1989.

48. Fall, *Anatomy*, 187.

49. The men were discussing funeral arrangements for the late King Sisavang Vong. Sisavang died in October 1959, but a funeral was postponed until an appropriate sandalwood cremation vessel could be found. Stevenson, *The End of Nowhere*, 92.

50. Ibid., 92–94.

51. Dommen, *Conflict*, 157.

52. Stevenson, *The End of Nowhere*, 95.

53. Brown and Zasloff, *Apprentice Revolutionaries*, 74–75.

54. Dommen, *Conflict*, 154–55. The blockade resulted in "the accumulation in Bangkok warehouses of 10,000 tons of U.S. aid goods destined for Laos." Fall, *Anatomy*, 191.

55. Hilsman, *To Move a Nation*, 124.

56. Brown and Zasloff, *Apprentice Revolutionaries*, 75–76.

57. Dommen, *Conflict*, 159–60. Souvanna later called Secretary Parsons "the most reprehensible and nefarious of men." Reported in Stevenson, *The End of Nowhere*, 105.

58. Dommen, *Conflict*, 160, and Brown and Zasloff, *Apprentice Revolutionaries*, 76.

59. Wing, *Case Study*, C16.

60. Bowers, *USAF in Southeast Asia: Tactical Airlift*. It is interesting to note that Bowers chose to use the word "royalist" in describing Phoumi's forces. Souvanna, after all, was the legitimate head of the Lao government and Phoumi, technically, was a "rebel." The remarkable nature of Lao politics is also reflected in the fact that General Phoumi, a commoner, was opposing two princes of the realm, Souvanna and Souphanouvong.

61. Dommen, *Conflict*, 154–55. The men had received their training in unconventional warfare and anti-guerrilla tactics under Project ERAWAN. Wing, *Case Study*, 28–9.

62. Dommen, *Conflict*, 164. See also Tilford's article "Two Scorpions in a Cup'', 3.

63. Dommen, *Conflict*, 167.

64. Goldstein, *American Policy*, 217.

65. Lee, *China's Policy Toward Laos*, 72–73. In fact, by this time the PEO had grown to more than five hundred men. Wing, *Case Study*, A30.

66. Bowers, *USAF Tactical Airlift*, 441, and Tilford, "Two Scorpions in a Cup,'' 154. See chapter three for details on the Thai involvement.

67. Dommen, *Conflict*, 166.

68. Stevenson, *The End of Nowhere*, 118. The Soviet Union and India continued to recognize the Souvanna government, while Canada, France, and Great Britain sided with the U.S. position. Dommen, *Conflict*, 175.

69. Fall, *Anatomy*, 198. See also Chalermnit Press Correspondent, *Battle of Vientiane 1960* 1–56. The writing is uneven, but the book contains rare photographs of Vientiane and other areas of Laos.

70. Toye, *Buffer State or Battleground*, 160.

71. Tilford, "Two Scorpions in a Cup,'' 156–57.

72. Vang Vieng is located about fifty-five miles north of Vientiane. Colonel Toland's pictures caused quite a stir among his superiors and were later released to the public. They appeared in a number of newspapers and magazines. Colonel Toland was rewarded with the Air Force Distinguished Flying Cross. My interview of November 30, 1990, with Colonel Toland. See also, Department of the Air Force. Oral History Interview. Lieutenant Colonel Butler B. Toland, Jr., 17–18, and 21–22. (Hereafter all such interviews will be referred to as an AF Oral History.) One of Colonel Toland's photographs is found in Tilford, "Two Scorpions in a Cup,'' 154.

73. AF Oral History, Toland, 23, and my interview with Toland, November 30, 1990. An official U.S. Air Force history errs in describing this incident. Earl H. Tilford, Jr., reports that Colonel Toland, who was in Saigon at the time, was flying the aircraft. Tilford, *Search and Rescue*, 33.

74. As indicated above, U.S. Air Force aircraft covertly flown by Civil Air Transport pilots were hit, with tragic results, by communist gunners while supporting the French at Dien Bien Phu (see chap. 1, n. 51). On December 28, 1960, the Air Attaché aircraft was struck by gunfire from an IL-14 as the Americans photographed Soviet airlift operations. The VC-47 landed safely and no injuries were reported. Tilford, "Two Scorpions in a Cup,'' 156.

75. Cited in Department of the Air Force, "United States Policy Toward Southeast Asia, 1943–1968,'' Futrell's Project Corona Harvest report, 119–20.

76. Marolda and Fitzgerald, *U.S. Navy*, II: 52

77. Eisenhower, *Waging Peace*, 609.

78. Schlesinger, *A Thousand Days*, 331.

152   3. Conflict, Diplomacy, and Covert Operations

3. Conflict, Diplomacy, and Covert Operations

1. Eisenhower, *Waging Peace*, 609–10.

2. Ibid., 612.

3. Schlesinger, *A Thousand Days*, 163. See also *Pentagon Papers: Gravel Edition*, II: 635–57. Eisenhower's actual comments, and how Kennedy and his advisors perceived this advice, are now under close historical scrutiny. U.S. diplomatic historians Richard H. Immerman and Fred I. Greenstein have recently located documentary evidence that indicates Eisenhower may not have recommended a unilateral U.S. response. Moreover, a number of people who attended the meeting have conflicting versions of what was said and by whom. Immerman and Greenstein, "What Did Eisenhower Advise Kennedy About Indochina?," unpublished (manuscript in my possession). A week earlier Eisenhower had dispatched to the Boun Oum government ten T-6 trainers modified to carry machine guns and rockets. Goldstein, *American Policy*, 231.

4. Following his election victory Kennedy is reported to have privately said of Laos: "An American invasion, a Communist victory or whatever, I wish it would happen before we take over and get blamed for it." Sorenson, *Kennedy*, 640.

5. The tag "action intellectuals," was coined by Theodore H. White. See Gibbons, *The U.S. Government and the Vietnam War, Part II*, 7.

6. Schlesinger, *A Thousand Days*, 329.

7. Rostow, *The Diffusion of Power*, 266.

8. *Pentagon Papers: Gravel Edition* II: 33.

9. Parmet, *JFK*, 133.

10. Goldstein, *American Policy*, 229.

11. Dommen, *Conflict*, 182–83, 186.

12. Goldstein, *American Policy*, 233, and Dommen, *Conflict*, 186–87.

13. Memorandum to the president, from Rostow, February 28, 1961 (document in my possession).

14. Gibbons, *U.S. and the Vietnam War, Part II*, 18–19, Hilsman, *To Move a Nation*, 128, and Schlesinger, *A Thousand Days*, 332.

15. Memorandum to the president, from Walt W. Rostow, March 10, 1961 (document in my possession).

16. Marolda and Fitzgerald, *U.S. Navy*, 60–62. Professor Gibbons, in his very valuable study on the Vietnam war, attributes these decisions to White House meetings of March 20 and 21. Gibbons, *U.S. and the Vietnam War, Part II*, 21. Arthur Schlesinger says that "neither the meeting on March 20 nor another session the next day reached a decision." Schlesinger, *A Thousand Days*, 333.

17. Schlesinger, *A Thousand Days*, 333.

18. Marolda and Fitzgerald, *U.S. Navy*, 60.

19. Ibid., 60–61. See also Tilford, *Search and Rescue*, 34. Udorn, like many other Thai airfields that would eventually host hundreds of American military aircraft, was officially a Royal Thai Air Force Base. The notable exception was the B-52 base at Utapao, which came under the control of the Royal Thai Navy.

20. *Air America Log,* Vol. VI No. 5, Kadena, Okinawa, 1972; my telephone interview with Abadie, August 26, 1987; and Fonburg letter of February 26, 1989. Abadie and Fonburg were two of the pilots who flew the helicopters to Udorn.

21. The "advisers" were, in fact, providing more than just leadership. A captured Vietnamese soldier, formerly assigned to the PAVN's 925th Independent Regiment, revealed that he "belonged to one of the two 42-man sections of mortar and machine gun specialists who had been ordered into Laos on February 19." Dommen, *Conflict,* 187–8.

22. Wing, *Case Study,* B41.

23. Ibid., B16.

24. Ibid., B18.

25. Ibid., B18–B19.

26. Dommen, *Conflict,* 187.

27. For a detailed account of the imprisonment of Captain Moon and Sergeant Ballenger see Wolfkill, *Reported to be Alive,* 144–198. On May 15, 1961, Wolf-kill, an NBC cameraman, and two "temporary" Air America employees, John McMorrow and Edward R. Shore, Jr., were captured by the Pathet Lao. In the "spirit" of the 1962 Geneva Agreements the communists released Ballenger, McMorrow, and Shore on August 17, 1962. See also Wing, *Case Study,* 32.

28. Hilsman, *To Move a Nation,* 127–29, and Wing, *Case Study,* E6.

29. Wing, *Case Study,* A31. See also Hilsman, *To Move a Nation,* 134. For an amusing account of how the PEO-turned-MAAG personnel scrambled to find uniforms in order to comply with the president's orders see Department of the Army, Senior Officers Debriefing Program, 23–24.

30. Goldstein, *American Policy,* 239.

31. Wing, *Case Study,* C27.

32. Ibid., C29.

33. Rostow memorandum, February 28, 1961.

34. AF Oral History, Toland, 24, and my interview with Toland on November 30, 1990.

35. AF Oral History, Von Platen, 53. At the time of the event Von Platen was a major serving as an assistant air attaché to Laos.

36. My telephone interview with Colonel Bailey, January 19, 1992; AF Oral History, Toland 35–38: my interview of November 30, 1990 with Toland; and AF Oral History, Von Platen, 53–4. See also Tilford, *Search and Rescue,* 33. Bailey was released with three other American prisoners on August 17, 1962.

37. Tilford, *Search and Rescue,* 34–35, and Futrell, *USAF in Southeast Asia. The Advisory Years,* 74.

38. Due to the time difference between Washington and Saigon it is unlikely the president knew of the SC-47 loss. When the aircraft did not arrive in Saigon by late afternoon Colonel Toland cabled Vientiane for confirmation of the crew's departure. Toland received verification the following morning and initiated a search. AF Oral History, Toland, 35.

39. Hall, "The Laos Crisis, 1960–61," 59.

40. Goldstein, *American Policy*, 236.

41. Mahajani, "President Kennedy and United States Policy in Laos, 1961–63," 91.

42. My interview on January 26, 1990, with Thomas G. Jenny, former Air America pilot and a "Millpond" participant.

43. Ibid. The active duty pilots reentered the Air Force following termination of the project. Leary letter of November 23, 1990.

44. Ibid. Another account indicates that some of the B-26s flew reconnaissance missions over eastern Laos from October to December 1961. Leary, letter of February 6, 1990.

45. My interview with Brigadier General Aderholt, May 2, 1988, and Leary letter of November 23, 1990. General Aderholt told me that his practical title from 1960 to 1962 was "Senior CIA Air Operations Officer." See also Bowers, *USAF Tactical Airlift*, 441.

46. Leary letter of November 23, 1990, and my interview with Jenny on January 26, 1990. The "blood chits" were silk cloths printed with messages in a variety of languages promising rewards to anyone who assisted downed American pilots.

47. Parmet, *JFK*, 148.

48. Marolda and Fitzgerald, *U.S. Navy*, 66. Admiral Felt recalled in a 1974 oral history interview that in 1961 the U.S. ambassador to Laos had requested B-26s. There is no specific date associated with this recollection, only the statement that the plea "was never granted." Felt "Reminiscences," 512. Admiral Felt has been unable to recall any details regarding the B-26 request. My interview with Felt, March 1, 1990.

49. Leary letter, November 23, 1990.

50. Ibid., and my interview with Jenny, January 26, 1990. Some aspects of "Millpond" remain classified by the U.S. government.

51. A detailed review of the Bay of Pigs invasion is found in *Operation Zapata: The "Ultrasensitive" Report.*

52. Sorenson, *Kennedy*, 644.

53. Randolph, *The U.S. and Thailand*, 36.

54. Ibid., 40.

55. Wing, *Case Study*, B42.

56. Ibid., B44.

57. Ibid., B47–B48.

58. Lobe, *U.S. Aid to the Thailand Police*, vol. 14, 2, 23.

59. My interview with General Saiyud Kerdphol, Bangkok, August 14, 1990. General Saiyud is a former supreme commander of the Thai Armed Forces and an acknowledged international expert on counterinsurgency operations. He was closely associated with the Hua Hin and Lop Buri training programs.

60. My interview with Shirley, Bangkok, August 1, 1990. Shirley was a CIA field agent operating undercover as an adviser to the Royal Thai Navy. He worked with the Thai counterinsurgency program for many years. In early 1951 Civil Air Transport began charter work for Sea Supply. Leary, *Perilous Missions*, 129, 199.

61. My interview with Lair, Bangkok, August 10, 1990. Lair, a CIA officer, joined the Thai police as a captain and eventually became a colonel. Professor Lobe says "to train and equip the new police units . . . the CIA gave $35 million to Sea Supply." Lobe, *Aid to the Thai Police,* 23. Lair reports his weapons and ammunition came from CIA-acquired World War II stockpiles, and that his yearly budget never exceeded $80,000 a year. I believe Lair's account to be accurate.

62. Lobe, *U.S. Aid to the Thailand Police,* 24, and my August 1990 interview with Shirley. From 1952 to 1958 Shirley was Lair's deputy at Lop Buri.

63. My interview with Shirley, August 1, 1990. The original Sea Supply training camp remains standing and symbolically "guards" the king's residence. Second Lieutenant Suriyoun Juntramanid of the Thai Border Patrol Police, in Hua Hin, Thailand, kindly allowed me to tour and photograph the Hua Hin compound on July 28, 1990.

64. The acronym PARU is also sometimes written out as Police Aerial Reconnaissance Unit or Police Aerial Resupply Unit.

65. My interview with Lieutenant Suriyoun, Hua Hin, Thailand, July 28, 1990, and my interview with General Saiyud on August 14, 1990. See also Saiyud Kerdphol, *The Struggle for Thailand,* 74–82.

66. My interview with Lair, Bangkok, August 14, 1990. See also Lobe, *U.S. Aid to the Thailand Police,* 34–37.

67. The CIA had previously organized an unconventional warfare program among some Laotian tribal groups. Wing, *Case Study,* B21.

68. My interviews with Shirley, Lair, and Landry, Bangkok, August 17, 1990. Over "the best Chinese fried noodles in Bangkok," the three men recounted to me the history of the establishment of CIA paramilitary operations in Laos. Tony Poe, born Anthony Posepny, is still living in Udorn, Thailand. Friends of Poe, however, advised me that he suffers from memory problems and would not be a useful source.

69. The Hmong had an uneasy and sometimes violent relationship with the French colonial administration. See Brown and Zasloff, *Apprentice Revolutionaries,* 10–11 and Lee, "Minority Policies and the Hmong," 200.

70. Scott, "Migrants Without Mountains," 141–42. These same sentiments have been expressed to me, often in very heated language, by scores of Hmong and lowland Lao.

71. My interviews with Shirley, Lair, and Landry, August 1990.

72. Ibid. The CIA teams were being transported around Laos in Air America helicopters and STOL U-10 Helio-Couriers. Among the pilots was Dien Bien Phu veteran Fred F. Walker.

73. Gibbons, *U.S. and the Vietnam War, Part II,* 24.

74. Opium was easily traded to Chinese merchants for guns and ammunition. Wekkin, "The Rewards of Revolution," 186.

75. Born in 1928, Vang Pao joined the French army as an enlisted man, served with distinction, and was the first Hmong commissioned into the Royal Lao Army. For a detailed review of Vang Pao's early life see Castle thesis "Alliance in a Secret War," 53–55. Vang Pao had a widespread reputation as a charismatic leader who

was dedicated to his people and ruthless with his enemies. My interview with Major Cherry, March 16, 1979. Cherry was an intelligence officer who served as a Vang Pao adviser from 1965 to 1966 and from 1972 to 1973. Vang Pao was also a close associate of Touby Lyfoung, the paramount Hmong leader of northeastern Laos and a member of the Boun Oum cabinet. Gary Y. Lee, "Minority Policies and the Hmong," in Stuart-Fox, ed., *Contemporary Laos*, 199–217 202. See also Quincy, *Hmong: History of a People*, 170–72.

76. My interview with Shirley, August 14, 1990.

77. D. Gareth Porter, "After Geneva: Subverting Laotian Neutrality," in Adams and McCoy, eds., *Laos: War and Revolution*, 183–84.

78. In early 1961 there were ninety-nine CIA-controlled PARU advisors assigned to Hmong units, according to *Pentagon Papers: Gravel Edition*, II: 646.

79. Bowers, *USAF Tactical Airlift*, 442.

80. Goldstein, *American Policy*, 238–39, and Stevenson, *The End of Nowhere*, 147.

81. Goldstein, *American Policy*, 241.

82. It was during this time that Team Moon was lost.

83. Gibbons, *U.S. and the Vietnam War, Part II*, 26.

84. Ibid., 25–26.

85. Ibid., 26–29.

86. Harriman, Kennedy Library Oral History Interview (unpublished), conducted by William H. Sullivan (second of two), August 5, 1970, 33. Rostow has recorded that Kennedy told him much the same thing about the advantages of fighting in Vietnam instead of Laos. See Rostows' paper "JFK and Southeast Asia," presented at a conference on November 14, 1980, 26.

87. Goldstein, *American Policy*, 247.

88. Stevenson, *The End of Nowhere*, 154.

89. My interview with Shirley, August 1, 1990. Shirley was assigned to Phadong during this time.

90. Dommen, *Conflict*, 207. Hugh Toye states that the gunners were members of Kong Le's army, trained by the Vietnamese. Toye, *Buffer State or Battleground*, 177–78. See also Thee, *Notes of a Witness*, 113–15. CIA officer Shirley recalls that the enemy used seventeen 75-mm guns during the attack on Phadong. Shirley, the "White Star" team, and the PARU accompanied the Hmong in their retreat to a safer location. Shirley interview, August 1, 1990.

91. Modelski, *International Conference the Laotian Question*, 65.

92. DOD, *U.S. Vietnam Relations*, 11: 247–49.

93. Stanton, *Green Berets at War*, 41.

94. The fighting at Phadong and the subsequent moves to Pha Khao and Long Tieng became the subject of a technically superior, one hour length, CIA-produced film called "Journey from Phadong." Originally, the movie was made to "sell" the Hmong assistance program to selected members of the U.S. Congress. Later, the film was dubbed in the Hmong language and shown in Laos. My interview with Lair, April 15, 1988. "Journey from Phadong" was held in the CIA archives until

a U.S. Air Force intelligence officer, who had formerly been assigned to Laos and requests anonymity, was given permission to copy the film. In 1987 a copy of the film was donated to the University of Minnesota refugee studies program. Through the efforts of Vang Yang, English and White Hmong language transcripts of the movie are available from the refugee studies program.

95. The ICA contract number was 39–007. USAF contracting records, June 7, 1961 (contracts in my possession).

96. During this period Air America was also flying fixed wing aircraft in Laos. According to Dr. Leary, "Air America's first permanent assignment in Laos began in July 1957 with a C-47 in Vientiane used by U.S. Embassy and CIA personnel." Leary letter of January 22, 1991.

97. U.S. Air Force contracting document, dated May 24, 1961 (document in my possession). Most of the Air America contracts for flying operations in Laos were negotiated and managed by U.S. Air Force contracting officers assigned to Japan and Thailand. Following termination of the program the Air Force records were stored at Hickam AFB, Hawaii, from 1973 to 1983, and then moved to permanent storage at the USAF Historical Research Center at Maxwell AFB, Alabama. Measuring some eighteen cubic feet, the materials remained sealed until reviewed by me in May 1989. Martin L. Kaufman, as a captain, served for nearly six years as one of the principal U.S. Air Force contracting officers assigned to oversee the Air America program and was the driving force behind the preservation of these invaluable records.

98. Doty and Widner thesis, "Logistics Support for the Royal Lao Air Force as Conducted by a MAAG in Exile," 95. I am indebted to Colonel Martin L. Kaufman, U.S. Air Force, for providing me with this document.

99. U.S. Air Force contracting document, June 30, 1961 (contract in my possession).

100. The contract period was July 1, 1961 through June 30, 1962. U.S. Air Force contracting document, July 1, 1961 (contract in my possession).

101. Air America accident investigation reports (documents in my possession). The ICA and USAF contracts required Air America to investigate and report to the U.S. Air Force all aircraft accidents. The "temporary" Air America designation indicates that the men were actually active-duty military personnel. About half of the original H-34 pilots and flight mechanics were active-duty members of the U.S. Navy, U.S. Marine Corps, or U.S. Army. Referred to as "sheep-dipped," most of these men served out their military time with Air America and then remained with the company upon discharge. Fonburg letter, February 26, 1989. Grant Wolfkill was the reporter.

102. Toye, *Buffer State or Battleground,* 174.

103. Goldstein, *American Policy,* 252–53.

104. Harriman's opinion of Souvanna was formed during personal talks between the two men and recommendations from French diplomats. Harriman, unpublished interview by Arthur M. Schlesinger on January 17, 1965, Kennedy Library Oral History Program, 56.

105. Goldstein, *American Policy,* 255.

106. Toye, *Buffer State or Battleground,* 182–83. Toye, a British military attache in Laos, personally observed Phoumi on numerous occasions.

107. Goldstein, *American Policy,* 256. Regarding the performance of Phoumi's army, an account by an American adviser (perhaps apocryphal), stated that "the morale of my battalion is substantially better than [in] our last engagement. The last time they dropped their weapons and ran. This time they took their weapons with them." *Pentagon Papers: Gravel Edition* 5: 264.

108. *New York Times,* May 7, 1962.

109. Stevenson, *The End of Nowhere,* 176–77, Gibbons, *U.S. and the Vietnam War, Part II,* 115–16, and Toye, *Buffer State or Battleground,* 184. For some interesting views on the decision making during this crisis see Pelz, "When Do I Have Time to Think?" 2: 215–29. Hilsman and Pelz. "When is a Document Not a Document—And Other Thoughts," 3: 345–48.

110. Stevenson, *The End of Nowhere,* 177.

111. Goldstein, *American Policy,* 262.

112. Stevenson, *The End of Nowhere,* 177, and Goldstein, *American Policy,* 263.

113. Dommen, *Conflict,* 213.

4. The Geneva Facade: See, Hear, and Speak No Evil

1. Rostow, *Diffusion of Power,* 290. In a letter to me Professor Rostow stated bluntly "not for one day did Hanoi honor the Laos 1962 Accords and stop transitting Laos en route to [South] Vietnam." Rostow, letter of February 28, 1990.

2. Modelski, *Settlement of the Laotian Question,* 144.

3. Hannah, *The Key to Failure* 37–38. See also Harriman interview by Schlesinger, 17 January 1965, p. 58.

4. My interview with Ambassador Unger, May 3, 1988.

5. Ibid.

6. USAID, *Facts,* 27. A small French military training mission was excepted.

7. Hilsman, *To Move a Nation,* 151.

8. Ibid., 151–52.

9. My interview with Felt, March 1, 1990.

10. Major General Tucker had succeeded Brigadier General Boyle in early 1962. Wing, *Case Study,* 22 and A38.

11. The Vientiane government, of course, had never made any such request. Dommen, *Conflict,* 240.

12. Colby, *Honorable Men,* 192.

13. Langer and Zasloff, *North Vietnam and the Pathet Lao,* 80–81.

14. My interviews with Ambassador Unger, May 3, 1988, and May 21, 1989. Unger would later serve as U.S. ambassador in both Thailand and the Republic of China.

15. As cited in Randolph, *The U.S. and Thailand,* 41.

16. Interview with Unger, May 3, 1988.

17. Colby, *Honorable Men,* 192–93, and my interview with Ambassador Colby, May 3, 1988.

18. Ibid. At the time there were two CIA case officers in Laos.

19. USAID, *Facts,* 28.

20. Senate, Committee on Foreign Relations, *United States Security Agreements and Commitments Abroad, Kingdom of Laos,* 441–43 (hereafter referred to as U.S., *Laos Hearings*).

21. USAID, *Facts,* 27.

22. Blaufarb, "Organizing and Managing Unconventional War in Laos," 19, and my telephone interview with Blaufarb, March 18, 1988.

23. St. Jean, McClain, and Hartwig, "Twenty-Three Years of Military Assistance to Laos," 35.

24. Wood letter, September 12, 1962.

25. CINCPAC letter, Admiral Felt to Colonel Munster, DEPCHIEF, March 8, 1963 (letter in my possession). The Military Assistance Program (MAP) was established under the U.S. Foreign Assistance Act of 1961.

26. Wood letter, September 12, 1962.

27. Doty and Widner, *MAAG in Exile,* 32–33, and U.S., *Laos Hearings,* 529.

28. Blaufarb, "Unconventional War in Laos," 45–46.

29. Schlesinger, *A Thousand Days,* 406–7.

30. Cited in Futrell, "United States Policy," 144.

31. Schlesinger, *A Thousand Days,* 428.

32. See, for example, testimony of Ambassador William H. Sullivan, U.S., *Laos Hearings,* 486–88, and 517–18.

33. Blaufarb, "Unconventional War in Laos," 20.

34. Brown and Zasloff, *Apprentice Revolutionaries,* 89–90, and Porter, "After Geneva," 188–92. According to Stevenson, on January 6, 1963 renegade neutralists shot down another Air America aircraft. Stevenson, *The End of Nowhere,* 189.

35. Dommen, *Conflict,* 247–48, and Stevenson, *The End of Nowhere,* 188–90.

36. Thee, *Notes of a Witness,* 325–26, 334.

37. Dommen, *Conflict,* 246–47.

38. Stevenson, *The End of Nowhere,* 191.

39. Brown and Zasloff, *Apprentice Revolutionaries,* 89.

40. Soviet Deputy Foreign Minister Georgi Pushkin, Harriman's Geneva confederate, was by this time dead. Harriman, Kennedy Library Oral History interview by Schlesinger, January 17, 1965, 59.

41. Senate Committee on Armed Services, *Hearing, Nomination of William E. Colby to be Director of Central Intelligence,* 28.

42. Colby, *Honorable Men,* 194.

43. Colby has referred to the Lao clandestine operation as "courage in civilian clothes." Remarks made during dedication of Air America-Civil Air Transport archives, Dallas, Texas, May 30, 1987 (videotape in my possession).

44. Kissinger also told the committee, "I do not believe in retrospect that it was

good national policy to have the CIA conduct the war in Laos. I think we should have found some other way of doing it. And to use the CIA simply because it is less accountable for very visible major operations is poor national policy." Church Committee Report, 1: 157. B. Hugh Tovar, chief of station in Vientiane from September 1970 until May 1973, vigorously challenges Kissinger's assertion that the agency was "less accountable." Tovar states that the CIA was subject to "rigorous internal auditing," and moreover, that Kissinger's after-the-fact comments are in conflict with his wartime direction to the CIA. Tovar letter of March 20, 1992.

45. Lair interview, April 15, 1988, and Leary letter, 22 January 1991.

46. Interview with Cherry, March 16, 1979, and interview with Yang Teng in San Diego, October 27, 1979. Yang Teng was a member of the original Hmong unit sent for training to Hua Hin. Over the ensuing years hundreds of Hmong would receive specialized training at Hua Hin and at a similar CIA-administered camp at Phitsanuloke, a small town in northwestern Thailand. My interview with Shirley, August 1, 1990.

47. Many of the Thailand-trained Hmong became instructors at a newly created military training school at Long Tieng. The program, aided by American and Thai advisers, followed the Hua Hin curriculum. My interview with Yang Teng, October 27, 1979.

48. My interview with Thao Pao Ly in San Diego, October 27, 1979. Thao Pao Ly was a Hmong battalion commander.

49. Blaufarb, "Unconventional War in Laos," 42.

50. St. Jean, McClain, and Hartwig, "Twenty-Three Years of Military Assistance to Laos," 164–65. The U-6, formerly designated the L-20, was a high-wing, all-metal monoplane capable of carrying a pilot and six passengers. Bowers, *Tactical Airlift*, 826.

51. As noted in ch. 3, n. 72, and Leary letter of January 22, 1991.

52. "Air Facilities Data, Laos," Flight Information Center, Vientiane, May 1970 (document in my possession).

53. My interviews with Lieutenant Colonel Stuart, March 24, 1988, MacFarlane, May 13, 1989; and Walker, May 14, 1989. All three men flew Air America fixed-wing transports throughout Southeast Asia. Military dispatches to Vang Pao from field units reveal that air-dropped supplies frequently struck people on the ground, causing serious injury and sometimes death. Despite Air America safety information campaigns, mountain people would often stand beneath the descending pallets. Likewise, villagers would occasionally run or walk into aircraft propeller or rotor blades. "Air Facilities Data, Laos."

54. Plattner, "Continental Air Lines Diversifies with Southeast Asia Operations," 37, and my interview with MacFarlane, May 13, 1989.

55. Plattner, "Continental Air Lines Diversifies with Southeast Asia Operations," 37. This article, however, mistakenly suggests that CASI had no connection with the CIA. According to William M. Leary, CASI did fly clandestine missions for the agency. Leary letter February 3, 1991.

56. "An Interview with Dr. John A. Hannah, Administrator of USAID," in Adams and McCoy, eds., *Laos: War and Revolution*, 408.

57. For a brief official explanation of USAID responsibilities in Laos, see USAID, *Facts*, v–vii.

58. Blaufarb, "Unconventional War in Laos," 42.

59. *Pentagon Papers: Gravel Edition* 5: 305, and U.S. Congress, Senate, *Thailand, Laos, and Cambodia: January 1972)*, Staff Report, 12 (hereafter cited as U.S., *Thailand, Laos, Cambodia: January 1972*). On September 30, 1988 I submitted a Freedom of Information Act request to the CIA asking for information on five areas having to do with the 4802d JLD. The CIA replied on April 20, 1989, saying that, in keeping with security provisions dealing with operational matters, they could not provide the requested information (letter in my possession).

60. After the Geneva Accords, Lair and Landry left Laos and moved their paramilitary support operations to Nongkai, the major river-crossing point between Thailand and Laos. Landry worked as Lair's deputy at the 4802d and succeeded him when Lair left Thailand in 1968 to attend the prestigious U.S. Army War College. My interviews with Shirley, Landry, and Lair, 17 August 1990, and my interview with Major General Thammarak Isarangura, September 13, 1990.

61. Ibid. The presence of Headquarters 333 and the 4802d JLD was never much of a secret in Thailand or Laos. A prominent Pathet Lao leader, Phoumi Vongvichit, wrote in 1969 "The whole system [of U.S. covert support to Laos] is directly under the U.S. "special forces" command, code-named H.Q. 333 and based in Oudone [Udorn]." Vongvichit, *Laos and the Victorious Struggle*, 99.

5. SECSTATE Theater of War

1. Menger, *Valley of the Mekong*, 150. Father Menger was a Catholic priest who for many years worked with Laotian refugees.

2. Dommen, *Conflict*, 257. For a detailed discussion of North Vietnamese military support to the Pathet Lao see Langer and Zasloff, *North Vietnam and the Pathet Lao*, 106–22.

3. Stevenson, *The End of Nowhere*, 193–94, and Brown and Zasloff, *Apprentice Revolutionaries*, 91.

4. See n. 3.

5. Lee, *China's Policy Toward Laos*, 112.

6. During the Hanoi visit Souvanna's aide was confined to his room. Dommen, *Conflict*, 259.

7. Brown and Zasloff, *Apprentice Revolutionaries*, 91, and Stevenson, *The End of Nowhere*, 195.

8. Dommen, *Conflict in Laos*, 261.

9. My interview with Unger on May 21, 1989, and Dommen, *Conflict*, 267. See also Stevenson, *The End of Nowhere*, 195–97.

10. Stevenson, *The End of Nowhere*, 195–97, and D. Gareth Porter, "After Geneva: Subverting Laotian Neutrality," in Adams and McCoy, eds., *Laos: War*

and Revolution, 203–4. The committee doled out important staff positions and appointed regional commanders.

11. Stevenson, *The End of Nowhere,* 199.

12. Ibid., 193. The T-28s were replacements for the older T-6 trainers provided in early 1961 by the Eisenhower administration. The T-28 "Trojan" is a two-seat, propeller-driven, single engine airplane. Two versions were sent to Laos, the reconnaissance RT-28 and the attack T-28D. Bowers, *Tactical Airlift,* 825.

13. Declassified Document Reference Service (hereafter cited as DDRS), 1981, document 205B, The American embassy in Vientiane retained the fuses for the T-28 ordnance, making it impossible for the Lao to conduct bombing operations without U.S. authority. Colonel Tyrrell, AF Oral History, 7–8. This precaution precluded the Lao Air Force from using the T-28s in any coup attempts.

14. Tyrrell, AF Oral History, 5.

15. DOD, "CINCPAC Command History, 1964," 285.

16. U.S. Army, Talking Paper for Chief of Staff, "Guidance for T-28 Aircraft Operations," March 9, 1964 (document in my possession); McShane letter of August 26, 1989. Mr. McShane was one of the original "Waterpump" pilots.

17. DDRS, 1990, document 248; DDRS, 1989, document 686; Tyrrell, AF Oral History, 23, 36–37, and Department of the Air Force, "Debriefing of LtCol Robert B. Melgard, Asst. Air Attaché, Vientiane, Laos." Washington, D.C., November 13, 1964 (document in my possession). Lieutenant Colonel Melgard was the first AOC commander in Savannakhet.

18. Stevenson, *The End of Nowhere,* 197–98.

19. Ibid., 201.

20. Tyrrell, AF Oral History, 33–34, and Stevenson, *The End of Nowhere,* 198. See DDRS, 1990, document 3311 for details on the Thai/Lao T-28 bombing.

21. DDRS, 1990, document 324, and DDRS, 1989, document 3543.

22. As recounted earlier, Washington was obtaining high-altitude U-2 photography of the communists' activities in Southeast Asia, but for diplomatic purposes and for reasons of national security preferred a dependable source of low-altitude tactical photography.

23. DDRS, 1990, document 3312.

24. DDRS, 1989, document 686.

25. U.S., *Laos Hearings,* 370.

26. DDRS, 1990, document 3312.

27. My interview with Unger, 21 May 1989.

28. DDRS, 1990, document 3312 and DDRS, 1989, document 686. The deleted portion appears to have been a reference to Thai involvement.

29. During the meeting there was no mention of compensation. Later, cash payments from the CIA to the pilots were received through the Air America general manager, Roy Stitt, and the Air America T-28 chief pilot, Edward Eckholdt. Jenny recalls the pay as being fifty dollars per mission. Interview with Jenny, January 26, 1990, and Hickler letter to the author, March 8, 1990. Hickler was a long-time Civil

Air Transport and Air America employee who, in August 1964, became general manager of the company's Vientiane office. He was administratively involved in some of the CIA cash payments.

30. DDRS, 1989, document 856. Although this cable mentions "Bird and Sons", all the initial T-28 pilots were Air America employees.

31. DDRS, 1989, document 857.

32. DDRS, 1990, document 3044. Although the name of the delivery point has been purged from this declassified document, it seems likely the aircraft were delivered by MACV to Vientiane.

33. My interview with Jenny, January 26, 1990.

34. DDRS, 1976, document 226A. William M. Leary relates that on the first day the Air America pilots were ordered to bomb a bridge in the northeastern corner of the Plain of Jars, but missed. Leary letter February 11, 1991.

35. The U.S. Air Force attaché in Vientiane suspected that other "Waterpump" pilots were flying unauthorized strike missions. The pilots felt an obligation to their Thai and Lao students and wanted to lead them into combat. Tyrrell, AF Oral History, 24.

36. My interview Hickler, June 15, 1989.

37. Leary letter, February 11, 1991, and Tilford, *Search and Rescue*, 48–49. Klusmann escaped from the Pathet Lao on August 29 and made contact with friendly Hmong soldiers on September 1. An Air America aircraft then transported Klusmann to Udorn, Thailand, and safety. An official debriefing of Klusmann's ordeal is found in DDRS, 1989, documents 2343 and 2344.

38. Tilford, *Search and Rescue*, 49.

39. Interview with Jenny, January 26, 1990.

40. Berger, *USAF in Southeast Asia*, 122.

41. DDRS, 1989, document 682.

42. Tilford, *Search and Rescue*, 51–52.

43. Stevenson, *The End of Nowhere*, 203. See also Langer, Rand Corporation Study "The Soviet Union, China, and the Pathet Lao," 69.

44. *Pentagon Papers: Gravel Edition*, 5: 268, and Lee, *China's Policy Toward Laos*, 116.

45. DDRS, 1989, document 2105.

46. Tyrrell, AF Oral History, 49.

47. Lee, *China's Policy Toward Laos*, 119, and Langer, Rand Corporation Study "The Soviet Union, China, and the Pathet Lao," 32.

48. U.S., *Laos Hearings*, 448–49.

49. Ibid., 412–13.

50. U.S., *Laos Hearings*, 372.

51. DDRS, 1989, document 2100.

52. U.S., *Laos Hearings*, 479; DDRS, 1990, document 1456; and DDRS, 1989, documents 2114 and 2115.

53. DDRS, 1989, document 2113.

54. U.S., *Laos Hearings,* 479. Tyrrell, AF Oral History, 51–52. The Pathet Lao view of Operation Triangle" is found in *Phoukout Stronghold* (n.p.: Neo Lao Haksat Publications, 1967), 6–9.

55. DDRS, 1990, document 684.

56. DDRS, 1990, document 1638; Air America Accident Board Investigation, September 20, 1964; and Air America communication from David H. Hickler to Air America president in Taipei, August 22, 1964 (documents in my possession). There is some confusion as to whether or not an Air America Filipino flight mechanic was killed in the H-34 crash. According to DDRS, 1990, document 1638, President Johnson was told on August 18 that "the pilot and crew . . . were rescued." This information was incorrect. Air Force historian Earl Tilford, who had access to a broad range of classified government documents, says a Filipino crewman was killed in the crash. It is instructive, however, that Tilford's account does not mention the use of Air America T-28s. See Tilford, *Search and Rescue,* 52. William M. Leary has also determined the Filipino flight mechanic was killed. See Leary letter of February 11, 1991.

57. DDRS, 1989, document 822.

58. Air America communication from Hickler to Air America president, August 22, 1964.

59. DDRS, 1989, document 822.

60. DDRS, 1990, document 1638.

61. The text is not available. An August 20, 1964 NSC memorandum to Bundy states "I understand that Mr. Rusk has had a NODIS exchange with Unger, the upshot of which is authorization only to use U.S. personnel on SAR helicopter operations unless Washington specifies otherwise in a response to a specific request." DDRS, 1990, document 1459.

62. DDRS, 1989, document 3403.

63. DDRS, 1989, document 823. This same cable was also released as DDRS, 1990, document 2637.

64. DDRS, 1990, document 3319.

65. DDRS, 1989, document 3404.

66. *Pentagon Papers: Gravel Edition,* 3: 552. The U.S. government's awkward and often puzzling declassification policy is demonstrated by comparing the text of this message in *Pentagon Papers* and the same message as it appears in DDRS, 1989, document 3406. In the *Pentagon Papers* version Rusk states "[SAR efforts should not] discriminate between rescuing Americans, Thais and Lao. . . . On the other side, we naturally recognize T-28 operations are vital both for their military and psychological effects in Laos and as a negotiating card in support of Souvanna's position." In the DDRS version both passages are deleted. Also, the DDRS documents in many cases, have been purged of any references to Thai participation in the Laos war.

67. My telephone interview with William M. Leary on May 9, 1988, and my interview with Hickler, on June 1, 1989.

68. Under his new authority to employ the Air America T-28s, Unger proposed

that the State Department upgrade his "air force" SAR capability by providing Air America with five of the U.S. Navy's heavily armored A-1H "Skyraider" attack aircraft. See DDRS, 1990, document 3320. Air America did not receive any A-1s, but a USAF Air Commando A-1E squadron would be deployed to Thailand in 1965 to support U.S. military and Air America rescue and special operations in Laos and Vietnam. See Tilford, *Search and Rescue*, 66.

6. William Sullivan's War

1. William H. Sullivan, *Obbligato*, 213.
2. Stevenson, *The End of Nowhere*, 208–9.
3. U.S., *Laos Hearings*, 309.
4. Presiding over a 1973 Senate Armed Services Committee hearing on the U.S. defense budget, Senator Stuart Symington referred to Sullivan as a satrap. See Senate. Committee on Armed Services, *Fiscal Year 1974 Authorization*, 5890 (hereafter cited as U.S., *Fiscal Year 1974*). The Random House College Dictionary defines *satrap* as "a subordinate ruler, often a despotic one."
5. U.S., *Laos Hearings*, 517–18.
6. Blaufarb, "Unconventional War in Laos," 61–62.
7. In my interview with Admiral U.S. Grant Sharp on March 6, 1990, he told me that Ambassador Sullivan was never reluctant, if he thought it expeditious, to deal directly with the JCS on military matters.
8. General Westmoreland's letter of March 3, 1990. General Westmoreland reaffirmed these same thoughts to me in a telephone interview on April 13, 1990.
9. Blaufarb, "Unconventional War in Laos," 60. Sullivan was referring to National Security Advisor MacGeorge Bundy, Secretary of Defense Robert S. McNamara, Chairman of the JCS Earle G. Wheeler, and CIA Director John A. McCone.
10. For an example of Westmoreland's irritation over Sullivan's involvement, see Westmoreland, *A Soldier Reports*, 449.
11. Ibid., 96–97; see also interview of Admiral Sharp conducted by Dr. Robert R. Kritt at the U.S. Naval Training Center, San Diego, on February 19, 1971 (transcript in my possession).
12. U.S., *Laos Hearings*, 518. Blaufarb, who attended the meetings, reports the daily presence of Sullivan "made the point that the Ambassador considered himself not only the Chief of Mission but also the operations manager." See Blaufarb, "Unconventional War in Laos," 66.
13. My interview with Vang Pao, Santa Ana, California, February 6, 1979; Blaufarb, "Unconventional War in Laos," 42.
14. The SGU "was a battalion composed of three line companies and a headquarters unit. Its arms were upgraded to include bazookas, medium-sized and even a few heavy mortars." Blaufarb, *The Counterinsurgency Era*, 157.
15. Ibid., 158–59; and paper by St. Jean, McClain, and Hartwig, "Twenty-Three Years of Military Assistance," 47–48.

16. CIA, "Intelligence Information Cable" (document in my possession).

17. Interview with Yang Teng; Leary, letter of March 6, 1991.

18. Interview with Cherry.

19. Interview with a respected Hmong source who wishes anonymity, San Diego, October 27, 1979.

20. Sullivan, *Obbligato*, 215–16.

21. Vang Pao, according to numerous accounts by knowledgeable observers, consistently risked danger so that he could personally view the battle and, if necessary, rally his forces. On the many occasions in 1979 and 1980 when I met personally with Vang Pao, or when I observed him with others, the general exuded a tremendous charismatic charm.

22. Tovar letter of March 20, 1992.

23. Sullivan, *Obbligato*, 213, and Ambassador Sullivan letter of November 9, 1990.

24. My interview with Colby, May 3, 1988.

25. Lieutenant Colonel Hartley, AF Oral History, 35.

26. Outgoing electrical message, "Special Operation," December 17, 1966 (document in my possession).

27. Outgoing electrical message, "Infiltration of CAS Road Watch Team," December 17, 1966 (document in my possession). Combined USAF/Air America air assaults were also used to "insert" large size SGUs into battle areas. Outgoing electrical message, "Operation Left Jab," June 19, 1969 (document in my possession). The CIA paid the Air America crews special "project pay" for these missions. Payment procedures were similar to those used to compensate the Air America T-28 Strike Force. Fonburg letter of January 8, 1989.

28. For example, "Twenty-five fish [Soviet trucks] moving. . . ." Transcription of "Journey from Pha Dong," Vang Yang, 1988, 14, and interview with Yang Teng, October 27, 1979. See also Ballard, *The United States Air Force in Southeast Asia. Development and Employment of Fixed-Wing Gunships 1962–1972*, 46.

29. Conboy, *The War in Laos, 1960–1975* 42–43.

30. Shackley, *The Third Option* 67–69.

31. Amazingly, the survivor was eventually repatriated in a prisoner exchange and, in 1979, was living in Minnesota. Interview with Yang Teng, October 27, 1979. Paramilitary specialist Kenneth Conboy has identified this failed team as part of an elite group called the "Commando Raiders." Kenneth Conboy in his letter to the author, April 18, 1988. See also Conboy, *War in Laos*, 19.

32. My interview with Cherry, March 16, 1979.

33. Senate, Committee on Foreign Relations, *Hearing, Activities of the U.S. Agency for International Development in Laos*, 4 (hereafter referred to as U.S., *AID Hearing*).

34. For a distinctly anti–U.S. essay on the IVS and their contributions in Laos see Lewallen, "The Reluctant Counterinsurgents: International Voluntary Services in Laos," Adams and McCoy, eds., *Laos: War and Revolution*, 357–71.

35. Buell's life is the subject of the undocumented and often erroneous book by

Don A. Schanche, *Mister Pop*. Schanche incorrectly reports that Buell participated in "blowing up bridges", 162–63. I have spoken with a number of Hmong soldiers, including Vang Pao, who deny Buell was involved in anything but humanitarian assistance. Numerous knowledgeable Americans agreed, describing Buell as invariably feisty, but "no commando." Buell was considered such a celebrity that the White House attempted in July 1964 to arrange a personal visit in Washington with President Johnson. DDRS, 1990, document 1637.

36. Blaufarb, "Unconventional War in Laos," 41–3.

37. CASI, Bird and Sons, and a few other smaller contractors also provided civilian airlift. Air America, however, performed the vast majority of the work.

38. Contract flying in Laos was not for the "rigid or timid." My interviews with Stuart, March 24, 1988, MacFarlane, May 13, 1989, Walker, May 14, 1989, and Colonel Leonard, February 19, 1988. Leonard was chief of the USAID Air Support Branch. Like most of the men working for the Requirements Office, Leonard was retired from the U.S. military.

39. My interview with Colonel Kaufman, May 19, 1989.

40. The Lao General Staff was the equivalent of the American Joint Chiefs of Staff. Doty and Widner, "MAAG in Exile," 35.

41. Blaufarb, "Unconventional War in Laos," 46.

42. Paper by St. Jean, McClain, and Hartwig, "Twenty-Three Years of Military Assistance to Laos," 49, and Doty and Widner, "MAAG in Exile," 35–36.

43. See n. 42.

44. U.S., *Laos Hearings,* 439.

45. The Ravens were administratively assigned to "Waterpump," but as TDY (temporary duty) personnel were selected for assignment under the USAF "Palace Dog" program. Scott, AF Oral History, 5–10.

46. U.S., *Laos Hearings,* 466–68.

47. Polifka, AF Oral History, 59–60. I am grateful to Colonel Polifka who, no less brash than when he returned from Laos, arranged a meeting between myself and a CIA case officer who served in Laos. This meeting, attended by Polifka and former Raven Michael D. Byers, provided me with considerable insight into the relationship between the Ravens, Vang Pao's army, and the CIA. My interview with Colonel Polifka, Byers, and an anonymous CIA source, May 25, 1989. For some excellent photographs, and a non-scholarly account of the Raven operation in Laos, see Robbins, *The Ravens.*

48. AF Oral History, Tyrrell, 111.

49. Major General James F. Kirkendall, letter to the author, July 25, 1988. General Kirkendall was deputy commander, 7/13th Air Force, Udorn, Thailand, from April to October 1970. These same sentiments were related to me by Lieutenant General James D. Hughes. Hughes interview (by audio tape response to author), November 25, 1988. General Hughes was deputy commander 7/13th Air Force, Udorn, Thailand, from September 1972 until April 1973.

50. Futrell, *USAF in SEA,* 256.

51. DDRS, 1990, document 3338.

52. The aircraft were stationed at Korat, Thailand, but due to Thai political sensitivities were staged from Da Nang, South Vietnam. "Three RF-101s served as pathfinders and damage-assessment craft. Eight F-100s flew combat air patrol to guard against MIG interference. Four F-105s carried 750-pound bombs, 2.75-inch rockets, and 20-mm ammunition." Futrell, *USAF in SEA,* 256.

53. Berger, *USAF in Southeast Asia,* 104–5.

54. Sullivan, *Obbligato,* 211.

55. U.S., *Laos Hearings,* 456.

56. Momyer, *Airpower in Three Wars,* 85–86. General Westmoreland, as a result of some of Ambassador Sullivan's targeting decisions, says he and his staff sometimes referred to the Ho Chi Minh trail as "Sullivan's Freeway." Westmoreland, *A Soldier Reports,* 256.

57. Hughes (audio tape) interview, November 25, 1988. Although General Hughes took command in Thailand after Ambassador Sullivan's departure, the air attaché functions in Vientiane remained the same.

58. Berger, *USAF in Southeast Asia,* 122.

59. Major General Charles R. Bond, letter to the author, May 1, 1988. In the course of my research I contacted all nine generals who served as deputy commander, 7/13th Air Force. Seven of these officers responded; they all indicated they found the job quite frustrating. General Bond served as deputy commander, 7/13th Air Force from January 1966 until March 1967.

60. Major General William C. Lindley, letter to the author, May 11, 1988. General Lindley served as Deputy Commander, 7/13th Air Force from June 1967 until May 1968.

61. Air Force end-of-tour report, "Major General Andrew J. Evans, Jr., 16 October 1970 to 30 June 1971," 2 (document in my possession).

62. My interview with Colonel Strathmore K. McMurdo, October 11, 1990, and my telephone interview with Lieutenant Colonel Stuart A. Beckley, October 20, 1990. Colonel McMurdo served in Thailand from 1967–69 as DEPCHIEF's chief of staff. Colonel Beckley served in Thailand and Laos from 1965–72 with DEPCHIEF, Project 404, and the U.S. Army Attaché office.

63. U.S., *Laos Hearings,* 528.

64. Lieutenant Colonel Stuart A. Beckley, letter to the author, October 25, 1990.

65. Sullivan letter, November 9, 1990.

66. Stevenson, *The End of Nowhere,* 209.

67. Major General Tucker, who had established DEPCHIEF in October of 1962, recommended in December 1962 that his position be downgraded to the rank of colonel. Three months later Colonel Daniel F. Munster was named DEPCHIEF. Outgoing electrical message, "Orders" (document in my possession), and DOD. "CINCPAC Command History, 1962," 221.

68. Sullivan letter, November 9, 1990.

69. See n. 68.

70. Ambassador Sullivan occasionally left Laos to attend diplomatic and military conferences and was hospitalized in the United States for several weeks in 1968. Sullivan, *Obbligato*, 233. Nevertheless, given the tight control Sullivan exercised within his embassy, it seems highly unlikely any subordinate would authorize operations like "Duck" unless he received clearance from the ambassador.

71. Outgoing electrical message, "Operation Duck," (document in my possession). See also Bowers, *Tactical Airlift*, 461.

72. Sullivan letter to author, August 18, 1991.

73. It is estimated that 70 percent of the bombs dropped on Laos were hitting targets along the "Ho Chi Minh" infiltration trails in eastern and southern Laos. See St. Jean, McClain, and Hartwig, "Twenty-Three Years of Military Assistance to Laos," 103–4.

74. *Phu* is the Lao word for mountain, making the literal translation *Pha Thi mountain*.

75. Department of the Air Force, Captain Edward Vallentiny, USAF, "The Fall of Site 85," Project CHECO report, viii (hereafter cited as Vallentiny, "Site 85"). There is some confusion as to the exact type of radar placed at Phu Pha Thi. In his authoritative study of air warfare, General William W. Momyer refers to the Pha Thi radar system as an "AN-MSQ-77 Radar Bomb Directing Central." Momyer, *Airpower*, 178. However, in a 1115Z, 24 November 1967, electrical message from the deputy commander, 7/13th AF, to General Momyer, Commander 7th AF in Saigon, "TSQ 81" is used to identify the equipment. "Combat Skyspot" was the nickname assigned to similar systems which were used throughout South Vietnam and Thailand. Additional details may be found in Department of the Air Force, Major Richard A. Durkee, USAF, "Combat Skyspot." Project CHECO report.

76. My interview with Yang Teng, October 27, 1979; Vallentiny, "Site 85," viii; and Momyer, *Airpower*, 178. The participation of Filipinos, presumably EC-COIL employees, was reported to me by Yang Teng.

77. Goldstein, *American Policy*, 310, and my interview with confidential sources, Eglin AFB, Florida, May 2, 1988. My confidential sources are U.S. Air Force Pararescue specialists who were involved in rescue operations from Pha Thi.

78. Moore letters to the author, June, 17 and July 12, 1988. and my telephone interview Moore, June 27, 1988.

79. Vallentiny, "Site 85," 12.

80. During the chase Captain Moore was assisted by Walt Darran, a Continental Air Services (CASI) pilot operating in the area. Darran relayed Moore's requests for assistance from U.S. Navy carrier-based aircraft in the Gulf of Tonkin. The Navy planes did not arrive. Moore letters of June 17 and July 12, 1988, and my interview with Moore, June 27, 1988.

81. Vallentiny, "Site 85," 12. One of the AN-2s was airlifted to Vientiane and placed on display near the That Luang temple. Goldstein, *American Policy*, 310. A photograph of the AN-2 is found in Berger, *USAF in Southeast Asia*, 128.

82. My interview with Moore, June 27, 1988.

83. Vallentiny, "Site 85," 39–40, and my interview with Vang Pao, February 6, 1979. Vang Pao is the source for the supposed use of "mine detectors."

84. Vallentiny, "Site 85," 41.

85. Ray Robinson, "Report Describes Loss of Secret Base," *The Sunday Oklahoman,* October 5, 1986, and McMurdo interview, October 11, 1990.

86. My interview with Vang Pao, February 6, 1979. Another source reports that the Hmong unit at the base of Phu Pha Thi had been involved in a disagreement with Vang Pao's local military commander. Consequently, they may not have provided a warning to the people at the site. My interview with a respected Hmong source who wishes anonymity, San Diego, October 27, 1979.

87. My interview with General Singkapo Sikhotchounamaly, Vientiane, August 21, 1990. This information was provided to appropriate officials in the U.S. State and Defense Departments. Several U.S. experts on the NVA have questioned the assertions of Vang Pao and Singkapo that the Vietnamese had mine detectors.

88. My interview with an official of the U.S. Joint Casualty Resolution Center (JCRC), Bangkok, September 10, 1990.

89. My telephone interview with Daniel W. Gray (a U.S. Department of Defense MIA/POW official), August 15, 1991.

7. Changing War; Changing Rules

1. Interview with Colby, May 3, 1988.

2. The subcommittee received classified testimony and limited attendance to those with a strict "need to know."

3. U.S., *Laos Hearings,* 365–66.

4. Stevenson, *The End of Nowhere,* 228. Since this study has already drawn extensively from these hearings, it is unnecessary to restate more than the principal topics. Over the past ten years the Senate Foreign Relations Committee has released to the National Archives a substantial amount of previously censored testimony on U.S. activity in Laos.

5. Senate, Committee on Foreign Relations, *Background Information Relating to Southeast Asia and Vietnam,* 359–61.

6. Stevenson, *The End of Nowhere,* 231–32.

7. Kissinger, *White House Years,* 456.

8. Paul, "Laos: Anatomy of an American Involvement," 545–46.

9. Arthur J. Dommen, "Laos in the Second Indochina War," 327–28.

10. Robbins, *The Ravens,* 132–33.

11. Stevenson, *The End of Nowhere,* 225. While attending a State Department-sponsored conference on Laos in Washington, D.C., I had lunch with Ambassador Godley, his niece Jinny St. Goar, and Lawrence Devlin, Godley's CIA station chief in Vientiane. The friendship and mutual admiration these men share for each other is still quite evident. Health problems have, unfortunately, affected Ambassador Godley's ability to speak without great difficulty. Nonetheless, Godley and Ms. St.

Goar are writing a book based on his experiences in Laos. Interview with Ambassador Godley and Ms. St. Goar, May 4, 1988. (Although Devlin participated in the conversation he requested that his remarks be kept off the record.)

12. Tyrrell, AF Oral History, 107–8.

13. Tovar letter, March 20, 1992.

14. U.S., *Laos Hearings,* 528.

15. My telephone interview with Colonel Russell, October 13, 1990.

16. I have corresponded with the principal attachés of this period, Colonel Robert L. F. Tyrrell, U.S. Air Force, and Lieutenant Colonel Edgar W. Duskin, U.S. Army. Colonel Tyrrell has been unable to accurately recall much of his long service in Laos. Tyrrell, letter to the author, April 18, 1988. I have, therefore, relied upon Tyrrell's 1969 Congressional testimony and his 1975 Air Force Oral History interview. Colonel Duskin, although initially amenable to written questions, has subsequently declined to answer my follow-up letters. Duskin, letter to the author, October 29, 1990. Colonel Duskin's silence is particularly disappointing, because he has been described by a knowledgeable confidential source as "the dominant military figure (except for the CIA) during his two years in Laos." Duskin also testified during the 1969 Congressional hearings.

17. Department of Defense. "CINCPAC Command History, 1971," 422.

18. DOD, "End-of-tour report, Colonel Russell, U.S. Army," 2–3 (document in my possession).

19. My telephone interview with General Vessey, May 31, 1989.

20. Jinny St. Goar, letter to the author, March 1, 1989.

21. Memorandum from General Vessey to Ambassador Godley, "Country Clearance for DEPCH Staff Members," September 30, 1972 (document in my possession).

22. St. Goar letter of March 1, 1989.

23. I make this observation after reviewing more than a dozen of General Vessey's lengthy inspection memorandums. These documents represent a small portion of declassified DEPCHIEF records provided to me by General Vessey's successor, Lieutenant General Richard G. Trefry, U.S. Army, retired.

24. My interview with Vessey, May 31, 1989, and Memorandum from Vessey to Major General Evans, "Thai SGU," February 23, 1973 (Document in possession).

25. U.S., *AID Hearing,* iv.

26. Ibid., 6.

27. Senate, Committee on Armed Services, *Hearings, Fiscal Year 1972,* 2021. MASF is defined by the U.S. government as "all defense articles and defense services transferred to foreign countries or international organizations under the authority contained in the Department of Defense Appropriations Act." Doty and Widner, "MAAG in Exile," 40.

28. Doty and Widner, "MAAG in Exile," 41.

29. Senate, Committee on Armed Services, *Hearings, Fiscal Year 1973,* 1603.

30. Colonel Kaufman, letter to the author, March 10, 1991. While assigned to DEPCHIEF Colonel Kaufman was a member of the Joint Agency Team.

31. Since 1968 a growing split had developed between some CIA veterans and younger, recently arrived CIA case officers. The "new breed" seemed insensitive to escalating Hmong casualties and the growing numbers of hill tribe refugees. My interview with Lair, April 15, 1988, and my telephone interview with Leary, March 2, 1991.

32. Berger, *USAF in Southeast Asia,* 130.

33. My telephone interview with Brigadier General Soutchay Vongsavanh, April 27, 1992. General Soutchay, who now works for the U.S. Department of Defense, has frequent contact with General Vang Pao and discussed the operation with him.

34. Thus began three years of B-52 "Arc Light" strikes on northern Laos. Berger, *USAF in Southeast Asia,* 131.

35. Fredric R. Branfman estimates that from May 1964 to September 1969 over seventy-five thousand tons of bombs were dropped on the plain. Branfman, *Voices From the Plain of Jars,* 3–4. No one is certain of the exact figure.

36. Berger, *USAF in Southeast Asia,* 134.

37. Blaufarb, *The Counterinsurgency Era,* 164.

38. Lofgren and Sexton, "Air War in Northern Laos," 88–89.

39. Berger, *USAF in Southeast Asia,* 134.

40. Soutchay Vongsavanh, *RLG Military Operations,* 37–38, and Conboy, *The War in Laos,* 18–19.

41. Hannah, *The Key to Failure,* 282–83.

42. Fulbrook, "Lam Son 719," 4.

43. Davidson, *Vietnam at War,* 585.

44. Soutchay Vongsavanh, *RLG Military Operations,* 60–61.

45. Kissinger, *White House Years,* 998. See also Hannah, *The Key to Failure,* 287.

46. Soutchay Vongsavanh, *RLG Military Operations,* 61.

47. Conboy, *The War in Laos,* 9–11. For an in-depth review see Vongsavanh, *RLG Military Operations,* 63–86.

48. Blaufarb, *The Counterinsurgency Era,* 164.

49. Lofgren and Sexton, "Air War in Northern Laos," 44, 86.

50. DOD, "CINCPAC Command History, 1969," 202.

51. My interview with Thammarak Isarangura, September 13, 1990.

52. Lofgren and Sexton, "Air War in Northern Laos," 46–47.

53. A Thai "volunteer" could expect to receive approximately three times his normal Thai army pay. For a private this came to about seventy-five dollars per month. The men also received, by Thai standards, very substantial reenlistment and end-of-tour bonuses. U.S., *Thailand, Laos, Cambodia: January 1972,* 20.

54. Lofgren and Sexton, "Air War in Northern Laos, 47."

55. During a five-week research visit to Thailand in the fall of 1990 I made several attempts to interview General Vithoon (or "Thep," as he was code-named during the Lao war). Despite the intercession of several senior Thai officers and a

former CIA colleague, General Vithoon declined my requests for an interview. The general is now an exceedingly wealthy man, has experienced some political problems resulting from a failed Thai coup attempt, and has no interest in discussing his past.

56. Cited in Dommen, *Conflict in Laos*, 284.

57. Lofgren and Sexton, "Air War in Northern Laos," 46–47.

58. Conboy, *The War in Laos*, 11.

59. The AN/PPN-118 beacon weighed only twenty pounds and could be easily transported and set-up by indigenous soldiers. Department of the Air Force, "End-of-tour report. Major General Hughes, USAF," 4–5.

60. Ibid., and Hughes audio tape interview response, November 25, 1988.

61. Hughes, "End of Tour," 4.

62. B. Hugh Tovar, CIA station chief in Vientiane at the time, strongly disagrees with this assessment. "At no time did I ever feel that I had 'control' of the air resources in Laos [other than Air America and Continental] . . . for U.S. Air Force resources we had to beg, plead, cajole and hope." Tovar letter, March 20, 1992. I must disagree with Mr. Tovar. Extant records, as well as the recollections of many senior military officers and the ambassadors themselves, clearly reflect the significant influence CIA exerted over all air operations in Laos.

63. Hughes, "End of Tour," 11, and Hughes audio tape interview response, November 25, 1988.

64. Hughes, "End of Tour," 14.

8. The Denouement of U.S. Military Aid to the Royal Lao Government

1. Brown and Zasloff, *Apprentice Revolutionaries*, 103.

2. Ibid., 104.

3. Kissinger, *Years of Upheaval*, 1231–32.

4. Ibid., 21.

5. According to Kissinger, "The purpose of my journey to Hanoi in February 1973 was to encourage any tendencies that existed to favor peaceful reconstruction over continued warfare, to stabilize the peace insofar as prospects of American goodwill could do so, and to warn of the serious consequences should these hopes be disappointed." Ibid., 23.

6. Ibid., 22.

7. Dommen, *Keystone of Indochina*, 94. Dommen bases this contention on the recollections of Lao Major General Oudone Sananikone. Sananikone says Souvanna Phouma was impatient for a cease-fire and John Gunther Dean, Deputy Chief of Mission, "was also very anxious that the negotiations not stall. He and his staff frequently urged members of the government to make more concessions to the Neo Lao Hak Sat [Pathet Lao]." Sananikone also claims the U.S. pressured the Lao army by threatening to cut off salary payments and fuel and rice shipments. Sananikone, *The Royal Lao Army*, 149–50.

8. Kissinger, *Years of Upheaval,* 34–35.

9. Dommen, *Keystone of Indochina,* 94.

10. Brown and Zasloff, *Apprentice Revolutionaries,* 365–66.

11. Ibid., 105–6.

12. Senate, Committee on Foreign Relations, *Thailand, Laos, Cambodia, and Vietnam: April 1973,* 18. My final combat mission over Laos was flown on February 8. I can still quite vividly recall the anger and disappointment of one young pilot who craved the danger and excitement of combat flying.

13. Berger, *USAF in Southeast Asia,* 135.

14. St. Jean, McClain, and Hartwig Study, "Twenty-Three Years of Military Assistance to Laos," 175–76. Anticipating the cease-fire's effect on their operations, in mid-March 1973 the President and Managing Director of Air America paid visits to DEPCHIEF at Udorn and the American embassy in Vientiane. Little could be done to change the situation. Air America was too closely linked to the CIA in Laos and the Thais were very anxious to takeover the lucrative Udorn facility. DEPCHIEF Memorandum for Record, "Visit of Mr. Grundy, President of Air America" (document in my possession).

15. DOD, "CINCPAC Command History, 1973," 489, and *New York Times,* July 13, 1975.

16. For several years I attempted to document the number of U.S. military pilots rescued by Air America crews. The job was made impossible by the passage of time, poor and intentionally misleading record keeping, and Air America employees who understandably continue to abide by past security oaths.

17. DOD, "End-of-Tour Report, Major General Trefry, U.S. Army," 27 (document in my possession).

18. See n. 10, this chapter.

19. Outgoing electrical message, "US–Thai Relations and Your Visit to Bangkok," January 31, 1973 (document in my possession). The vice-president was sent the message in preparation for his stop in the Thai capital.

20. Outgoing electrical message, "Thai SGU Future," February 17, 1973 (document in my possession).

21. Electrical message, "US–Thai Relations and Your Visit to Bangkok."

22. Electrical message, "Thai SGU Future."

23. Outgoing electrical message, "Thai SGU," SECSTATE WASHDC, April 7, 1973 (document in my possession).

24. Outgoing electrical message, "Thai SGU," AFSSO, March 1, 1973, and "Thai SGU," DEPCHJUSMAG, March 8, 1973 (documents in my possession).

25. Outgoing electrical message, "Thai SGU: New Funds Required," April 19, 1973. (Retransmittal of electrical message sent April 19 from U.S. embassy in Vientiane) (Document in my possession).

26. Outgoing electrical message, "Thai SGU," SECDEF, June 28, 1973 (document in my possession). See also *Bangkok Post,* September 18, 1973.

27. U.S., *Thailand, Laos, Cambodia, Vietnam: April 1973,* 13–15. Since fiscal year 1973 all military funding for Laos was included in the Defense Department

budget. The DOD then transferred money for the Thai and Lao irregulars to the CIA, which physically disbursed the payments. Beginning in fiscal year 1974 the money was no longer transferred from the DOD to CIA budget, but CIA case officers continued to make the field payments. U.S., *Fiscal Year 1974,* 5887–88.

28. DEPCHIEF Memorandums for Record, "Visit to Long Tieng on 20 March 1973," and "Visit to Long Tieng on 21 June 1973" (documents in my possession). General Trefry had succeeded General Vessey in late February 1973.

29. Lee, "Minority Policies and the Hmong," 203, and my interview with Vang Pao, February 6, 1979.

30. DEPCHIEF Memorandum from General Vessey to Ambassador Godley, "Organization for Post Cease-fire U.S. Military Assistance to Laos," February 14, 1973 (document in my possession).

31. Blaufarb, "Unconventional War in Laos," 63–64.

32. DEPCHIEF Memorandum, "Organization for Post Cease-fire U.S. Military Assistance to Laos."

33. DEPCHIEF Memorandum, "Meeting Concerning Reorganization of the Laotian Attache Office, RO, Project 404, and DEPCH," February 20, 1973 (document in my possession).

34. My interview with General Trefry, May 19, 1989. Lao Major General Oudone Sananikone has suggested that an overhaul of the Lao military supply system would have upset the financial interests of many powerful Lao families. Sananikone, *The Royal Lao Army,* 161.

35. My interview with Trefry, May 19, 1989, and outgoing electrical message, "SGU and FY74 Air Services Contracts—Laos," July 4, 1973 (document in my possession). The State Department message was 2217Z, March 8, 1973, with a State Department assigned number of 060000. The message was commonly known as "SECSTATE 60,000."

36. My interview with Trefry, May 19, 1989.

37. Whitehouse arrived in August and, in contrast to previous ambassadors to Laos, was immediately at ease with the U.S. military. He and General Trefry enjoyed a very warm relationship in the midst of Washington's somewhat conflicting political and military guidance. My interview with Ambassador Whitehouse, May 24, 1989.

38. St. Jean, McClain, and Hartwig, "Twenty-Three Years of Military Assistance to Laos," 63, and DOD. "CINCPAC Command History, 1973," 58. (document in my possession).

39. Dommen, *Keystone of Indochina,* 98.

40. Brown and Zasloff, *Apprentice Revolutionaries,* 108–9.

41. Ibid., 107.

42. Zasloff and Brown, eds., *Communism in Indochina,* 265.

43. Outgoing electrical message, "Withdrawal of Thai Forces from Laos" May 22, 1974 (Document in my possession). See also *Bangkok Post,* May 22, 1974.

44. St. Jean, McClain, and Hartwig, "Twenty-Three Years of Military Assistance to Laos," 66.

45. According to a senior Hmong official in the Souvanna government, Souvanna later told the French Ambassador to Laos that "the Hmong had served his purpose well, but it was a pity that peace in the country had to be achieved at the expense of their extinction." Lee, "Minority Policies and the Hmong," 204–5.

46. Yang Dao, "Why Did the Hmong Leave Laos?," in *The Hmong in the West: Observations and Papers,* Bruce T. Downing and Douglas P. Olney, eds. (Minneapolis: Center for Urban and Regional Affairs, University of Minnesota, 1982) 13–14; Lee, "Minority Policies and the Hmong," 206; and my interview with Moua Thong, November 6, 1979. Moua Thong was the manager of the Long Tieng radio station.

47. Brown and Zasloff, *Apprentice Revolutionaries,* 118.

48. Henry Kamm, "U.S. Involvement in Laos is Virtually Over," *New York Times,* June 20, 1975. General Round assumed his duties in December 1974.

49. My telephone interview with General Round, March 16, 1992.

50. DOD. "CINCPAC Command History, 1975," 616–17, and my interview with Major Litvinas, February 20, 1991. Major Litvinas' father, Clement P. Litvinas, worked for the U.S. Federal Highway Administration in Savannakhet and "negotiated" with the students. Mr. Litvinas convinced the revolutionaries to sign receipts for all the U.S. equipment they seized.

51. Department of the Air Force. "PACAF Command History, July–December, 1974–5," 475, and DOD, "CINCPAC Command History, 1973," 58. The former USAID compound in Vientiane is now office space for the Council of Ministers. In August and September of 1990 I conducted a number of interviews in the main building. The offices are still furnished with U.S. government issue desks, chairs, and file cabinets.

52. Kamm, "U.S. Involvement," *New York Times,* June 20, 1975.

53. "CINCPAC Command History, 1975," 619–20.

54. General Round, letter to the author, March 30, 1991 and my telephone interview with him on March 16, 1992.

55. "CINCPAC Command History, 1975," 41, 621.

56. Brown and Zasloff, *Apprentice Revolutionaries,* 119.

BIBLIOGRAPHY

U.S. Government Documents

United States Agency for International Development

Facts on Foreign Aid to Laos. Embassy of the United States, Vientiane. April 1971.
——2d ed., July 1973.
——"Fact Sheet, Laos," September 1, 1967.

United States Central Intelligence Agency

"Intelligence Information Cable," Foreign Broadcast Information Service Vienna, February 27, 1964.
——"Journey from Phadong," video tape, n.d.

United States Congress

House. Committee on Appropriations. *Foreign Assistance and Related Agencies Appropriations for 1973. Hearings before a Subcommittee of the Committee on Appropriations,* pt. 2, 92d Cong., 2d sess., 1972.

House. Committee on Foreign Affairs. *United States Aid to Indochina*. Report of a Staff Survey Team to South Vietnam, Cambodia, and Laos for the Committee on Foreign Affairs, 93d Cong., 2d sess., 1974.

House. Committee on Government Operations. *U.S. Aid Operations in Laos*. H. Rept. 546, 86th Cong., 1st sess., 1959.

Senate. Committee on Armed Services. *Fiscal Year 1972 Authorization for Military Procurement, Research and Development, Construction and Real Estate Acquisition for the Safeguard ABM, and Reserve Strengths: Hearings before the Committee on Armed Services*, pt. 2 and supp., 92d Cong., 1st sess., 1971.

——*Fiscal Year 1973 Authorization for Military Procurement, Research and Development, Construction Authorization for the Safeguard ABM, and Active Duty and Selected Reserve Strengths: Hearings before the Committee on Armed Services*, pt. 3, 92d Cong., 2d sess., 1972.

——*Fiscal Year 1974 Authorization for Military Procurement, Research and Development, Construction Authorization for the Safeguard ABM, and Active Duty and Selected Reserve Strengths: Hearings before the Committee on Armed Services*, pt. 8, 93d Cong., 1st sess., 1973.

——*Nomination of William E. Colby to be Director of Central Intelligence: Hearing before the Committee on Armed Services*, 93d Cong., 1st sess., 1973.

Senate. Committee on Foreign Relations. *Aid Activities in Laos. Hearing before the Subcommittee on U.S. Security Agreements and Commitments Abroad of the Committee on Foreign Relations*, 92d Cong., 2d sess., 1972.

——*Background Information Relating to Southeast Asia and Vietnam*. 6th ed., 91st Cong., 2d sess., 1970.

——*Foreign Assistance Act of 1974*. Report No. 93-1299 prepared by Mr. Humphrey for the Committee on Foreign Relations. 93d Cong., 2d sess., 1974.

——*Laos: April 1971*. Staff Report Prepared for the Use of the Subcommittee on U.S. Security Agreements and Commitments Abroad, 92d Cong., 1st sess., 1971.

——*Postwar Southeast Asia. A Search for Neutrality and Independence*. A Report by Senator Mike Mansfield for the Committee on Foreign Relations, 94th Cong., 2d sess., 1976.

——*Security Agreements and Commitments Abroad*. Report to the Committee on Foreign Relations by the Subcommittee on U.S. Security Agreements and Commitments Abroad, 91st Cong., 2d sess., 1970.

——*Thailand, Laos, and Cambodia: January 1972*. Staff Report Prepared for the Use of the Subcommittee on U.S. Security Agreements and Commitments Abroad of the Committee on Foreign Relations, 92d Cong., 2d sess., 1972.

——*Thailand, Laos, Cambodia, and Vietnam: April 1973*. Staff Report Prepared for the Use of the Subcommittee on U.S. Security Agreements and Commitments Abroad of the Committee on Foreign Relations, 93d Cong., 1st sess., 1973.

——*United States Security Agreements and Commitments Abroad: Kingdom of Laos. Hearings before the Subcommittee on U.S. Security Agreements and Commitments Abroad*, pt. 2, 91st Cong., 1st sess., 1969.

——*United States Security Agreements and Commitments Abroad: Kingdom of Thailand. Hearings before the Subcommittee on U.S. Security Agreements and Commitments Abroad,* pt. 3, 91st Cong., 1st sess., 1969.
——*Winds of Change. Evolving Relations and Interests in Southeast Asia.* A Report by Senator Mike Mansfield to the Committee on Foreign Relations, 94th Cong., 1st sess., 1975.
Senate. Select Committee to Study Governmental Operations with Respect to Intelligence Activities. *Foreign and Military Intelligence.* Final Report of the Select Committee. S. Rept. 94-755, Books I and IV, 94th Cong., 2d sess., 1976.

United States Department of Defense

Assistant Secretary of Defense, Director of Military Assistance. Letter from General Robert J. Wood, U.S. Army, to Major General C. V. Clifton, U.S. Army, military aide to the president, September 12, 1962.
Commander in chief Pacific. "CINCPAC Command History, 1962," Camp Smith, Hawaii: Office of the Command Historian.
——"CINCPAC Command History, 1964," Camp Smith, Hawaii: Office of the Command Historian, 1964.
——"CINCPAC Command History, 1969," Camp Smith, Hawaii: Office of the Command Historian, 1969.
——"CINCPAC Command History, 1971," Camp Smith, Hawaii: Office of the Command Historian, 1971.
——"CINCPAC Command History, 1973," Camp Smith, Hawaii: Office of the Command Historian, 1973.
——"CINCPAC Command History, 1975," Camp Smith, Hawaii: Office of the Command Historian, 1975.
——CINCPAC letter, from Admiral H. D. Felt to Colonel D. F. Munster, Executive Officer, DEPCHIEF, March 8, 1963.
——Deputy Chief, Joint United States Military Advisory Group Thailand. End-of-tour report of Colonel Peter T. Russell, U.S. Army. July 27, 1971.
——Deputy Chief, Joint United States Military Advisory Group Thailand. "Final Report of Military Assistance and Advisory Group, Laos." December 11, 1962.
Defense Intelligence Agency. End-of-tour report of Brigadier General Roswell E. Round, Jr., U.S. Army, Defense Attaché, Vientiane. July 29, 1975.
——End-of-tour report of Major General Richard G. Trefry, U.S. Army, Defense Attaché, Vientiane. December 12, 1974.
Department of the Air Force. "Air War in Northern Laos 1 April–30 November 1971." Project CHECO report. Major William W. Lofgren, USAF, and Major Richard R. Sexton, USAF. Hickam AFB, Hawaii: Headquarters Pacific Air Forces, June 22, 1973.
——"Combat Skyspot." Project CHECO report. Major Richard A. Durkee, USAF. Hickam AFB, Hawaii: Headquarters Pacific Air Forces, August 9, 1967.

——"Debriefing of LtCol Robert B. Melgard, Asst. Air Attaché, Vientiane, Laos."
Washington, D.C., November 13, 1964.

——Headquarters 7/13AF Udorn, Thailand. End-of-tour report of Major General
Andrew J. Evans, Jr., October 16, 1970 to June 30, 1971. Udorn, Thailand.
June 30, 1971.

——Headquarters 7/13AF End-of-tour report of Major General DeWitt R. Searles,
USAF. July 1, 1971 to September 8, 1972. Udorn, Thailand. September 9,
1972.

——Headquarters 7/13AF End-of-tour report of Major General James D. Hughes,
USAF. September 10, 1972 to April 19, 1973. Nakhon Phanom, Thailand.
April 20, 1973.

——"MAP Aid to Laos 1959–1972." Project CHECO report. Captain Peter A.
W. Liebchen, USAF. Hickam AFB, Hawaii: Headquarters Pacific Air Forces,
June 25, 1973.

——Negotiated contracts with Air America, Inc., May 24, 1961, June 7, 1961,
June 30, 1961, and July 1, 1961.

——Oral History Interview (OHI). Lieutenant Colonel Howard K. Hartley, USAF,
retired. July 14, 1974. Maxwell AFB, Alabama.

——OHI. Lieutenant General James D. Hughes, USAF. September 21 and 22,
1982. Maxwell AFB, Alabama.

——OHI. Lieutenant Colonel Billie R. Keeler, USAF. February 5, 1973. Maxwell
AFB, Alabama.

——OHI. Colonel Roland K. McCoskrie, USAF. July 14, 1975. Maxwell AFB,
Alabama.

——OHI. Captain Karl L. Polifka, Jr., USAF. December 17, 1974. Maxwell AFB,
Alabama.

——OHI. Major Donald Randle, USAF. December 1974. Maxwell AFB, Alabama.

——OHI. Major Jesse E. Scott, USAF. April 6, 1973. Maxwell AFB, Alabama.

——OHI. Lieutenant Colonel Butler B. Toland, Jr., USAF. November 18, 1974.
Maxwell AFB, Alabama.

——OHI. Colonel Robert L. F. Tyrrell, USAF. May 12, 1975. Maxwell AFB,
Alabama.

——OHI. Colonel William Von Platen, USAF. May 10, 1975. Maxwell AFB,
Alabama.

——"PACAF Command History, July–December, 1974–5." Hickam AFB, Hawaii: Office of PACAF History, 1975.

——"Short Rounds." Project CHECO report. Lieutenant Colonel Frank J. Adamcik, USAF. Hickam AFB, Hawaii: Headquarters Pacific Air Forces, July 15,
1972.

——"The Fall of Site 85." Project CHECO report. Captain Edward Vallentiny,
USAF. Hickam AFB, Hawaii: Headquarters Pacific Air Forces, August 9,
1968.

——"The Royal Lao Air Force 1954–1970." Project CHECO report. Major John

C. Pratt, USAF. Hickam AFB, Hawaii: Headquarters Pacific Air Forces, September 15, 1970.

——"United States Policy Toward Southeast Asia, 1943–1968: A Chronological Compendium." Project Corona Harvest report. Robert F. Futrell. Maxwell AFB, Alabama: Air University, October 1, 1968.

Department of the Army. *Laos: A Country Study*. Donald P. Whitaker, et al. D.A. Pam 550-58, 2d ed., Washington, D.C.: GPO, 1979.

——Senior Officers Debriefing Program. Lieutenant General Andrew J. Boyle, U.S. Army. March 1971. Reprinted by Dalley Book Service, Christiansburg, Virginia.

——Talking Paper for Chief of Staff, U.S. Army, "Guidance for T-28 Aircraft Operations," March 9, 1964.

United States–Vietnam Relations, 1945–67 (12 books). Washington, D.C.: GPO, 1971.

United States Department of State

Department of State Bulletin, 1954.
——*Department of State Bulletin, 1961.*
——*The Situation in Laos.* September 1959.

Electrical Messages

Outgoing electrical message, "Orders," CINCPAC, Hawaii, 1300Z, March 8, 1963.

——"Infiltration of CAS Road Watch Team," DEP CMDR 7/13AF Udorn RTAFB, Thailand, 1100Z, December 17, 1966.

——"Special Operation," DEP CMDR 7/13AF Udorn RTAFB, Thailand, 1245Z, December 17, 1966.

——Deputy Commander, 7/13th AF, to General Momyer, Commander 7th AF, 1115Z, November 24, 1967.

——"Operation Duck," DEP CMDR 7/13AF Udorn AFLD, Thailand, 0826Z, March 20, 1969.

——"Operation Left Jab," 7/13AF Udorn RTAFB, Thailand, 1112Z, June 19, 1969.

——"US–Thai Relations and Your Visit to Bangkok," U.S. Embassy Bangkok, 0808Z, January 31, 1973.

——"Thai SGU Future," U.S. Embassy, Bangkok, 0329Z, February 17, 1973.

——"Thai SGU," AFSSO Udorn RTAFB, 1030Z, March 1, 1973.

——"Thai SGU," DEPCHJUSMAG Udorn RTAFB, Thailand, 0915Z, March 8, 1973.

——"Thai SGU," SECSTATE WASHDC, 2152Z, April 7, 1973.

——"Thai SGU: New Funds Required," SECSTATE WASHDC, 0629Z, April 19, 1973 (re-transmittal of electrical message sent April 19 from U.S. Embassy Vientiane).

——"Thai SGU," SECDEF WASHDC, 2154Z, June 28, 1973.
——"SGU and FY74 Air Services Contracts—Laos," CINCPAC, Hawaii, 0504Z, July 4, 1973.
——"Withdrawal of Thai Forces from Laos," U.S. Embassy Vientiane, 1055Z, May 22, 1974.

Memoranda

Memorandum to the president from Walt W. Rostow. February 28, 1961.
——March 10, 1961.
Memorandum from Brigadier General Vessey to Ambassador Godley, "Country Clearance for DEPCH Staff Members." September 30, 1972. Udorn, Thailand.
DEPCHIEF memorandum from Brigadier General Vessey to Ambassador Godley, "Organization for Post Cease-fire U.S. Military Assistance to Laos." February 14, 1973. Udorn, Thailand.
DEPCHIEF memorandum from Vessey, "Meeting Concerning Reorganization of the Laotian Attaché Office, RO, Project 404, and DEPCH." February 20, 1973. Udorn, Thailand.
Memorandum from Vessey to Major General Evans, "Thai SGU." February 23, 1973. Udorn, Thailand.
DEPCHIEF memorandum for record from Vessey, "Visit to Long Tieng on 20 March 1973." March 26, 1973. Udorn, Thailand.
——"Visit to Long Tieng on 21 June 1973." June 26, 1973.

Declassified Documents Reference System (DDRS) Sources

Woodbridge, Conn.: DDRS Research Publications, 1976, document 226A.
——1981, document 205B.
——1989, documents 686, 822–23, 856–57, 2100, 2105, 2113–15, 2343–44, 3403–4, 3406, and 3543.
——1990, documents 248, 324, 684, 1456, 1459, 1637–38, 3044, and 3311–12.

Interviews By Author

Abadie, Clarence J. Houston. August 26, 1987 (by telephone).
Aderholt, Harry C. Brigadier general, U.S. Air Force, retired. Ft. Walton Beach, Florida. May 2, 1988.
Anthony, Victor B. Major, U.S. Air Force, retired. Colorado Springs. March 18 and 19, 1988.
Bailey, Lawrence R., Jr. Colonel, U.S. Army, retired. Atlanta. January 19, 1992 (by telephone).

Beckley, Stuart A. Lieutenant colonel, U.S. Army, retired. San Antonio. October 20 and 21, 1990 (by telephone).

Blaufarb, Douglas S. Lehew, West Virginia. March 18, 1988 (by telephone).

Byers, Michael D. Falls Church, Virginia. May 25, 1989.

Cherry, Don T. Major, U.S. Air Force, retired. San Diego. March 16, 1979.

Colby, William E. Former Director, Central Intelligence Agency. Washington, D.C. May 3, 1988.

——Colorado Springs. February 20, 1992.

Conboy, Kenneth J. Washington, D.C. May 3, 1988.

Confidential Interview. San Diego. October 27, 1979.

——Bangkok. September 17, 1990.

Felt, Harry D. Admiral, U.S. Navy, retired. Honolulu. March 1 and 9, 1990.

Godley, G. McMurtrie. Former ambassador to Laos. Washington, D.C. May 4, 1988.

Gray, Daniel Warren. Washington, D.C. August 15, 1991 (by telephone).

Guilmartin, John F., Jr. Lieutenant colonel, U.S. Air Force, retired. Columbus, Ohio. November 11 and 12, 1987.

Hansel, Jack H. Honolulu. October 27, 1990.

Hickler, David H. Escondido, California. June 1, 1989.

Hughes, James D. Lieutenant general, U.S. Air Force, retired. Audio tape interview, Newburgh, New York. November 25, 1989.

Jenny, Thomas G. Honolulu. January 26, 1990.

Kaufman, Martin L. Colonel, U.S. Air Force. Alexandria, Virginia. May 19, 21, and 25, 1989.

Khamouan Boupha. Vice minister of the Lao People's Democratic Republic and former general of the Lao People's Liberation Army. Vientiane. September 6, 1990.

Klingaman, Jerome W. Lieutenant colonel, U.S. Air Force, retired. Maxwell AFB, Alabama. March 2, 1988.

Kong Le. Former general, Lao Neutralist Army. Honolulu. April 15, 17, and 18, 1989.

Lair, James W. Colorado Springs. April 15, 1988.

——Hua Hin, Thailand. July 28, 1990.

——Bangkok. August 10, 13, 14, and 17, 1990.

Landry, Lloyd. Bangkok. August 17 and September 13, 1990.

Leary, William M. Athens, Georgia. May 9, 1988 (by telephone).

Lee Khue. San Diego. November 6, 1979.

Leonard, William R. Lieutenant colonel, U.S. Air Force, retired. Colorado Springs. February 19, 1988.

Litvinas, Anthony J. Major, U.S. Army. Honolulu. February 20, 1991.

MacFarlane, James M. Portsmouth, New Hampshire. May 13, 1989.

Mayoury Ngaosyvathn. Honolulu. December 4, 1990.

McMurdo, Strathmore K. Colonel, U.S. Army, retired. Honolulu. October 11, 1990.

Moore, Theodore H. Reno, Nevada. June 27, 1988 (by telephone).

Moua Thong. San Diego. October 6 and November 6, 1979.

Nantana Sribunnak. Bangkok. August 13 and September 12, 1990.

Polifka, Karl L. Colonel, U.S. Air Force. Falls Church, Virginia. May 25, 1989.

Round, Roswell E., Jr. Brigadier general, U.S. Army, retired. Sarasota. March 16, 1992 (by telephone).

Russell, Peter T. Colonel, U.S. Army, retired. Washington, D.C. October 13, 1990 (by telephone).

Saiyud, Kerdphol. General, Royal Thai Army, retired. Bangkok. August 14, 1990.

Sharp, U. S. Grant. Admiral, U.S. Navy, retired. Honolulu. March 6, 1990.

Sherwood, Michael H. Bangkok. August 16, 1990.

Shirley, John E. Bangkok. August 1, 14, and 17, 1990.

Singkapo Sikhotchounamaly. President, Peace Committee, Lao People's Democratic Republic and former general, Lao People's Liberation Army. Vientiane. August 21 and September 4, 1990.

Sisana Sisane. Director, Social Science Research Committee, Lao People's Democratic Republic. Vientiane. August 20 and September 5, 1990.

Smith, Felix. Honolulu. January 2, 1990.

Soutchay Vongsavanh. Brigadier general, Royal Lao Army, retired. Washington, D.C. April 27, 1992 (by telephone).

Srichow Manitayakoon. Bangkok. August 12 and 14, 1990.

Stuart, Richard E. Lieutenant colonel, U.S. Air Force, retired. Colorado Springs. February 19 and March 24, 1988.

Suriyoun Juntramanid. Second lieutenant, Thai Border Patrol Police. Hua Hin, Thailand. July 28, 1990.

Thammarak Isarangura. Major general, Royal Thai Army. Bangkok. September 13, 1990.

Thao Pao Ly. San Diego. October 27, 1979.

Thompson, Macalan. Bangkok. September 15, 1990.

Trefry, Richard G. Lieutenant general, U.S. Army, retired. Alexandria, Virginia. May 18, 19, and 26, 1989.

Unger, Leonard. Former ambassador to Laos. Washington, D.C. May 3, 1988.

——Rockville, Maryland. May 21, 1989 and September 12, 1991.

United States Joint Casualty Resolution Center official, Bangkok. September 10, 1990.

Vang Pao. Major general, Royal Lao Army, retired. Santa Ana, California. February 6 and April 28, 1979.

Vessey, John W., Jr. General, U.S. Army, retired. Garrison, Minnesota. May 31, 1989 (by telephone).

Walker, Fred F. Freyburg, Maine. May 14, 1989.

Westmoreland, William C. General, U.S. Army, retired. Charleston, South Carolina. April 13, 1990 (by telephone).

Whitehouse, Charles S. Former ambassador to Laos. Washington, D.C. May 24, 1989.

Yang Dao. Minneapolis. May 30, 1987.
Yang Teng. San Diego. October 27, 1979.

Personal Correspondence with Author

Ankerberg, David L. Letter of March 26, 1988.
Bailey, Lawrence R., Jr. Colonel, U.S. Army, retired. Letter of January 30, 1992.
Beckley, Stuart A. Lieutenant colonel, U.S. Army, retired. Letter of October 25, 1990.
Bond, Charles R. Major general, U.S. Air Force, retired. Letter of May 1, 1988.
Burke, Marius. Letter of May 8, 1988.
Carroll, George. Letter of March 31, 1988.
Cates, Allen E. Letter of March 16, 1988.
Conboy, Kenneth J. Letter of April 18, 1988.
Crews, P. T. Letter of June 1, 1988.
Darran, Walt. Letter of July 6, 1988.
Duskin, Edgar W. Colonel, U.S. Army, retired. Letter of October 29, 1990.
Fonburg, John. Letters of January 8, and February 26, 1989.
French, Dick. Letter of March 23, 1988.
Godley, G. McMurtrie. Former ambassador to Laos. Letter of April 4, 1988.
Hall, Robert E. Colonel, U.S. Air Force, retired. Letter of January 15, 1989.
Hartwig, Ronald C. Lieutenant colonel, U.S. Air Force, retired. Letter of February 2, 1989.
Hickler, David H. Letter of March 8, 1990.
Hildreth, James R. Major general, U.S. Air Force, retired. Letter of January 10, 1989.
Hughes, James D. Lieutenant general, U.S. Air Force, retired. Letter of August 22, 1988.
Jennings, Phillip E. Letter of April 4, 1988.
Kaufman, Martin L. Colonel, U.S. Air Force. Letters of December 19 and 23, 1988, March 29, 1989, and March 10, 1991.
Keeler, Billie R. Lieutenant colonel, U.S. Air Force, retired. Letter of December 0, 1988.
Kirkendall, James F. Major general, U.S. Air Force, retired. Letter of May 12, 1988.
Knight, Wayne. Letters of April 24, 1988, and January 23, 1989.
Leary, William M. Letters of February 6 and November 23, 1990, and of January 22, February 3 and 11, and March 6, 1991.
Lindley, William C. Major general, U.S. Air Force, retired. Letter of May 11, 1988.
MacFarlane, James M. Letters of April 24, 26, 29, 30, and May 13, 1988.
McCauley, John J. Letter of April 8, 1988.

McShane, William E. Letter of August 26, 1989.

Moore, Theodore H. Letters of June 17 and July 12, 1988.

Munsell, Elmer L. Letter of June 4, 1988.

Pettigrew, Paul A. Colonel, U.S. Air Force, retired. Letter of February 11, 1989.

Polifka, Karl L., Jr. Colonel, U.S. Air Force. Letters of January 3, and March 13, 1989.

Rostow, Walt W. Letters of January 19 and February 28, 1990.

Round, Roswell E., Jr. Brigadier general, U.S. Army, retired. Letter of March 30, 1991.

Russell, Peter T. Colonel, U.S. Army, retired. Letter of October 23, 1990.

Sanchez, Pete H. Letter of January 6, 1989.

Searles, DeWitt R. Major general, U.S. Air Force, retired. Letter of April 23, 1988.

St. Goar, Jinny. Letter of March 1, 1989.

Stergar, Frank E. Letters of March 17 and July 5, 1988.

Sullivan, Emmet R. Letter of April 1, 1988.

Sullivan, William H. Former ambassador to Laos. Letters of April 10, 1988, January 16, 1989, November 9, 1990, and August 18, 1991.

Tovar, B. Hugh. Letter of March 20, 1992.

Trefry, Richard G. Lieutenant general, U.S. Army, retired. Letter of December 26, 1988.

Tyrrell, Robert L. F. Colonel, U.S. Air Force, retired. Letter of April 18, 1988.

United States Central Intelligence Agency. Letter of April 20, 1989.

Van Etten, Benjamin. Letter of April 20, 1988.

Walker, Fred F. Letter of March 8, 1989.

Westmoreland, William C. General, U.S. Army, retired. Letter of March 10, 1990.

Dissertations, Theses, and Unpublished Documents

Blaufarb, Douglas S. "Organizing and Managing Unconventional War in Laos." Rand Corporation, 1972, reprinted by Dalley Book Service, Christiansburg, Virginia.

Castle, Timothy N. "Alliance in a Secret War: The United States and the Hmong of Northeastern Laos." M.A. thesis, San Diego State University, 1979.

——"At War in the Shadow of Vietnam: United States Military Aid to the Royal Lao Government, 1955–75." Ph.D. diss., University of Hawaii, 1991.

Dilbert, Thomas F., and Timothy N. Castle. "Chemical Warfare in Indo-China and Afghanistan: Implications for Low-Intensity Conflict." Paper presented to 9th Air University Airpower Symposium, Maxwell AFB, Alabama, 1985.

Doty, Edouard R. L., and Rodney C. Widner. "Logistics Support for the Royal Lao Air Force as Conducted by a MAAG in Exile." M.A. thesis, Air Force Institute of Technology, Wright-Patterson AFB, Ohio, 1974.

Harriman, W. Averell. Interview conducted by Michael V. Forrestal on April 13, 1964, for the John F. Kennedy Library Oral History Program.

——Interviews conducted by Arthur M. Schlesinger, on January 17 and June 6, 1965, for the John F. Kennedy Library Oral History Program.

Immerman, Richard H., and Fred I. Greenstein. "What Did Eisenhower Advise Kennedy About Indochina?" Unpublished manuscript.

Langer, Paul F. "The Soviet Union, China, and the Pathet Lao: Analysis and Chronology." Santa Monica: Rand Corporation, 1972.

Leary, William M. "Air America: Myth and Reality." Paper presented at University of Texas at Dallas, on February 1, 1992.

McKeithen, Edwin T. "The Role of North Vietnamese Cadres in the Pathet Lao Administration of Xieng Khouang Province." Xieng Khouang, Laos: April 1970.

"Reminiscences of Admiral Harry Donald Felt, U.S. Navy, Retired." Vol II. U.S. Naval Institute, Annapolis, 1974.

Rostow, Walt W. "JFK and Southeast Asia." Paper presented at the Conference on the Presidency of John Fitzgerald Kennedy in Los Angeles on November 14, 1980.

Sarasin Viraphol. "Directions in Thai Foreign Policy." Occasional Paper No. 40. Singapore: Institute of Southeast Asian Studies, May 1976.

Scott, George M., Jr. "Migrants Without Mountains: The Politics of Sociocultural Adjustment Among the Lao Hmong Refugees in San Diego." Ph.D. diss., University of California, San Diego, 1986.

Sharp, U.S. Grant. Interview conducted by Dr. Robert R. Kritt, U.S. Naval Training Center, San Diego, on February 19, 1971.

St. Jean, Frederick J., Terrance W. McClain, and Ronald C. Hartwig. "Twenty-Three Years of Military Assistance to Laos." Air War College, Air University, Maxwell AFB, Alabama, March 1975.

Thak Chaloemtiarana. "The Sarit Regime, 1957–1963: The Formative Years of Modern Thai Politics." Ph.D. diss., Cornell University, 1974.

Tuttle, Vanida Trongyounggoon. "Thai-American Relations, 1950–1954." Ph.D. diss., Washington State University, 1982.

United Nations. "Salient Features of Lao PDR." n.d.

Westermeyer, Joseph P. "The Use of Alcohol and Opium Among Two Ethnic Groups in Laos." M.A. thesis, University of Minnesota, 1968.

Wing, Roswell B., et al. "Case Study of US Counterinsurgency Operations in Laos, 1955–1962." McLean, Virginia: Research Analysis Corporation, 1964.

Books

Adams, Nina S. and Alfred W. McCoy, eds. *Laos: War and Revolution*. New York: Harper & Row, 1970.

Allen, Douglas. and Ngo Vinh Long, eds. *Coming to Terms: Indochina, the United States, and the War*. Boulder: Westview, 1991.

Ballard, Jack S. The United States Air Force in Southeast Asia. *Development and Employment of Fixed-Wing Gunships, 1962–1972*. Washington, D.C.: Office of Air Force History, 1982.

Berger, Carl, ed. The United States Air Force in Southeast Asia, *1961–1973: An Illustrated Account*. 2d ed. Washington D.C.: Office of Air Force History, 1984.

Berman, Larry. *Lyndon Johnson's War: The Road to Stalemate in Vietnam*. New York: Norton, 1989.

Blaufarb, Douglas S. *The Counterinsurgency Era*. New York: Free Press, 1977.

Blazhenkov, Stanislav. *Laos*. Moscow: Planeta Publishers, 1985.

Blechman, Barry M. and Stephan S. Kaplan, eds. *Force Without War: U.S. Armed Forces as a Political Instrument*. Washington: Brookings Institute, 1978.

Blum, Robert M. *Drawing the Line: The Origin of the American Containment Policy in East Asia*. New York: Norton, 1982.

Bowers, Ray L. The United States Air Force in Southeast Asia, *Tactical Airlift*. Washington, D.C.: Office of Air Force History, 1983.

Brace, Ernest C. *A Code To Keep*. New York: St. Martin's, 1988.

Brailey, Nigel J. *Thailand and the Fall of Singapore: A Frustrated Asian Revolution*. Boulder: Westview, 1986.

Branfman, Fredric R. *Voices from the Plain of Jars: Life Under an Air War*. New York: Harper & Row, 1972.

Brown, MacAlister and Joseph J. Zasloff. *Apprentice Revolutionaries: The Communist Movement in Laos, 1930–1985*. Stanford: Hoover Institution Press, 1986.

Cady, John F. *The History of Post-War Southeast Asia: Independence Problems*. Athens, Ohio: Ohio University Press, 1980.

Caldwell, J. Alexander. *American Economic Aid to Thailand*. Lexington, Mass.: D. C. Heath, 1974.

Cameron, Allan W., ed. *Vietnam Crisis: A Documentary History*. 2 vols. Ithaca: Cornell University Press, 1971.

Chalermnit Press Correspondent. *Battle of Vientiane 1960*. Bangkok: Chalermnit, 1961.

Clarke, Jeffrey J. *Advice and Support: The Final Years, 1965–1973*. Washington, D.C.: Center of Military History, U.S. Army, 1988.

Clodfelter, Mark. *The Limits of Airpower: The American Bombing of North Vietnam*. New York: Free Press, 1989.

Colby, William E. *Honorable Men*. New York: Simon & Schuster, 1978.

——*Lost Victory*. Chicago: Contemporary Books, 1989.

Conboy, Kenneth. *The War in Laos, 1960–1975*. London: Osprey, 1989.

Concerning the Situation in Laos. Peking: Foreign Language Press, 1959.

Davidson, Phillip B. *Vietnam at War: The History, 1946–1975*. Novato, Cal.: Presidio, 1988.

Dommen, Arthur J. *Conflict in Laos*. 2d ed. New York: Praeger, 1971.

——*Laos: Keystone of Indochina*. Boulder: Westview, 1985.

Downing, Bruce T. and Douglas P. Olney, eds. *The Hmong in the West: Observations and Papers*. Minneapolis: Center for Urban and Regional Affairs, University of Minnesota, 1982.

Duiker, William J. *China and Vietnam: The Roots of Conflict*. Berkeley: Institute of East Asian Studies, University of California, 1986.

——*The Communist Road to Power in Vietnam*. Boulder: Westview, 1981.

Eisenhower, Dwight D. *Mandate for Change, 1953–1956*. Garden City, N.Y.: Doubleday, 1963.

——*The White House Years: Waging Peace, 1956–1961*. Garden City, N.Y.: Doubleday, 1965.

Errington, Elizabeth J. and B. J. C. McKercher, eds. *The Vietnam War as History*. New York: Praeger, 1990.

Fall, Bernard B. *Anatomy of a Crisis: The Laotian Crisis of 1960–1961*. Garden City, N.Y.: Doubleday, 1969.

——*Street Without Joy*. New York: Schocken, 1972.

——*Hell in a Very Small Place: The Siege of Dien Bien Phu*. New York: Da Capo, 1967.

Fifield, Russell H. *The Diplomacy of Southeast Asia: 1945–1958*. New York: Harper & Row, 1958.

——*Americans in Southeast Asia: The Roots of Commitment*. New York: Crowell, 1973.

Futrell, Robert F. *The United States Air Force in Southeast Asia. The Advisory Years to 1965*. Washington, D.C.: Office of Air Force History, 1981.

Geddes, William R. *Migrants of the Mountains*. Oxford: Clarendon Press, 1976.

Gelb, Leslie H. and Richard K. Betts. *The Irony of Vietnam: The System Worked*. Washington, D.C.: Brookings Institute, 1979.

George, Alexander L., David K. Hall, and William E. Simons. *The Limits of Coercive Diplomacy*. Boston: Little, Brown, 1971.

Gibbons, William C. *The U.S. Government and the Vietnam War: Executive and Legislative Roles and Relationships. Part I, 1945–1960*. Princeton: Princeton University Press, 1986.

——*The U.S. Government and the Vietnam War: Executive and Legislative Roles and Relationships. Part II, 1961–1964*. Princeton: Princeton University Press, 1986.

——*The U.S. Government and the Vietnam War: Executive and Legislative Roles and Relationships. Part III, January–July 1965*. Princeton: Princeton University Press, 1989.

Girling, John L. S. *Thailand: Society and Politics*. Ithaca: Cornell University Press, 1981.

Goldstein, Martin E. *American Policy Toward Laos*. Teaneck, N.J.: Farleigh Dickinson University Press, 1973.

Gunn, Geoffrey C. *Political Struggles in Laos (1930–1954)*. Bangkok: Editions Duang Kamol, 1988.

Gurtov, Melvin. *China and Southeast Asia: The Politics of Survival*. Lexington, Mass.: D. C. Heath, 1971.

Hannah, Norman. *The Key to Failure: Laos and the Vietnam War*. New York: Madison Books, 1987.

Hayes, Samuel P., ed. *The Beginning of American Aid to Southeast Asia*. Lexington, Mass.: D. C. Heath, 1971.

Heimbach, Ernest E. *White Meo-English Dictionary*. Data Paper No. 75. Ithaca: Cornell University Press, 1969.

Hendricks, Glenn L., Bruce T. Downing, and Amos S. Deinard, eds. *The Hmong in Transition*. New York: Center for Migration Studies of New York and Southeast Asian Refugee Studies Project of the University of Minnesota, 1986.

Herring, George C. *America's Longest War: The United States and Vietnam, 1950–1975*. New York: Wiley, 1979.

Herring, George C., ed. *The Secret Diplomacy of the Vietnam War: The Negotiating Volumes of the Pentagon Papers*. Austin: University of Texas Press, 1983.

Hess, Gary R. *The United States' Emergence as a Southeast Asian Power, 1940–1950*. New York: Columbia University Press, 1987.

Hilsman, Roger. *To Move a Nation: The Politics of Foreign Policy in the Administration of John F. Kennedy*. Garden City, N.Y.: Doubleday, 1967.

Indorf, Hans H., ed. *Thai-American Relations in Contemporary Affairs*. Singapore: Executive Publications, 1982.

Iron Man of Laos: Prince Phetsarath Ratanavongsa. By "3349." Translated by John B. Murdoch and edited by David K. Wyatt. Data Paper No. 110. Ithaca: Southeast Asia Program, Cornell University, 1978.

Isaacs, Arnold R. et al., ed. *Pawns of War: Cambodia and Laos*. Boston: Boston Publishing, 1987.

Jackson, Karl D. and Wiwat Mungkandi. *United States–Thailand Relations*. Berkeley: Institute of East Asian Studies, University of California, 1986.

Jha, Ganganath. *Foreign Policy of Thailand*. New Delhi: Radiant, 1979.

Kahin, George McTurnan. *Intervention: How America Became Involved in Vietnam*. New York: Knopf, 1986.

Kaplan, Lawrence, Denise Artaud, and Mark R. Rubin, eds. *Dien Bien Phu and the Crisis of Franco-American Relations, 1954–1955*. Wilmington: Scholarly Resources, 1990.

Kaysone Phomvihane. *Revolution in Laos*. Moscow: Progress Publishers, 1981.

Kennedy, Paul M. *The Rise and Fall of the Great Powers*. New York: Random House, 1987.

Kissinger, Henry A. *White House Years*. Boston: Little, Brown, 1979.

——*Years of Upheaval*. Boston: Little Brown, 1982.

Kunstadter, Peter, ed. *Southeast Asian Tribes, Minorities, and Nations*. Princeton: Princeton University Press, 1967.

LaFeber, Walter. *America, Russia, and the Cold War, 1945–1984*. 5th ed. New York: Knopf, 1985.

Langer, Paul F. and Joseph J. Zasloff. *North Vietnam and the Pathet Lao: Partners in the Struggle for Laos*. Cambridge: Harvard University Press, 1970.

Leary, William M. *Perilous Missions: Civil Air Transport and CIA Covert Operations in Asia*. University, Ala.: University of Alabama Press, 1984.

LeBar, Frank M., Gerald C. Hickey, and John K. Musgrave. *Ethnic Groups of Mainland Southeast Asia*. New Haven, Conn.: Human Relations Area Files Press, 1964.

Lee, Chae-Jin. *Communist China's Policy Toward Laos: A Case Study, 1954–67.* Lawrence, Kan.: Center for East Asian Studies, 1970.

Lobe, Thomas. *United States National Security and Aid to the Thailand Police.* Monograph Series in World Affairs, vol. 14, bk. 2. Denver: University of Denver Graduate School of International Studies, 1977.

Marolda, Edward J. and Oscar P. Fitzgerald. *The United States Navy and the Vietnam Conflict. Volume 2, From Military Assistance to Combat, 1959–1965.* Washington, D.C.: Naval Historical Center, 1986.

McCoy, Alfred W. *The Politics of Heroin: CIA Complicity in the Global Drug Trade.* Brooklyn: Lawrence Hill, 1991.

Menger, Matt J. *In the Valley of the Mekong.* Patterson, N.J.: St. Anthony's Guild, 1970.

Modelski, George. *International Conference on the Settlement of the Laotian Question, 1961–1962.* Canberra: The Australian National University, 1962.

Modelski, George, ed. *SEATO: Six Crises.* Melbourne: F. W. Cheshire, 1962.

Momyer, William W. *Airpower in Three Wars.* Washington D.C.: Office of Air Force History, 1985.

Moseley, George V. H. *The Consolidation of the South China Frontier.* Berkeley: University of California Press, 1973.

Muscat, Robert J. *Thailand and the United States: Development, Security, and Foreign Aid.* New York: Columbia University Press, 1990.

Navarre, Henri. *Agonie de l'Indochine.* Paris: Plon, 1956.

Nixon, Richard M. *No More Vietnams.* New York: Avon, 1985.

Nuechterlein, Donald E. *Thailand and the Struggle for Southeast Asia.* Ithaca: Cornell University Press, 1965.

Operation Zapata: The "Ultrasensitive" Report and Testimony of the Board of Inquiry on the Bay of Pigs. Frederick, Md.: University Publications of America, 1981.

Oudone Sananikone. *The Royal Lao Army and U.S. Army Advice and Support.* Washington, D.C.: Center of Military History, U.S. Army, 1978.

Parmet, Herbert S. *JFK: The Presidency of John F. Kennedy.* New York: Dial, 1983.

Patti, Archimedes L. A. *Why Viet Nam?: Prelude to America's Albatross.* Berkeley: University of California Press, 1980.

Pentagon Papers, The, as Published by the New York Times. New York: Quadrangle, 1971.

Pentagon Papers, The: The Senator Gravel Edition. 5 vols. Boston: Beacon, 1973.

Phoukout Stronghold. n.p.: Neo Lao Haksat Publications, 1967.

Phoumi Vongvichit. *Laos and the Victorious Struggle of the Lao People Against U.S. Neo-Colonialism.* Sam Neua, Laos: Neo Lao Haksat, 1969.

Phuangkasem, Corrine. *Thailand and SEATO.* Bangkok: Thai Watana Panich, 1973.

Pike, Douglas. *History of Vietnamese Communism, 1925–1976.* Stanford: Hoover Institution Press, 1978.

——*PAVN: People's Army of Vietnam.* Novato, Cal.: Presidio, 1986.

Prados, John. *Presidents' Secret Wars: CIA and Pentagon Covert Operations from World War II Through Iranscam*. New York: Quill, 1986.

Prouty, L. Fletcher. *The Secret Team: The CIA and Its Allies in Control of the World*. New York: Ballantine, 1973.

Quincy, Keith. *Hmong: History of a People*. Cheney, Wash.: Eastern Washington University Press, 1988.

Randle, Robert F. *Geneva 1954: The Settlement of the Indochinese War*. Princeton: Princeton University Press, 1969.

Randolph, R. Sean. *The United States and Thailand: Alliance Dynamics, 1950–1985*. Berkeley: Institute of East Asian Studies, University of California, 1986.

Robbins, Christopher. *Air America*. New York: Avon, 1979.

——*The Ravens: The Men Who Flew in America's Secret War in Laos*. New York: Crown, 1987.

Rostow, Walt W. *The Diffusion of Power: An Essay in Recent History*. New York: Macmillan, 1972.

Rotter, Andrew J. *The Path to Vietnam: Origins of the American Commitment to Southeast Asia*. Ithaca: Cornell University Press, 1987.

Roy, Jules. *La bataille de Dien Bien Phu*. Paris: Julliard, 1963.

Rust, William J. *Kennedy in Vietnam*. New York: Scribner's, 1985.

Saiyud Kerdphol. *The Struggle for Thailand: Counter-insurgency, 1965–1985*. Bangkok: S. Research Center, Co., 1986.

Schaller, Michael. *The American Occupation of Japan: The Origins of the Cold War in Asia*. New York: Oxford University Press, 1985.

Schanche, Don A. *Mister Pop*. New York: David McKay, 1970.

Schlesinger, Arthur M., Jr. *A Thousand Days: John F. Kennedy in the White House*. Boston: Houghton Mifflin, 1965.

Schlight, John. The United States Air Force in Southeast Asia, *The War In South Vietnam: The Years of the Offensive, 1965–1968*. Washington, D.C.: Office of Air Force History, 1988.

Schulzinger, Robert D. *Henry Kissinger: Doctor of Diplomacy*. New York: Columbia University Press, 1989.

Scott, Peter D. *The War Conspiracy: The Secret Road to the Second Indochina War*. Indianapolis: Bobbs-Merrill, 1972.

Shackley, Theodore. *The Third Option: An American View of Counterinsurgency Operations*. New York: Dell, 1981.

Short, Anthony. *The Origins of the Vietnam War*. Essex, England: Longman Group, 1989.

Sisouk Na Champassak. *Storm over Laos: A Contemporary History*. New York: Praeger, 1961.

Smith, R. B. *An International History of the Vietnam War: The Kennedy Strategy*. New York: St. Martin's, 1975.

——*An International History of the Vietnam War: Revolution Versus Containment, 1955–61*. New York: St. Martin's, 1983.

Sorenson, Theodore C. *Kennedy*. New York: Harper & Row, 1965.

Soutchay Vongsavanh. *RLG Military Operations and Activities in the Laotian Panhandle.* Washington, D.C.: Center of Military History, U.S. Army, 1978.

Spector, Ronald H. *Advice and Support: The Early Years, 1941–1960.* Washington, D.C.: Center of Military History, U.S. Army, 1983.

Stanton, Shelby L. *Green Berets at War.* New York: Dell, 1985.

Steinberg, David J., ed. *In Search of Southeast Asia: A Modern History.* New York: Praeger, 1971.

Stevenson, Charles A. *The End of Nowhere: American Policy Toward Laos Since 1954.* Boston: Beacon, 1972.

Stuart-Fox, Martin, ed. *Contemporary Laos: Studies in the Politics and Society of the Lao People's Democratic Republic.* St. Lucia, Queensland: University of Queensland Press, 1982.

——*Laos: Politics, Economics, and Society.* Boulder: Lynne Rienner, 1986.

Sullivan, William H. *Obbligato: Notes on a Foreign Service Career.* New York: Norton, 1984.

Surachart Bamrungsuk. *United States Foreign Policy and Thai Military Rule, 1947–1977.* Bangkok: Editions Duang Kamol, 1988.

Thee, Marek. *Notes of a Witness: Laos and the Second Indochinese War.* New York: Random House, 1973.

Tilford, Earl H., Jr. *Search and Rescue in Southeast Asia, 1961–1975.* Washington, D.C.: Office of Air Force History, 1980.

Toye, Hugh. *Laos: Buffer State or Battleground.* 2d ed. New York: Oxford University Press, 1971.

20 Years of Lao People's Revolutionary Struggle. n.p.: Neo Lao Haksat, 1966.

Vo Nguyen Giap. *Dien Bien Phu.* Hanoi: Foreign Languages, 1962.

Westmoreland, William C. *A Soldier Reports.* New York: Dell, 1976.

Wiens, Herold J. *China's March Toward the Tropics.* Hamden, Conn.: Shoe String Press, 1954.

Wise, David and Thomas B. Ross. *The Invisible Government.* New York: Bantam, 1965.

Wolfkill, Grant. *Reported to Be Alive.* New York: Simon & Schuster, 1965.

Yang Dao. *Les Hmong du Laos face au developpement.* Vientiane: Siaosavath, 1975.

Zasloff, Joseph J. *The Pathet Lao: Leadership and Organization.* Lexington, Mass.: D. C. Heath, 1973.

Zasloff, Joseph J. and MacAlister Brown, eds. *Communism in Indochina.* Lexington, Mass.: D. C. Heath, 1975.

Zasloff, Joseph J. and Leonard Unger, eds., *Laos: Beyond the Revolution.* New York: St. Martin's, 1991.

Articles

Air America Log, vol. 7 no. 5, Kadena, Okinawa, 1972.

Baltimore Sun, December 4, 1975.

Bangkok Post, March 12, 13 and 15, 1968.

——November 18, 1973.

——May 22, 1974.

Cheney, Dick. "The POW-MIA Effort: Our Fullest Support." *Defense 92* (January–February 1992), 3–13.

Crozier, Brian. "Peking and the Laotian Crisis: A Further Appraisal." *China Quarterly* (July–September 1962), 116–23.

——"Peking and the Laotian Crisis: An Interim Appraisal." *China Quarterly* (July–September 1961), 128–37.

Dommen, Arthur J. "Laos in the Second Indochina War." *Current History* (December 1970).

Fulbrook, Jim E. "Lam Son 719, Part III: Reflections and Values." *United States Army Aviation Digest* (August 1986), 3–13.

Haase, David. "Long Cheng: From Bastion to Forward Base." *Far Eastern Economic Review* (January 22, 1972), 8–9.

Hamilton-Merritt, Jane. "Gas Warfare in Laos: Communism's Drive to Annihilate a People." *Reader's Digest* (October 1980), 81–88.

——"Tragic Legacy from Laos." *Reader's Digest* (August 1981), 96–100.

Harriman, W. Averell. "What We Are Doing in Southeast Asia." *New York Times Magazine* (May 27, 1962).

Heibert, Murray. "The Road to Reform." *Far Eastern Economic Review* (February 16, 1989), 18–23.

Helms, Richard. "Readers Forum." *International Journal of Intelligence and Counterintelligence* Vol. 3, 4: 563–65.

Herring, George C. "America and Vietnam." *Foreign Affairs* (Winter 1991/92), 104–19.

——"The Truman Administration and the Restoration of French Sovereignty in Indochina." *Diplomatic History* (1977), 1: 97–117.

Herring, George C. and Richard H. Immerman. "Eisenhower, Dulles, and Dien Bien Phu: The Day We Didn't Go To War Revisited." *Journal of American History* (September 1984), 71: 343–63.

Hess, Gary R. "Franklin Roosevelt and Indochina." *Journal of American History* (September 1972) 59: 353–68.

Hilsman, Roger and Stephen E. Pelz. "When is a Document Not a Document—And Other Thoughts." *Diplomatic History* (1979), 3: 345–48.

Jenkins, David. "Death by a Thousand Pin-Pricks." *Far Eastern Economic Review* (March 21, 1975), 26–27.

Kamm, Henry. "U.S. Involvement in Laos is Virtually Over." *New York Times* (June 20, 1975), 3.

Kerby, Robert L. "American Military Airlift During the Laotian Civil War, 1958–1963." *Aerospace Historian* (March 1977), 24: 1–9.

Kozicharow, Eugene. "Assets of Air America Totaled $50 Million During Peak Years." *Aviation Week & Space Technology* (May 3, 1976), 15–16.

La Feber, Walter. "Roosevelt, Churchill, and Indochina: 1942–45." *American Historical Review* (December 1975), 80: 1277–95.

"Laos: Climbing the Last Small Hills." *Far Eastern Economic Review* (May 30, 1975), 13–14.

"Laos: The Silent Surrender." *Far Eastern Economic Review* (May 1975), 23: 10–11.

Leary, William M. "CAT at Dien Bien Phu." *Aerospace Historian* (Fall 1984), 177–84.

Leary, William M. and William W. Stueck. "The Chennault Plan to Save China: U.S. Containment in Asia and the Origins of the CIA's Aerial Empire, 1949–1950." *Diplomatic History* (1984), 4: 349–64.

Los Angeles Times, March 22, 1972.

———August 1, 1974.

Mahajani, Usha. "President Kennedy and United States Policy in Laos, 1961–63." *Journal of Southeast Asian Studies* (September 1971), 2: 87–99.

Murphy, Charles J. V. "Thailand's Fight to the Finish." *Fortune* (October 1965), 122–274.

New York Times, July 23, 1951.

———May 7, 1962.

———October 26, 27, and 28, 1969.

———March 12, 1971.

———June 8, 1971.

———July 13, 1975.

Paul, Roland A. "Laos: Anatomy of an American Involvement." *Foreign Affairs* (April 1971), 49: 533–47.

Pelz, Stephen E. "When Do I Have Time to Think? John F. Kennedy, Roger Hilsman, and the Laotian Crisis of 1962." *Diplomatic History* (1979), 2: 215–29.

Phelan, Brian. "Thailand: Plight of the Meo." *Far Eastern Economic Review* (August 29, 1975), 20–22.

Plattner, C. M. "Continental Air Lines Diversifies with Southeast Asia Operations." *Aviation Week & Space Technology* (August 30, 1976), 37.

Pringle, James. "A Symbolic Change of Heart in Laos." *Bangkok Post* (April 2, 1991).

Robinson, Ray. "Report Describes Loss of Secret Base." *The Sunday Oklahoman* (October 5, 1986).

Simmonds, E. H. S. "The Evolution of Foreign Policy in Laos Since Independence." *Modern Asian Studies,* vol. 2, part I (January 1968), 1–30.

Starner, Frances. "Flight of the CIA." *Far Eastern Economic Review* (October 1972), 7: 23–26.

——"Watch Your Neighbor." *Far Eastern Economic Review* (June 1973), 18: 31–33.

——"The Lost World of Laos," *The Economist,* December 7, 1991, 37–38.

Tilford, Earl H., Jr. "Two Scorpions in a Cup: America and the Soviet Airlift to Laos." *Aerospace Historian* (September 1980), 27: 151–162.

Wall Street Journal, April 18, 1980.

Washington Evening Star, April 20, 1970.

Washington Post, March 16, 1972.

——July 10, 1977.

Wilson, David A. "Bangkok's Dim View to the East." *Asian Survey* (June 1961), 4: 13–17.

Other Sources

Air America. "A Short History of the Flight Information Center." Vientiane, October 12, 1964.

——Accident Board Investigation. September 20, 1964, Udorn Thailand.

——"Air Facilities Data, Laos." Flight Information Center, Vientiane: May 1970.

——Communication from David H. Hickler to Air America President, Taipei, August 22, 1964.

Air America Club. Video tape of dedication ceremonies for Air America/Civil Air Transport memorial and archives, Dallas, Texas, May 30, 1987.

INDEX

Text: 10/12.5 Times Roman
Compositor: Maple-Vail
Printer: Maple-Vail
Binder: Maple-Vail

28 DAYS